SIMON & SCHUSTER
Thesaurus
for
Children

Jonathan P. Latimer and Karen Stray Nolting

Simon & Schuster Books for Young Readers

STAFF

Editor in Chief	Jonathan P. Latimer
Managing Editor	Karen Stray Nolting
Art Director	Manuel Valdivia III
Copy Editors / Proofreaders	Lelia W. Mander, *JaBS Media;* Dorothy Gribbin
Cover Designer	Paula Winicur

SIMON & SCHUSTER BOOKS FOR YOUNG READERS
An imprint of Simon & Schuster Children's Publishing Division
1230 Avenue of the Americas, New York, New York 10020

Produced by Jonathan P. Latimer Publishing Group

CIP data for this book is available from the Library of Congress.
ISBN 0-689-84322-4

Manufactured in the United States of America
First Edition
2 4 6 8 10 9 7 5 3 1

WELCOME

Have you ever known what you wanted to say but were not able to find the right words? Or have you written something and used the same word over and over? The *Simon & Schuster Thesaurus for Children* can help you find just the right word. It can help you to express yourself more clearly and exactly in your writing. It can also help you make your writing more interesting and exciting for your readers.

HOW TO USE THIS THESAURUS

A thesaurus is a collection of words that mean almost the same thing. Words that share meanings are known as **synonyms**. For example, if you want to describe someone **laughing**, you have many choices. They could **chuckle**, **giggle**, **guffaw**, **roar**, or **snicker**. Each of these words is a **synonym** for **laugh**, but each also means a slightly different kind of laughter. The *Simon & Schuster Thesaurus for Children* can help you choose the word that best describes the kind of laughter you mean.

USING THIS THESAURUS

The words in a thesaurus are listed in alphabetical order. You look up words in a thesaurus as you do in a dictionary.

THE ENTRY

When a word is listed in the thesaurus, you will find an entry like this one:

right *adjective*	Free from mistakes; true:	*It turned out that there was only one **right** answer to the problem.* *Telling the truth is the **right** thing to do.*
correct	Not having any mistakes:	*Sydney gave the correct answer.* *Alex fumbled through his pocket looking for correct change.*
definite	Certain, clear:	*Her answer was a definite no.*
faultless	Without anything wrong; unspoiled:	*After checking for every possible error, Walt was sure that his computer program was faultless.*
precise	Clearly and accurately said or shown:	*The science teacher asked the class to measure the precise amount the jar would hold.* *The precise time the bus arrived was 4:38.*
specific	Exact; particular:	*We need to set a specific time for our meeting.*

For more choices see the entries for PERFECT and TRUE.
Antonyms: See the entries for INCORRECT and WRONG.

The word right is called an *entry word*. An *entry word* is printed in red letters. It is followed by its part of speech, a definition, and example sentences to help you understand how the *entry word* is commonly used. The part of speech for each *entry word* is also listed in red letters.

Synonyms are listed in blue letters beneath the *entry word*. Each synonym is followed by a definition and one or more example sentences.

Sometimes you will find cross-references at the end of an entry. For example, the cross-reference for right tells you to look under perfect and true for more synonyms.

You may also find information about antonyms at the end of an entry. These are words that mean the opposite of the *entry word*. The note at the entry for right tells you that its antonyms are found at the entries for incorrect and wrong.

SPECIAL FEATURES

This thesaurus has several special features to help you select the words that say what you want to say.

WORD BANKS

Sometimes the word that comes to mind is so general it doesn't tell your reader what you really mean. *Word Banks* are found at entries such as **cat**, **dog**, or **ship**. They contain lists of particular kinds of things that you may want to name instead of using a more general term. For example, here is the *Word Bank* for **color**.

WORD BANK

Sometimes you can make things clearer and more interesting for your reader by naming the particular **COLOR** you mean. Some **colors** are:

black	gray	pink	violet
blue	green	purple	white
brown	orange	red	yellow

WORDS FROM WORDS

Common words are often combined with other words to form new words or phrases with new meanings. For example, **key** means something that solves or explains. However, **keyed up** means very excited, and **to key in** means to enter information on a computer. *Words from Words* features list these combinations with their definitions, one or more example sentences, and some synonyms that you may want to consider using. For example, here is the *Words from Words* feature for **key**.

WORDS from Words

KEY can be combined with other words to form expressions that have special meanings. These expressions also have synonyms. *For example:*

keyed up means very excited: *The children were so **keyed up**, they couldn't stand still. If you get too **keyed up** before bedtime, you won't sleep well.* Useful synonyms are **agitated** and **stimulated**.

to key in means to enter information into a computer: *I had to **key in** my report all over again after the computer crashed.* Useful synonyms are **enter**, **input**, and **type in**.

WORD ALERT

When there is something special about a word that will help you use it,
its entry is followed by a *Word Alert*. Some *Word Alert* features note special
usage problems you should be aware of, others tell you where to find other
meanings and synonyms for a word. For example, **trip** means ***traveling*** or ***going
from one place to another***. But **trip** also has another common meaning,
which does not have its own entry. Instead, it is given in the *Word Alert*.

<table>
<tr><td>Word Alert</td></tr>
</table>

TRIP also means to lose one's balance: *I tripped over my shoelaces*. Synonyms for this meaning of **trip** are
fall and ***stumble***.

THE INDEX

If the word you want to look up isn't an *entry word,* check the *index,* which starts on
page 265. Every **synonym** mentioned in the thesaurus is also listed alphabetically in
the *index.* In the *index,* all words in CAPITAL LETTERS are *entry words.* These are
the words that are listed alphabetically and defined in the thesaurus. Every synonym
found in the thesaurus is listed in the index in lowercase letters. Under each word in
lowercase letters is the word *See* followed by an *entry word* in CAPITAL LETTERS.
This is the *entry word* under which you will find the synonym you are looking up. If
the synonym doesn't appear in the entry itself, it can be found in the special feature
that accompanies that entry.

ADMIT¹ *(to let in)*
ADMIT² *(to confess)*
adolescence
   See YOUTH
adorable
   See PRETTY
adore
   See LOVE

adorn
   See DECORATE
ADULT *(adjective)*
ADULT *(noun)*
advance
   See MOVE
adventurous
   See DARING

Some words have more than one meaning. When they are the same part of
speech, as with **admit**, small numbers are used to indicate the difference.
For example, ADMIT¹ is a *verb* meaning **to let in** and ADMIT² is a *verb* meaning
to confess. Words that are used as more than one part of speech are given
separate entries, as with the *adjective* ADULT and the *noun* ADULT.

WORDS FOR STORY WRITERS

The words in the main part of this thesaurus are commonly found in ordinary conversation or writing. However, if you want to write a story about a faraway or imaginary time or place, you may need some special words. Although most of the words listed here are rarely heard in everyday conversation, they are commonly used in their settings. These words will help you make your story or report more accurate and interesting. These words can also inspire your imagination by suggesting other words — or even ideas. If you are unfamiliar with a word on these lists, you can find its meaning in a dictionary.

MYSTERY STORY

If you want to write a *mystery* story, try some of these words:

accomplice	detective	loot	safecracker
chase	getaway car	police station	scene of the crime
clue	gumshoe	precinct	siren
cops	inspector	private eye	squad car
crook	judge	reward	stickup

SCIENCE FICTION

If you want to write a report on *space travel* or a *science fiction* story, some words you may want to use include:

alien	launch	planet	space suit
asteroid	light speed	ray gun	spaceship
beam	moon	rocket	star
comet	nebula	satellite	warp speed
galaxy	orbit	space station	weightlessness

WESTERN

Here are some words that you may want to use if you want to write a report on the Old West or a *western* story:

buckaroo	chaps	hideout	sagebrush
buckboard	corral	lariat **or** lasso	scout
cactus	cowboy	outlaw	sheriff **or** marshal
cantina	doggie	rodeo	stagecoach
cavalry	gunfight	saddle	wagon train

MEDIEVAL TIMES

If you want to write a report or story about *medieval* times, try these words:

archer	castle	lady	shield
armor	charger	lance	siege
banquet	flagon	mace	sword
battle-ax	helmet	moat	tournament
boon	knight	quest *or* crusade	tower

FANTASY

It can be fun to imagine what things would be like if there was magic in the world. If you want to write a story about imaginary events, here are some words that you may want to use:

cauldron	curse	secret passage	wishing well
cloak	oracle	spell *or* charm	witch
crystal ball	potion	wand	wizard

Many *fantasy* stories include **mythological creatures**. Some examples are:

centaur	gremlin	mermaid	siren
dragon	griffin	phoenix	sphinx
giant	leprechaun	sea serpent	unicorn

Fantasy stories often take place in **imaginary places**. Some examples are:

Atlantis	El Dorado	Narnia	Shangri-la
Camelot	Middle-Earth	Oz	Wonderland

PREHISTORIC TIMES

If you want to write a report or story about *prehistoric* times, here are some words that you may want to use:

bow and arrow	cave painting	flint	saber-toothed tiger
cave	cave woman	giant sloth	scraper
cave man	fire	mammoth	stone spear point

Although **dinosaurs** lived millions of years before humans appeared, they were important **prehistoric** creatures in their own time. Some *dinosaurs* are:

allosaurus	archaeopteryx	diplodocus	triceratops
apatosaurus	compsognathus	stegosaurus	tyrannosaurus

ability *noun*   The power to do something: *Sarah has the **ability** to run fast.*
*Humans have the **ability** to speak.*

capability   The quality of being capable of doing something well; ability: *Jane has the capability of winning the chess tournament.*

knack   A special ability or skill for doing something easily: *Sherry seems to have a knack for designing clothes.*
Paul has the knack for making us laugh.

skill   The power to do something: *You will gain skill if you practice.*

For more choices see the entry for TALENT.

---

able *adjective*   Having the power to do something: *He was an **able** hockey player.*
*A cheetah is an **able** hunter.*

capable   Having skill or power: *A capable teacher can help students learn better.*

competent   Able to perform basic skills: *A competent plumber should be able to fix the clogged drain in your sink.*

qualified   Meeting the requirements: *We need a qualified candidate for the election.*

---

about *adverb*   Very close to: *The school had **about** twenty singers.*
***About** two inches of rain fell last night.*

approximately   Nearly exact: *There were approximately eighty people in the audience.*

around   Somewhere near: *There must have been around two hundred marbles in the jar.*

nearly   Almost: *There were nearly a dozen birds sitting in the tree.*

roughly   Approximately but not exactly: *It takes roughly fifteen minutes to walk to school from my house.*

about *preposition*	Having to do with:	*The movie was **about** dinosaurs.* *Rachel told us **about** her visit to the museum.*
concerning	Having to do with:	*The teacher wanted to talk with us* *concerning our project.*
regarding	Relating to:	*We wrote the television network regarding* *the cancellation of our favorite show.*

absent *adjective*	Not present:	*The two **absent** members of our class have colds.* *The **absent** teacher was replaced by a substitute.*
away	Distant; gone:	*My brother is away at summer camp.*
gone	Away from a place:	*The cookies are gone from the kitchen table.*
missing	Not there:	*Ben had to hunt all over for his missing sock.*

absolute *adjective*	Not limited; whole:	*The witness told the **absolute** truth.* *This sweater was an **absolute** bargain.*
complete	Having all its parts:	*I read the complete works of Jane Austen last summer.*
total	All there is:	*The total amount of the bill is twenty-three dollars.*
utter	Complete or perfect:	*Some animals have adapted to living in the utter darkness* *of caves.*

ache *verb*	To hurt with a dull or constant pain:	*My foot **ached** after I banged it.* *My tooth was **aching** so I went to the dentist.*
hurt	To be painful:	*The bruise on my elbow hurt for a few days.*
smart	To feel a sharp, stinging pain:	*Stephanie's eyes smarted whenever she spent* *too much time in the pool.*
throb	To pound rapidly:	*My thumb throbbed after I accidentally struck it* *with a hammer.*

act *noun*	Something done; a deed:	*Saving the struggling swimmer was an **act** of bravery.* *His good **acts** earned him the community's respect.*
accomplishment	Something accomplished; achievement:	*Finding a new planet is a great scientific* *accomplishment.* *Her accomplishments included winning a scholarship.*
achievement	Something accomplished or achieved:	*The teacher was proud of the achievements of her class.*
deed	Something done; an act:	*Sissy did a good deed by helping a child find his mother.*
feat	An act or deed that shows courage, strength, or skill:	*Swimming across the lake was quite a feat.*

Word Alert

ACT also means a law: *Congress passed several acts to protect endangered species.* Synonyms for this meaning of **act** can be found at the entry for *LAW*. **Act** can also mean a short performance or a part of a play: *The comedian's act was hilarious. We drank sodas between the first and second acts.*

---

act *verb*	To do something:	*The lifeguard acted quickly to pull the frightened boy out of the pool.* *If you don't act, nothing will get done.*
function	To work or serve:	*A calculator functions best when it has new batteries.* *I don't function well in cold weather.*
operate	To go or to run:	*The washing machine operated smoothly once the water was turned on.* *Jack doesn't know how to operate his camera.*
perform	To carry out to completion:	*You must perform each step in the right order or the magic trick won't work.* *The doctor performed the operation.*
work	To act or make act properly; to do the job:	*Megan can work on your computer after she finishes fixing mine.*

For more choices see the entry for DO.

WORDS from Words

ACT is often combined with other words to form expressions that have special meanings. These expressions also have synonyms. *For example:*

to act on or **act upon** means to behave according to or follow something: *The reporter acted on a tip from a reader. The principal acted upon the ruling of the school board.* Useful synonyms are **follow**, **heed**, and **obey**. **Act on** or **act upon** can also mean to have an effect upon something else: *Acid acts on metal.*

to act out means to perform as in a play or drama: *Each of us had to act out our favorite story for the class.* A useful synonym is **perform**.

to act up means to behave poorly in a playful way: *The mischievous boy acted up during class.* A useful synonym is **misbehave**. **Act up** can also mean to cause discomfort or to malfunction: *My stomach ache acted up after dinner. Our computer is acting up, and I can't finish my assignment.*

action *noun*   The process of doing something: *Actions include throwing a ball, writing a letter, and reading a book.*
The student government discussed what action to take.

   exertion   The act of making use of something; an effort: *After much exertion, everything was loaded in the car.*

   motion   The act of changing place or position: *The motion of the train made it hard to read.*
She lifted the heavy suitcase in one motion.

   movement   The act of changing the place or direction of something: *The slow movement of the traffic made us late.*
The fan caused movement of the air in the room.

For more choices see the entry for WORK¹.

WORDS from Words

ACTION is often combined with other words to form expressions that have special meanings. These expressions also have synonyms. *For example:*

actions means behavior or conduct: *How do you account for her actions? There are a number of actions we can take to correct this situation.* Useful synonyms can be found at the entry for **BEHAVIOR**.

out of action means unable to function: *Your bicycle will be out of action until the chain is replaced. The football player was out of action because of an injury.*

to take action means to do something when it is very important: *We had to take action during the emergency. The electrical workers took action to repair the power lines during the blackout.* Useful synonyms can be found at **ACT** and **DO**.

admit¹ *verb*   To allow to enter; let in: *They will admit everyone who has a ticket.*
Lou hopes he will be admitted into the club.

   allow to enter   To admit; let in: *Only children older than twelve are allowed to enter.*

   give access   To admit to something: *The security guards wouldn't give us access to the star's dressing room.*

   let in   To allow to enter; admit: *I let in the cat when it scratched on the door.*
Please unlock the door and let me in.

admit² *verb*   To make known that something is true: *She admitted that her dog ate the birthday cake.*
I must admit that you have done an excellent job.

   acknowledge   To admit the truth of something: *The coach acknowledged her part in losing the game.*

   concede   To admit as true: *After they showed us all the evidence, we had to concede that their story was true.*

   confess   To admit to something: *I have to confess that I didn't like that movie.*
The suspect confessed to the crime.

adult *adjective* — Having grown to full size and strength:
An **adult** whale can weigh over 100 tons.
An **adult** robin takes care of its young until they are grown.

   full-grown — Grown to full size:
A *full-grown* panda is huge compared to its newborn baby.

   grown-up — Fully grown; like an adult:
A *grown-up* colt is called a horse.

   mature — Having reached full growth:
Although it is small, a newly hatched rattlesnake is just as dangerous as a *mature* one.

---

adult *noun* — A person, plant, or animal that is fully grown:
We need an **adult** to drive us to the mall.
No **adults** came to the theater for the cartoon festival.

   grown-up — An adult:
The *grown-ups* watched the children on the playground.

For more choices see the entries for MAN and WOMAN.

---

afraid *adjective* — Feeling fear, often for a long time:
Jerry is **afraid** of the dark.
An elephant is supposed to be **afraid** of a mouse.
Are you **afraid** of lightning?

   fearful — Filled with fear:
Donna was *fearful* of the thunder.

   frightened — Suddenly afraid:
The *frightened* cat jumped when the loud music came on.

   scared — Frightened or alarmed:
She got *scared* when she heard a noise.

   terrified — Extremely afraid; filled with terror:
Roy was *terrified* when he watched the movie.
The *terrified* child woke up from his nightmare.

For more choices see the entry for SHY.
Antonyms: See the entries for BRAVE and DARING.

---

agree *verb* — To have the same opinion or feeling:
My best friend and I **agree** on the video games we like.
We **agreed** to eat first and then go to the movie.
Dana and I **agreed** not to watch television.

   assent — To express agreement:
The class *assented* to sponsoring a raffle to earn money for a class trip.

   concur — To have the same opinion:
The judges *concurred* in awarding the trophy to our team.

   consent — To give permission:
My parents *consented* to let me stay overnight with a friend.

For more choices see the entry for LET.
Antonyms: See the entries for FORBID and PREVENT.

agreement *noun* — An understanding between people or groups: — *By the end of the meeting we had reached an* **agreement**. *The* **agreement** *was written down and signed by all the participants.*

    bargain — An agreement to trade or exchange: — *We made a* bargain *to trade my old bike for his comic book collection.*

    contract — A written agreement: — *The basketball player signed a three-year* contract.

    deal — An arrangement: — *According to our* deal, *you will make the beds and I will do the dishes.*

    pact — An agreement between persons or countries: — *They had a* pact *not to reveal each other's secrets. Two nations signed a peace* pact.

    treaty — A formal agreement among nations: — *Many nations signed a* treaty *to limit pollution in the oceans.*

---

alert *adjective* — Watching carefully: — *The* **alert** *mouse was on the lookout for our cat. A night watchman must stay* **alert** *for trouble.*

    attentive — Paying attention: — *The audience was* attentive *throughout the play.*

    vigilant — Alert or watchful for possible danger: — *The* vigilant *forest ranger looked for signs of fire.*

    watchful — Watching carefully: — *The* watchful *mother let her child play on the swings.*

---

alive *adjective* — Having life: — *You have to water plants if you want them to stay* **alive**. *Nicole felt very* **alive** *when she was dancing.*

    active — Doing something; lively: — *Brian took an* active *interest in the drama club. Susan played an* active *role in the debate team.*

    animated — Full of life: — *She was an* animated *speaker, smiling and waving her hands.*

    living — Having life: — *The aquarium was filled with* living *creatures from the sea. Kyle found a book about famous* living *musicians.*

---

almost *adverb* — Very close to: — *After riding for an hour, we were* **almost** *there. I* **almost** *made a goal, but the goalie was too quick.*

    nearly — All but; not quite: — *We* nearly *forgot your birthday. It was* nearly *noon before we had breakfast.*

    practically — Nearly; just about: — *I'm* practically *finished with my homework.*

alone *adjective* — Apart from anything or anybody else: — *An owl perched **alone** in an empty tree.* / *I had to go **alone** to get my hair cut.*

isolated — Placed or set apart: — *The **isolated** beach was perfect for finding shells.* / *Brittany was **isolated** from her sisters when she had measles.*

lone — Away from others: — *A **lone** star twinkled in the twilight.*

solo — Made or done by one person or thing alone: — *A flute played a **solo** part during the concert.* / *A **solo** airplane flew overhead.*

For more choices see the entry for LONELY.

---

amaze *verb* — To surprise greatly: — *I was **amazed** by the beautiful view from the mountain.* / *Her story **amazed** all of us.*

astonish — To surprise very much: — *The news that we had won the contest **astonished** everyone.*

astound — To surprise greatly: — *The discovery of a cure for yellow fever **astounded** the world.*

impress — To have a strong effect on the mind or feelings: — *The size of the huge building **impressed** me.*

For more choices see the entry for SURPRISE.

---

amount *noun* — The sum of two or more numbers or quantities: — *What is the **amount** of money you spent on books?* / *The **amount** of water that bottle will hold is one liter.*

number — The total amount of things in a group: — *The **number** of students in this class is twenty-four.*

quantity — A number or amount: — *We only had a small **quantity** of sugar left.*

sum — The number that results from adding two or more numbers together. — *The **sum** of all the votes determines who will win the student body elections.*

---

ancient *adjective* — Of great age; very old; of times long past: — *The ruins of an **ancient** city were discovered buried in the desert.*

antique — Of old times: — *We saw **antique** automobiles at the museum.*

old-fashioned — No longer in fashion: — *We laughed at the **old-fashioned** clothes my grandparents were wearing in the old photos.* / *The antique car club has a parade of **old-fashioned** cars every year.*

out-of-date — No longer in style or use: — *The covered wagon is an **out-of-date** method of traveling.*

For more choices see the entry for OLD.
Antonyms: See the entries for NEW and YOUNG.

anger *noun* — A strong feeling caused by a person or thing that opposes, displeases, or hurts one: — *She felt **anger** when a mean classmate insulted her best friend.*

    irritation — Anger or impatience: — *Playing loud music late at night can cause irritation for your neighbors.*

    outrage — Great anger: — *Alex felt outrage when he found out the contest was fixed.*

    temper — A tendency to become angry: — *Dave has quite a temper when someone insults him.*

For more choices see the entry for RAGE.

---

angry *adjective* — Feeling or showing anger: — *I was **angry** when the power went out for the third time. The **angry** fans booed the opposing team.*

    enraged — Filled with rage; angry beyond control: — *The enraged mother elephant drove the lions away from her baby.*

    furious — Extremely angry; fierce or violent: — *Jason was furious at me for losing his glove. A furious wind rattled the windows.*

    irate — Very angry: — *The irate crowd booed when the referee made a bad call.*

    mad — Feeling or showing anger; crazy or reckless: — *Her insult made me mad. Jumping down a whole flight of stairs was a mad thing to do.*

---

animal *noun* — A living thing that takes in food and moves about: — *Butterflies, birds, zebras, lions, and humans are all **animals**.*

    beast — An animal that has four feet: — *The zoo displays tigers, monkeys, and other beasts of the jungle in their natural habitat.*

    creature — A living animal: — *Deer and bears are creatures of the forest. A shark is a creature of the sea.*

    organism — A living thing: — *Bacteria and amoebas are organisms you can only see with a microscope.*

---

answer[1] *noun* — Something said or written in reply: — *She was waiting for an **answer** to her e-mail.*

    reply — Something said, written, or done in answer: — *I received a reply to the letter I wrote to my favorite movie star. How many replies have we received to the party invitations?*

    response — Something said or done in answer: — *The student gave an unexpected response to the teacher's question.*

    retort — A sharp or witty reply: — *Jason's quick retort made everyone laugh.*

answer² *noun* · The correct solution to a problem: · *There is only one right **answer** when you multiply 3 times 12.*

result · Something that happens because of something else: · *The results of your test will be in tomorrow.*
The accident was a result of carelessness.

solution · The answer to a problem: · *It took us hours to find the solution to the puzzle.*

---

answer *verb* · To speak or write as a reply: · *I **answered** the teacher's questions when he called on me.*

reply · To answer in speech, writing, or action: · *I will reply to her later.*
Everyone has replied to our invitations.

respond · To give an answer: · *The bus driver responded to my question.*

retort · To reply quickly or sharply: · *"Not in my house!" she retorted angrily.*

---

appreciate *verb* · To understand the value of something: · *I **appreciated** the gifts that my parents gave me for my birthday.*

cherish · To love and treat tenderly: · *Jenny always cherished her little dog.*

prize · To think very highly of: · *Jose prized his new bicycle.*

treasure · To think of as being of great value: · *I treasure our friendship.*

value · To think highly of: · *Danny valued his father's advice.*

---

appropriate *adjective* · Suitable for the occasion: · *He wore the **appropriate** clothes for going swimming.*

correct · Agreeing with the approved way; proper: · *It is correct to thank the hostess for inviting you to her party.*
The correct line for buying tickets is over there.

fit · Right or suitable for: · *This spoiled food is not fit to eat.*
It seemed fitting that the citizenship award should be given to Julie after all the volunteer work she had done.

proper · Suitable for a certain occasion: · *You must wear proper clothing to attend the opera.*
A mechanic needs proper tools to fix a car.

---

argue *verb* · To express a difference of opinion: · *They **argued** about what to eat for dinner.*
*We almost never **argue** because we like the same things.*

bicker · To quarrel noisily about something unimportant: · *The sisters bickered about who would wear the new sweater.*

quarrel · To have a disagreement: · *The children quarreled over who should go first.*

For more choices see the entries for CONTRADICT, DISAGREE, and DISCUSS.

argument *noun* — A discussion between people who do not agree: — *We had an **argument** about which team was going to win. The speaker's **arguments** sounded illogical to me. I felt miserable after a silly **argument** with my best friend.*

controversy — A disagreement: — *The new rules caused much controversy.*

debate — A discussion between persons or groups who disagree: — *The debate about how to deal with pollution has gone on for years.*

disagreement — A difference of opinion: — *There is no disagreement about the need for clean air and water.*

For more choices see the entry for QUARREL.

---

arrange *verb* — To put in order or position: — *Please **arrange** the chairs in a circle for the next lesson. They **arranged** the books by size.*

classify — To arrange in groups: — *Most libraries classify fiction by the author's name.*

organize — To put together in an orderly way: — *I organized my desk so everything is within easy reach.*

set — To place; to put in a useful order: — *Please set the packages on the back seat of the car. Kelsey set the table.*

sort — To separate according to kind or type: — *We sort our socks by color after they are washed.*

For more choices see the entry for PUT.
Antonyms: See the entries for JUMBLE and MIX.

---

art *noun* — An activity by which one creates a work that is beautiful or has special meaning: — *She learned the **art** of weaving over the summer.*

craft — A trade or art requiring special skill: — *It takes time to learn the craft of carpentry.*

skill — The ability to do something well: — *Study and practice are needed to develop a skill.*

technique — A way of bringing about a desired result in art, science, or sport: — *The concert pianist practiced her technique every day. The coach helped Anna develop her riding technique.*

WORD BANK

ARTIST means a person who is skilled in painting, music, literature, or other form of art: *An artist showed us how she paints when we visited the museum.* There is no exact synonym for **artist**, but you may want to consider using one of the following terms:

actor **or** *actress*	*creator*	*musician*	*sculptor*
artisan	*dancer*	*painter*	*singer*
author	*designer*	*playwright*	*virtuoso*
composer	*illustrator*	*poet*	*writer*

---

ask *verb* — To question about something: *Jeremy **asked** for directions to the video store.*
*The children **asked** many questions, and the teacher answered them all.*

inquire — To ask for information: *We **inquired** about the schedule of events at the fair.*

interrogate — To question harshly and in great detail: *The detectives **interrogated** the suspect.*

question — To ask questions about: *The teacher **questioned** the students about their project.*

request — To ask for: *We **requested** mustard for our hot dogs.*

---

assist *verb* — To do something useful or helpful: *The students were asked to **assist** in collecting cans for recycling.*

aid — To give help or support: *The volunteers **aided** the flood victims.*

help — To give or do something useful or needed: *We **helped** the outfielder find the lost ball.*

Antonyms: See the entry for RESTRICT.

---

atom *noun* — The smallest particle of a chemical element: *You can't see an **atom** because it is so small. All matter is made up of **atoms**.*

bit — A small piece or part: *A **bit** of mud stuck to my shoe. The vase fell and broke to **bits**.*

grain — A tiny, hard piece of something: *My mother used a handkerchief to get a **grain** of sand out of my eye.*

particle — A very small bit of something: *You can sometimes see **particles** of dust floating in the air.*

speck — A very small bit, spot, or mark: *There was a **speck** of ink on his shirt.*

For more choices see the entry for PIECE.

attack *verb*

	To fight against or use violence on something or someone:	The soldiers will **attack** the enemy at dawn. The firefighters **attacked** the blaze and put it out.
ambush	To make a surprise attack:	Our cat ambushed our dog when it came into the bedroom.
assault	To attack suddenly:	The soldiers assaulted the fort.
charge	To rush at:	The buffalo put its horns down and charged at the lion.
invade	To attack in order to conquer:	The enemy invaded but had to retreat. Ants invaded our kitchen.

For more choices see the entries for ARGUE and FIGHT.
Antonyms: See the entry for DEFEND.

---

avoid *verb*

	To keep away from:	We took a shortcut and **avoided** the traffic.
dodge	To keep away by stepping aside quickly:	Samantha dodged a snowball that was thrown at her.
evade	To escape from:	Our cat evaded capture until two of us cornered it.
sidestep	To avoid by stepping out of the way:	I sidestepped to avoid bumping into a pole.

For more choices see the entry for ESCAPE.

---

awful *adjective*

	Causing fear, dread, or awe:	The squealing brakes made an **awful** noise. The sound of the badly tuned violin was **awful**.
dreadful	Very frightening:	We heard a dreadful scream.
frightening	Causing alarm and fear:	The darkness was frightening.
horrible	Causing great fear or shock:	The eerie sound of the wind was horrible.
scary	Causing fear:	The scary movie made the audience scream.
terrible	Causing fear or terror:	Our dog hid in a closet during the terrible thunderstorm. The child made a terrible face when he tasted the sour lemonade. Luckily no one was hurt in the terrible accident on the highway.

---

awkward *adjective*

	Lacking grace or poise:	A giraffe looks **awkward**, but it can run very fast.
clumsy	Not graceful:	Sometimes I'm so clumsy, I break things by mistake. The clumsy puppy stumbled over its own ears.
uncoordinated	Not working together smoothly:	Swans are graceful on water but uncoordinated on land.
ungainly	Clumsy:	His long arms and legs made him look ungainly.

Antonyms: See the entry for GRACEFUL.

back *noun* — The part of anything opposite of the front: *Put your name on the back of the application. The kitchen is at the back of the house.*

    rear — The part behind or in back: *I sat at the rear of the class.*

For more choices see the entry for END.
Antonyms: See the entry for FRONT.

WORDS from Words

BACK is often combined with other words to form expressions that have special meanings. *For example:*

back and forth means first in one direction and then the other: *The windshield wipers moved back and forth. The band marched back and forth across the football field.* Useful synonyms are **from side to side** and **sideways**.

behind one's back means without someone's knowledge or approval: *We planned the party behind your back. I hope you are not spreading rumors behind my back.* A useful synonym is **secretly**.

in back of means at the rear of: *I sit in back of Heidi in math class.* Useful synonyms are **at the rear of** and **behind**.

to back down means to give up a claim on something: *She said she wouldn't go to the library but backed down when we asked her nicely.* Useful synonyms are **take back** and **withdraw**.

to back out or **back out of** means not to keep a promise or agreement: *Don't back out of your promise to visit.* Useful synonyms are **abandon** and **quit**.

to back up means to give support to: *He backed up his statements with facts.* Useful synonyms are **strengthen** and **support**. **To back up** can also mean to save computer files: *I backed up my work on a floppy disk.* Useful synonyms are **file**, **save**, and **store**.

---

bad[1] *adjective* — Having little quality or worth; undesirable: *The movie was so bad that my friends and I walked out. We have bad television reception where we live.*

    defective — Having a flaw; not perfect: *The defective paint on my bike rusted.*

    inadequate — Not enough; not good enough: *There is an inadequate food supply for this many people.*

    inferior — Poor quality; below average: *This restaurant serves inferior food.*

For more choices see the entry for CHEAP[2].
Antonyms: See the entry for GOOD.

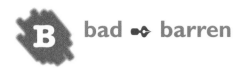

bad² *adjective* | Not good or moral: | *He had **bad** thoughts about getting even.*
*Committing a crime is a **bad** thing to do.*

evil | Wicked or harmful: | *The evil plan to take over the world was foiled by the quick action of the heroes.*

wicked | Mean and very bad: | *The villain in the story was a wicked giant.*

wrong | Not moral or good: | *It is wrong to steal.*

Antonyms: See the entry for GOOD.

---

bad³ *adjective* | Having a harmful effect: | *Reading in **bad** light is not good for your eyes.*
*A **bad** snowstorm caused a blackout.*

damaging | Making something less valuable or useful: | *The damaging flood left people without homes.*

harmful | Causing injury: | *We must try to avoid the harmful effects of pollution.*

hurtful | Causing harm or damage: | *She told hurtful lies about her sister.*

For more choices see the entry for UNFAVORABLE.

---

bad⁴ *adjective* | Behaving badly: | *The **bad** dog was sent to obedience school.*
*You can expect to be punished if you are **bad**.*

disobedient | Refusing to obey: | *The disobedient child refused to behave in the restaurant.*

impudent | Shamelessly bold and rude: | *The impudent boy made faces at strangers and talked back when asked to stop.*

rowdy | Disorderly; quarrelsome: | *The crowd became rowdy when the coach pulled the star player out of the game.*

unruly | Hard to control: | *The class was unruly when the teacher left the classroom.*

For more choices see the entry for NAUGHTY.
Antonyms: See the entries for GOOD and NICE.

---

barren *adjective* | Not able to produce anything: | *No plants could grow on the **barren** soil.*
*The **barren** trees bent in the winter wind.*

desolate | Without people; deserted: | *We enjoyed walking on a desolate stretch of beach.*

infertile | Not useful for farming: | *This infertile desert was covered with flowers after an unusual thunderstorm.*

For more choices see the entry for EMPTY.
Antonyms: See the entry for PRODUCTIVE.

basic *adjective*	Forming the basis or most important part:	*Addition and subtraction are basic parts of math. Sharing is a basic rule of friendship.*
elementary	Dealing with the simple parts or beginning of something:	*Leslie thought the lesson was too elementary for her because it was so easy.*
fundamental	Serving as a basis:	*Knowing the alphabet is fundamental to learning how to read.*
introductory	Serving as an introduction; preliminary:	*The speaker began her talk with a few introductory remarks about her childhood.*
preliminary	Coming before the main part:	*After a few preliminary announcements, the principal introduced the main speaker.*
primary	First in order of time:	*Our project is still in its primary stage of development.*

bear *verb*	To put up with patiently:	*I cannot bear being last all the time. He bore the responsibility for the whole project by himself.*
endure	To put up with:	*The first colonists had to endure many hardships.*
stand	To put up with; be patient about:	*How do you stand all this mess? I can't stand that song.*
tolerate	To put up with:	*I can't tolerate people who talk during a movie.*

For more choices see the entry for TAKE².

Word Alert

TO BEAR WITH means to be patient toward someone or something: *Please bear with me for a few moments while I get organized.* Useful synonyms are **put up with** and **tolerate**.

beautiful *adjective*	Pleasing to look at, hear, or think about; full of beauty:	*The ballet was beautiful. Where is that beautiful music coming from? What a beautiful sunset!*
exquisite	Of great beauty and perfection:	*The view over the lake was exquisite. He gave her an exquisite diamond ring.*
gorgeous	Extremely beautiful or richly colored:	*The roses look gorgeous this year.*
lovely	Beautiful in a soothing or peaceful way:	*This garden is lovely in the afternoon sunlight.*

For more choices see the entries for HANDSOME, MAGNIFICENT, and PRETTY.
Antonyms: See the entry for UGLY.

begin *verb* To do the first part of something: *It is time to **begin** your homework.*
*The show **began** at eight o'clock.*

    initiate To be the first to do: *The music teacher initiated a series of free concerts.*

    originate To bring into being: *Paige originated the idea for the presentation.*

    set off To start to go or begin: *We set off on our trip early in the morning.*

For more choices see the entry for START.
Antonyms: See the entry for END.

---

beginning *noun* The point at which something begins: *The **beginning** of this path is over that hill.*
*At the **beginning** of the story, Goldilocks got lost.*

    commencement A beginning; start: *January 1 marks the commencement of the new year.*

    opening The first time something is performed or open for business: *We saw many celebrities at the opening of the new movie.*

    origin The cause or source of something: *Scientists are trying to explain the origin of the moon.*
The origin of their quarrel had been forgotten.

    source A person, place, or thing from which something comes or begins: *The source of the river is high in the mountains.*
This book is the source of that idea.

    start Beginning to act, move, or happen: *We got an early start.*
The runners were bunched up at the start of the race.

Antonyms: See the entry for END.

---

behavior *noun* A way of acting or doing things: *Her cheery **behavior** showed she was in a good mood.*
*Our teacher complimented us on our good **behavior**.*

    conduct The way someone behaves: *I was annoyed by his childish conduct.*

    manner A way of acting or behaving: *My friend has an easygoing manner.*
The librarian greeted us in a friendly manner.

---

belief *noun* The certainty that something is true, real, or worthwhile: *My grandfather has a strong **belief** in exercise.*
*Equality under the law is one of the important **beliefs** that form the basis of democracy.*

    conviction A firm belief: *It is my conviction that everyone should vote.*

    judgment An opinion or estimate: *In your teacher's judgment, your drawings are very good.*

    opinion A belief based on what someone thinks or guesses is true: *When Jeffrey heard all the facts, he had to change his opinion.*
What is your opinion of that book?

    view A way of thinking about something: *What is your view on the candidates for class president?*

For more choices see the entries for IDEA and STAND.

bend *verb* — To make or become curved or crooked: — The gym teacher made us **bend** over and touch our toes. / We **bent** wire to make sculptures.

curve — To move in a curved line: — The river **curves** after it goes under the bridge. / The road **curved** around the park.

twist — To turn around something: — The string in my yo-yo **twisted** into a knot.

wind — To wrap something around: — If you will **wind** the hose, I'll put the garden tools away. / The vine **wound** around the porch.

For more choices see the entry for TURN.

---

between *preposition* — In the space or time separating or joining two things: — There is a good highway **between** here and the next city. / We can have a snack **between** classes.

amid — In the middle of: — The cabin was located **amid** tall trees.

among — In the middle of; surrounded by: — Our school is **among** the best in the state. / I stood **among** the rocks and looked at the view.

in between — In the middle: — A cat crawled **in between** the fence and our house.

Word Alert

BETWEEN is usually used when you are writing or talking about just two people or things: *I sit between Peter and Bruce in music class.* **Amid** and **among** are only used when you are writing or talking about more than two people or things: *The small house looked out of place amid the tall buildings. I found this sweater among the ones in my drawer.*

---

big *adjective* — Great size or amount: — There are **big** buildings in the city. / The farmer has a **big** herd of cows.

enormous — Much greater than the usual size: — We saw an **enormous** mushroom on the front lawn.

gigantic — Huge and powerful: — Engineers built a **gigantic** dam across the river.

huge — Extremely big: — That is a **huge** tree, but not as **huge** as a skyscraper.

immense — Of great size; very large: — The blue whale is an **immense** animal that can grow more than 100 feet long.

For more choices see the entries for GIANT and LARGE.
Antonyms: See the entries for LITTLE, SMALL, and TINY.

blame *verb* — To find fault with:

The boy **blamed** the dog for eating his lunch.
The boat captain **blamed** the storm for the accident.

accuse — To say a person has done something wrong:

The truck driver was accuse of speeding.

criticize — To find fault:

Don't criticize our decision until you know all the facts.

fault — To hold responsible:

I fault the owner for the bite because he didn't keep his dog on a leash.

For more choices see the entries for DISAPPROVE and OBJECT.

---

boast *verb* — To talk too much or with too much pride about oneself:

He **boasted** about how good he was at chess until she beat him.
After hearing him **boast** so often, people just didn't listen anymore.

brag — To speak with too much praise about what one does or owns:

They bragged about their school team.

exaggerate — To make something seem more important than it is:

Fishermen often exaggerate the size of the fish that got away.

gloat — To think about something with great satisfaction:

It makes me mad to see the other team gloat over beating us.

---

boat *noun* — A small vessel used for traveling on water:

We rowed the **boat** out to where the fish were biting.
Miranda started the motor and steered the **boat** back to shore.

craft — A boat:

The harbor was filled with sailing craft.

For more choices see the entry for SHIP.

WORD BANK

Sometimes you can make things clearer and more interesting for your reader by naming the particular **BOAT** you mean. Some **boats** are:

cabin cruiser	gondola	mailboat	sailboat
canal boat	gunboat	outboard	sampan
canoe	houseboat	outrigger	skiff
dinghy	hydrofoil	patrol boat	speedboat
diving boat	junk	PT boat	steamboat
dugout	kayak	punt	umiak
fishing boat	lifeboat	raft	whaleboat
flatboat	longboat	rowboat	yacht

body *noun* The whole physical structure that makes up a person, an animal, or a plant: | *His body has become very slim since he started jogging every day.*

build	Body shape:	*The stranger had a heavy build.*
figure	The shape of a person:	*I couldn't make out the figure in the shadows.*
silhouette	A dark outline:	*I was barely able to make out the silhouette of the woman in the dim light.*

boss *noun* A person who watches over and plans work for others: | *The boss gave everyone a bonus for working so hard. He had to check with his boss before he could make the sale.*

employer	A person or business that pays workers:	*My employer wants to hire more workers.*
head	The person above others in rank:	*The head of this organization is the president.*
manager	A person who directs or controls something:	*The manager of a baseball team sets up the batting order.*
supervisor	A person who watches over or directs:	*The supervisor on this project reports to the head of the company.*

bother *verb* To give trouble to: | *Those mosquitoes bothered me all night. Don't bother to cook; I'll pick up something for dinner.*

annoy	To make somewhat angry:	*The child's repeated questions began to annoy me.*
disturb	To make uneasy or nervous:	*The loud noise disturbed my cat.*
irritate	To make angry or impatient:	*Don't let little things irritate you.*

For more choices see the entry for TEASE.

box *noun* A stiff container made of cardboard, wood, or other material. | *We packed everything in boxes when we moved. I kept my old photos in a box in the closet.*

carton	A container made of cardboard, paper, plastic, or other material:	*We bought a carton of eggs at the market.*
case	A container to hold or protect something:	*I took a CD out of its plastic case.*
container	A box, can, or jar that holds something:	*Nat took a container of juice for his lunch.*
crate	A box made of slats of wood:	*My new bicycle came in a large crate.*

For more choices see the entry for PACK.

brave *adjective* | Being able to face danger or pain without being overcome by fear: | The **brave** firefighter raced into the burning house to rescue a child.

bold | Showing courage: | The **bold** explorer marched through the dark forest.

courageous | Having courage: | A **courageous** woman jumped into the icy water to save the young girl.

heroic | Very brave: | The **heroic** lifeguard pulled a swimmer out of the surf.

For more choices see the entry for DARING.
Antonyms: See the entries for AFRAID and SHY.

---

break *noun* | A short rest period: | We took a **break** before we continued the test. After our **break** we worked for several hours.

interlude | Something filling time between two things: | We enjoyed an **interlude** of sunshine during the rain.

intermission | A time of rest or stopping between periods of activity: | There was a short **intermission** between each act of the play.

lull | A short period of calm or quiet: | There was a **lull** in the proceedings while the broken microphone was replaced.

For more choices see the entry for PAUSE.

WORDS from Words

BREAK is often combined with other words to form expressions that have special meanings. These expressions also have synonyms. *For example:*

to break down means to stop working: *Our car broke down. The elevator always seems to break down on the weekend.* Useful synonyms are **fail** and **cease to work**.

to break off means to stop suddenly: *The speaker broke off to take a drink of water.* Useful synonyms are **end**, **pause**, and **stop**.

to break out means to start suddenly: *A fire broke out in the basement.* Useful synonyms are **begin** and **happen suddenly**. **Break out** also means to escape or emerge: *Our dog broke out of the yard and chased the neighbor's cat.* Useful synonyms are **escape**, **flee**, and **run away**. **Break out** can also mean to become covered with a rash or pimples: *Poison ivy made my skin break out in a rash.* A useful synonym is **erupt**.

to break up means to separate or scatter: *The ice on the pond breaks up in spring. We use a shovel to break up the soil in our garden.* Useful synonyms are **disperse**, **separate**, and **scatter**. **Break up** also means to come to or bring to an end: *The meeting broke up very late.* Useful synonyms are **conclude**, **finish**, and **end**. **Break up** can also mean to laugh: *The comedian made the audience break up. Your story broke me up.* Useful synonyms are **laugh** and **roar**.

break *verb* | To come apart or make something come apart by force: | *He is so clumsy he seems to **break** everything he touches. The glass fell to the floor and **broke**.*

crack | To make a small break in something: | *The case on my CD player cracked but didn't break. I cracked two eggs to make an omelet.*

shatter | To break into pieces: | *The window pane shattered when the ball hit it.*

smash | To break violently: | *I dropped a plate by accident and smashed it.*

For more choices see the entry for DESTROY.
Antonyms: See the entries for BUILD and MAKE¹.

---

bright *adjective* | Filled with light; shining: | *The sun was so **bright** I had to wear sunglasses.*

brilliant | Shining or sparkling: | *The dark sky was filled with brilliant stars.*

gleaming | Shining or glowing: | *The gleaming lights of the city lit up the night sky.*

glowing | Shining with a warm light: | *A glowing fire burned in the fireplace.*

shiny | Reflecting brightly: | *I could see shiny coins in the fountain.*

Antonyms: See the entry for DARK.

---

bring *verb* | To cause something or someone to come with you: | *I want to **bring** marshmallows to the picnic. Put what you **brought** on the table.*

deliver | To take to the proper place or person: | *A mail carrier delivers mail to our home.*

transfer | To move from one person or place to another: | *All the books have been transferred to the new library.*

transport | To take from one place to another: | *Bread is transported from the bakery to the market by truck.*

For more choices see the entries for CARRY and MOVE.

WORDS from Words

BRING is often combined with other words to form expressions that have special meanings. These expressions also have synonyms. *For example:*

to bring about and **to bring on** mean to lead to: *The flood was **brought about** by heavy rains. Reading in poor light can **bring on** a headache.* Useful synonyms are **cause** and **produce**.

to bring out means to make clear: *That shirt **brings out** the color of your eyes.* Useful synonyms are **reveal** and **show**. **Bring out** also means to offer to the public: *The studio is **bringing out** a new movie this summer.* Useful synonyms are **offer**, **present**, and **show**.

to bring up means to take care of during childhood: *My grandparents **brought up** three boys and two girls.* Useful synonyms are **raise** and **rear**. **Bring up** also means to offer as a subject for discussion: *Nick **brought up** his plan at the meeting. Please don't **bring up** that old joke again.* Useful synonyms are **mention**, **offer**, and **suggest**.

build *verb* — To make by putting parts or materials together: — *We are going to **build** a sand castle when we get to the beach.*
*They **built** the new library next to our school.*

  assemble — To put or fit together: — *We assembled my model airplane from a kit.*

  construct — To make by putting parts together: — *Constructing a tall building can take months.*
That house was constructed over 100 years ago.

  erect — To build: — *We erected a tent in our backyard.*

For more choices see the entry for MAKE[1].

---

burn *verb* — To set or be on fire: — *We **burn** a fire at night to keep warm.*
*The candle **burned** for hours.*

  blaze — To burn brightly: — *The campfire blazed while we told scary stories.*

  ignite — To set on fire: — *My father ignited the gas heater with a match.*

  scorch — To burn slightly on the surface: — *The iron scorched my shirt.*

  singe — To burn a little: — *A spark singed the rug in front of the fireplace.*

business[1] *noun* — The work a person does to earn a living: — *Joel's father is in the real estate **business**.*

  industry — A branch of business, trade, or manufacturing: — *Melissa's uncle used to work in the entertainment industry.*

  occupation — The work a person does to earn a living: — *Her mother's occupation is selling insurance.*

  profession — An occupation requiring special education and training: — *Someday I want to join the medical profession.*

---

business[2] *noun* — An activity or organization that buys and sells goods and services to earn money: — *Some friends of my mother want her to go into **business** with them.*
*We will need an office for our **business**.*

  company — A business firm or organization: — *The company across town develops software.*

  firm — A company in which two or more people go into business together: — *There are more than twenty lawyers in this law firm.*

  store — A place where goods are sold: — *Tomorrow we have to go to the shoe store and the grocery store.*

busy *adjective* — Doing something; having plenty to do: — *Janice is a **busy** person.* / *You seem to be **busy** all the time.*

employed — In use; busy: — *After the blizzard all the snow plows were fully employed cleaning the streets.*

engaged — Taking part; involved: — *The class was so engaged in a discussion they didn't hear the bell.*

occupied — Keeping busy: — *The children were occupied playing a game.*

Antonyms: See the entry for LAZY.

Word Alert

BUSY also means in use: *Her phone was busy*. Synonyms for this meaning of **busy** are *in use* and *occupied*.

---

but *conjunction* — On the other hand; in contrast: — *My brother is a fast runner, **but** I am faster.* / *Most of the time I like movies, **but** this one was awful.*

although — In spite of the fact that: — *I ordered caramel ice cream although I usually have chocolate.*

however — In spite of that: — *We thought we had everything ready for our trip; however we forgot to pick up our tickets.*

yet — However; but: — *I thought I knew my way, yet I soon became lost.* / *We read the manual, yet we couldn't get the computer to work.*

---

but *preposition* — Other than: — *Everyone **but** those who have not turned in their work can go out for recess.* / *I finished the test **but** didn't have time to check my answers.*

except — Not including: — *The mail is delivered every day except Sunday.* / *I ate everything except the carrots.*

cabin *noun*

A small, simple house often built of rough boards or logs:

*I love my **cabin** in the woods, but it doesn't have electricity.*
*At summer camp everyone slept in **cabins**.*

bungalow — A small house: — *One summer we stayed in a bungalow near the beach.*

cottage — A small house: — *The old lady lived in a quaint cottage surrounded by trees.*

lodge — A small house, cottage, or cabin: — *Before we hiked into the woods, we spent the night in a mountain lodge.*

For more choices see the entries for HOUSE and HUT.

---

call *verb*

To speak or say in a loud voice:

*Alexander searched the neighborhood, **calling** for his lost puppy.*
*She **called** to her friend across the street.*

cry — To call loudly: — *We heard a frantic cry for help.*

exclaim — To speak or shout suddenly: — *"Great to see you!" my friend exclaimed when she returned after a month away.*

hail — To greet by calling or shouting: — *My friends hailed me from down the block.*
We tried to hail a cab in the downpour.

For more choices see the entries for TALK and YELL.

calm *adjective* — Not excited or nervous; peaceful:

Jennifer was very **calm** before her speech because she felt well prepared.
It was a **calm** day after the wind died down.
Everyone remained **calm** during the fire drill.

collected — Not confused or disturbed:

Jill remained cool and *collected* throughout the emergency.

composed — Not excited; quiet:

Although Brian was nervous about performing, he looked very *composed*.

cool — Not excited:

Walter's *cool* behavior during the crisis helped keep everyone calm.

relaxed — Less tense:

The *relaxed* atmosphere of the playground was welcome after the difficult test.

serene — Calm and peaceful:

The sound of the ocean gave her a *serene* feeling.
The park was *serene* after the thunderstorm.

For more choices see the entry for QUIET.
Antonyms: See the entries for NERVOUS and UPSET.

---

careful *adjective* — Paying close attention, trying to avoid mistakes:

The teacher warned us to be **careful** and to check our work on the math test.
A **careful** driver obeys the traffic laws.

cautious — Watching closely:

The *cautious* puppy peered down the dark stairway.
You should be *cautious* when crossing the street.

exact — Without mistakes:

Laura needed *exact* measurements to make the costumes.

wary — Watching carefully, alert:

The *wary* rabbit scampered nervously across the open field.
You should be *wary* when you are out at night.

Antonyms: See the entry for CARELESS.

---

careless *adjective* — Not paying close attention:

I made **careless** mistakes on the math test.
He was so **careless** he lost his new jacket.

mindless — Without thought or care:

His *mindless* chatter interrupted my train of thought.

negligent — Not showing proper care:

The *negligent* waiter forgot to bring our drinks.

thoughtless — Doing things without thinking:

Thoughtless people leave litter in the park.

For more choices see the entry for RECKLESS.
Antonyms: See the entry for CAREFUL.

carry *verb* — To hold something while moving it: *We had to **carry** the heavy tent up the hill. Debbie **carried** the groceries into the kitchen.*

    bear — To hold up; support: *The tree's branches are too small to **bear** your weight. We **bore** the heavy load without complaining.*

    lug — To carry or drag with much effort: *Victor **lugged** his heavy suitcase up to his room.*

    tote — To carry or haul: *We **toted** our school books home in our backpacks.*

For more choices see the entries for BRING and MOVE.

WORDS from Words

CARRY is often combined with other words to form expressions that have special meanings. These expressions also have synonyms. *For example:*

to carry on means to go on: *We must **carry on** our effort to protect the environment. The teacher told us to carry on with our work while she stepped outside.* Useful synonyms are **continue**, **persist**, and **proceed**.

to carry out means to obey: *The soldier **carried out** his orders.* Useful synonyms are **follow** and **observe**. **Carry out** also means to get done or complete: *We **carried out** our plans for the parade successfully.* Useful synonyms are **accomplish**, **conclude**, and **finish**.

---

cat *noun* — A small furry animal with short ears and a long tail, often kept as a pet or for catching rats or mice: *My **cat** never goes outside. We haven't seen any signs of mice since we got a **cat**.*

    kitten — A young cat: *Our cat had five **kittens**. The **kitten** played with a ball of yarn.*

    tomcat — A male cat: *Our **tomcat** comes and goes as he pleases.*

WORD BANK

Sometimes you can make things clearer and more interesting for your reader by naming the particular **CAT** you mean. Some **cats** are:

Angora	*Egyptian*	*Persian*	*Siamese*
calico	*Manx*	*shorthair*	*tabby*

CAT can also refer to any animal in the **cat** family. Many of these are ferocious predators often seen in zoos. Some of these **cats** are:

bobcat	*jaguar*	*lynx*	*panther*
cheetah	*leopard*	*mountain lion*	*tiger*
cougar	*lion*	*ocelot*	*wildcat*

catch *verb* — To take hold of something or someone that is moving: *Can your dog catch a ball? I didn't go into his house because I didn't want to catch a cold. The police caught the robber red-handed.*

apprehend — To capture and arrest: *The criminals were apprehended after a long search.*

arrest — To catch and hold; stop: *The sheriff arrested the suspect. We hope to arrest the spread of air pollution in the next ten years.*

capture — To catch and hold a person, animal, or thing: *We tried to capture a squirrel, but it was too smart for us.*

trap — To catch in a trap: *Rangers trapped a wolf in town and released it in the forest.*

For more choices see the entry for SEIZE.
Antonyms: See the entry for MISS.

WORDS from Words

CATCH is often combined with other words to form expressions that have special meanings. These expressions also have synonyms. *For example:*

to catch on means to get the idea: *Julia caught on to the joke before I had finished telling it. I thought I would never catch on to the algebra problem, until my teacher explained it.* Useful synonyms are **grasp**, **see**, and **understand**.

to catch up means to move fast enough to come up from behind: *Kyle had to run to catch up with his friends.* A useful synonym is **overtake**. **Catch up** also means to bring up-to-date: *I've got to catch up on my homework tonight.* Useful synonyms are **complete** and **finish**.

---

caution *noun* — Close care or watchfulness: *Use caution when you cross the street.*

attention — The act of watching carefully: *The movie captured our attention.*

care — Close and serious attention: *Antonio dried the dishes with care.*

vigilance — Alertness and watchfulness: *Constant vigilance at crosswalks can prevent accidents.*

---

cave *noun* — A natural hole or hollow in the ground or the side of a mountain: *The huge cave had many tunnels. Early humans decorated the walls of caves with drawings of animals.*

burrow — A hole dug in the ground by an animal: *Rabbits, gophers, and woodchucks live in burrows.*

cavern — A large cave: *Some caverns have many miles of tunnels.*

tunnel — A long passage underneath the ground or water: *We drove through a tunnel to get to the city.*

celebrate *verb*	To observe a special day or event with a celebration or party:	The whole family got together to **celebrate** my grandfather's birthday. Calvin **celebrates** every time his favorite team wins.
commemorate	To honor the memory of:	Postage stamps often commemorate famous people or events. President's Day commemorates the birthdays of George Washington and Abraham Lincoln.
honor	To show respect for a person or thing:	The town honored its victorious team with a parade.
observe	To celebrate:	We observed my mother's birthday on Saturday even though it was really on Thursday.

ceremony *noun*	A formal act done on a special occasion:	The senior class sang the school song at the graduation **ceremony**. The opening **ceremonies** for the Olympics were very impressive.
celebration	Ceremonies performed to observe or honor a special day or event:	The family held a celebration when my sister graduated. Our town holds a special celebration on Veteran's Day.
rite	A solemn ceremony:	Most religions have special rites for celebrating the birth of a child.
ritual	A system of rites in a ceremony:	The rite of marriage is part of the ritual of most religions.
service	A religious ceremony:	The family arrived late for the Sunday church service. The funeral service will be held on Friday.

champion *noun*	A person or thing that wins a contest or game:	The governor presented the trophy to the state **champion**. Last year's **champions** are going to try to win again this year.
victor	The winner of a struggle, battle, or contest:	The trophy went to the victor. The North was the victor over the South in the Civil War.
winner	A person or thing that wins:	Madeline was the winner of the spelling bee.

change *verb* | To make or become different: | *Jamal looked completely different after he changed his clothes.* *We change our opinions as we learn more.*

adapt	To change in order to make suitable:	*My family adapted to our new home.* *The authors adapted their novel for television.*
alter	To make or become different:	*We altered our plans so we could stay longer.* *I am having my coat altered so it will fit better.*
amend	To change formally:	*The Constitution has been amended several times during its history.*
convert	To change something into something different:	*They converted the old barn into an artist's studio.*
modify	To change in some way:	*They modify car designs every year.*
transform	To change in form or appearance:	*The spring wildflowers transformed the empty field into a colorful garden.* *The magician transformed an egg into a rabbit.*

For more choices see the entries for CORRECT and FIX.

---

cheap[1] *adjective* | Low priced: | *My car was cheap, but it is very reliable.* *We found a store where you can buy cheap shoes.*

economical	Avoiding waste; thrifty:	*Traveling by bus is economical.*
inexpensive	Low-priced:	*Zachary bought an inexpensive lunch so he would have money for the movie.* *The hotel we stayed in was inexpensive but nice.*
reasonable	Not asking too much; fair:	*The price for those oranges seems reasonable.*

Antonyms: See the entry for EXPENSIVE.

---

cheap[2] *adjective* | Not worth very much or not of good quality: | *My new shirt was so cheap it fell apart the first time it was washed.* *The cheap wristwatch doesn't keep accurate time.*

poor	Below standard:	*Lack of rain and poor soil ruined this year's crop.* *The bag broke because it was of poor quality.*
shabby	Worn out:	*My old coat looks shabby.*
worthless	Not good or useful; without value:	*My skateboard is worthless because the wheel came off.*

For more choices see the entry for BAD[1].
Antonyms: See the entries for GOOD and LUXURIOUS.

child ⇥ choice

child *noun* A son or daughter; a young person: *The child was too small to go on the carnival ride alone, so her father held her in his lap.*

baby A very young child; infant: *The baby cries because he is hungry.*

kid A word for child used in informal conversation: *All the kids want to go swimming.*
"No kids allowed," the mean teenager said.

youngster A young person: *Those youngsters live down the street.*

For more choices see the entry for YOUTH.

WORD BANK

The plural of **CHILD** is **CHILDREN.** The **children** or young of other animals often have special names. Some examples of these names are:

calf — a young cow or bull, deer, elephant, seal, or whale

chick — a young chicken or other bird

colt — a young horse, donkey, or zebra

cub — a young bear, fox, or lion

fawn — a young deer

joey — a young kangaroo

kid — a young goat or human

kitten — a young cat

lamb — a young sheep

piglet — a young pig

pup — a young dog, coyote, fox, wolf, or seal

puppy — a young dog

childish *adjective* Like a child, or suitable only for a child: *His childish behavior included making faces.*
The movie was too childish for my parents.

babyish Like a baby: *His round face gave him a babyish appearance.*

childlike Of or like a child: *She had a childlike curiosity about everything around her.*

immature Foolish or childish: *It is immature to expect everyone to do things your way all the time.*

infantile Of or like an infant: *Refusing to try new foods is infantile.*

For more choices see the entry for YOUNG.

choice *noun* The act or result of choosing: *Sarah had the choice of either staying home or going to her friend's house.*
You made your choice, now you have to stick with it.

alternative A choice between two or more things: *You have the alternative of seeing a movie or going shopping.*

option A choice; alternative: *Going to the beach on a school day is not an option.*

selection A choice: *The bookstore has a good selection of mysteries.*

choose *verb* — To decide to take from what is available: — *You can **choose** to ride your bike to school or go on the bus.*
*The team captains **chose** the best players first.*

determine — To decide or settle: — *The judges **determined** the winner.*

elect — To choose by voting: — *We **elect** a president every four years.*

select — To make a choice: — *Each coach **selected** players from the class.*
*Which book did you **select**?*

For more choices see the entry for PICK.

---

city *noun* — An area where people live and work that is larger than a town: — *Georgia liked living in the **city** better than her small hometown in the country.*
*Many **cities** have their own symphony orchestras.*

metropolis — A large and important city: — *The **metropolis** of Los Angeles covers hundreds of square miles.*

municipality — A city or town with a local government: — *Our **municipality** has its own recycling program.*

For more choices see the entry for TOWN.

---

clean *adjective* — Free from dirt; not soiled: — *I put on **clean** socks this morning, but I didn't realize they had holes in them.*
*It's important to keep a **clean** kitchen.*

fresh — Clean or refreshing: — *My clothes smelled **fresh** after they were washed.*
*The air was **fresh** after the rain.*

spotless — Without any mark or stain: — *Her room was **spotless** when she finished cleaning it.*

unsoiled — Clean; not dirty: — *Even though he had been hiking all day, his clothes were **unsoiled**.*

washed — Free of dirt: — *All my clothes are **washed** and ready to be packed for our trip.*
*The **washed** glasses sparkled.*

For more choices see the entry for NEAT.
Antonyms: See the entries for DIRTY, MESSY, and UNTIDY.

---

clean *verb* — To remove dirt from something or make it neat: — *My room is such a mess, I have to **clean** it before I can go out.*
*They **cleaned** the chalkboard after school.*

cleanse — To make clean: — *You should **cleanse** a cut before you bandage it.*

scrub — To rub in order to clean: — *They had to **scrub** hard to get the kitchen floor clean.*

wash — To make free of dirt: — *It is best to use soap when you **wash** your hands.*

climb ◆ clothes

climb *verb*	To move upward or across something using the hands and feet:	*We **climbed** the mountain and stood on its peak.*
ascend	To move or go up:	*The flag ascended to the top of the pole. The teacher ascended the stairs to make her announcement.*
mount	To go up:	*The athletes mounted the victory stand to receive their medals.*
rise	To move from a lower to a higher place:	*Everyone rose to say the pledge of allegiance. The elevator slowly rose to the top floor.*
scale	To climb to or over the top:	*The firefighters scaled their ladders to get to the fire.*

close *verb*	To shut an opening with a door or lid:	*I **closed** the window to keep the rain out. Please **close** the peanut butter jar before you put it away.*
fasten	To close so that it will not come open:	*Please fasten the screen door.*
seal	To close tightly and completely:	*Be sure to seal the envelope before you mail it. The mummy was sealed in its tomb.*
secure	To fasten firmly:	*The guard secured the lock on the jail cell.*

For more choices see the entries for LOCK and SHUT.
Antonyms: See the entry for OPEN.

Word Alert

CLOSE can mean almost equal or nearly even: *That was a very close race.* Synonyms for this meaning of **close** can be found at the entry for **SIMILAR**. **Close** can also mean near: *The library is close to our house.* Synonyms for this meaning of close can be found at the entry for **NEAR**.

clothes *noun*	Things worn to cover the body:	*She put on her school **clothes** in the morning but changed to her casual **clothes** when she got home.*
apparel	Clothing; clothes:	*That store sells children's apparel.*
attire	Clothing:	*They went to the prom in formal attire.*
clothing	Things worn to cover the body:	*We bought warm clothing for the winter.*
costume	Clothes worn to look like someone or something else:	*He dressed up in a clown costume. The dancers wore ballet costumes.*
garment	A piece of clothing:	*His garments were worn from use.*

cold *adjective* — Having a low temperature; not warm or hot: — *The desert has hot days and **cold** nights.*
*The **cold** wind made her shiver.*

chilly — Uncomfortably cool: — *The first day of spring was wet and chilly.*

cool — Somewhat cold: — *A glass of cool lemonade can be refreshing on a hot summer day.*

freezing — Cold enough for water to freeze: — *My fingers stuck to the freezing metal pole.*

frigid — Extremely cold: — *The North Pole is frigid all year long.*

frosty — Cold enough for frost: — *Trees often glisten with ice on frosty mornings.*

icy — Very cold: — *An icy wind stung our faces.*

For more choices see the entry for RAW.
Antonyms: See the entries for HOT and WARM.

---

color *noun* — A quality of light we see with our eyes: — *The **color** of something depends on how it reflects light.*
*Whenever she had to pick a **color**, she always chose blue.*

hue — A color or shade of color: — *The sunset had a bright orange hue.*

shade — A particular color: — *Roses come in many shades of pink.*

tint — A shade of color: — *Adding blue and yellow gave our paint a green tint.*

tone — A shade of color: — *The artist used a mix of colors to get the right tone.*

WORD BANK

Sometimes you can make things clearer and more interesting for your reader by naming the particular **COLOR** you mean. Some **colors** are:

black	*gray*	*pink*	*violet*
blue	*green*	*purple*	*white*
brown	*orange*	*red*	*yellow*

---

come *verb* — To move toward something: — *The teacher told them to **come** to the front of the class.*
*Toni's aunt **came** for dinner.*
*What time are you **coming** over?*

appear — To come into sight: — *The plane appeared right on time.*

approach — To come near: — *The puppy was too scared to approach me.*

arrive — To come to a place: — *What do you want to do when we arrive?*

reach — To come to: — *The boat reached the shore, and we got out.*

Antonyms: See the entry for VANISH.

WORDS from Words

COME is often combined with other words to form expressions that have special meanings. These expressions also have synonyms. *For example:*

to come across and **to come upon** mean to meet by chance: *I came across some old clothes in the basement. We came upon a rabbit in the woods.* Useful synonyms are **find**, **locate**, and **uncover**.

to come at means to rush forward or attack: *The angry bulldog came at us, but we got away.* Useful synonyms can be found at the entry for **ATTACK**.

to come back means to return: *My friends came back to our house after the game.* Useful synonyms can be found at the entry for **RETURN**[1].

to come down means to become sick: *Jeremy came down with a cold last winter.* A useful synonym is **catch**.

to come in or **to come into** means to enter: *We came in from the rain. Please come into the house for lunch.* Useful synonyms can be found at the entry for **ENTER**. **To come in** also means to arrive: *What time does the plane come in?* Useful synonyms can be found at the entry for **COME**.

to come off means to take place or happen: *The homecoming game comes off in two weeks.* Useful synonyms can be found at the entry for **HAPPEN**.

to come off also means to turn out or result in: *The meeting didn't quite come off the way we expected.* Useful synonyms are **end** and **turn out**.

to come out means to become known: *The truth finally came out.* Useful synonyms are **disclose**, **reveal**, and **tell**. **To come out** can also mean to be presented in public: *The new movie will come out next week.* A useful synonym is appear. **To come out** also means result: *Everything will come out all right.* Useful synonyms are **end** and **turn out**. The noun form of this meaning is **outcome**.

to come through means to accomplish something: *My friends always come through for me. The fire department really came through in the emergency.* Useful synonyms are **perform** and **succeed**.

to come to means to become conscious again: *When did he come to?* A useful synonym is **wake up**. **To come to** can also mean to add up to: *Our bill comes to four dollars.* Useful synonyms are **equal** and **total**.

to come up means to move to a higher place: *She came up the mountain on her horse.* Useful synonyms can be found at the entry for **CLIMB**. **To come up** also means arise or develop: *The sun comes up in the east. Your suggestion never came up.* A useful synonym is **arise**.

---

comfortable *adjective*	Giving ease or comfort:	*The comfortable sofa had big, soft pillows.* *The friendly children made the new student feel comfortable.*
cozy	Warm and comfortable:	*It is hard to get out of my cozy bed in winter.*
pleasant	Giving pleasure:	*The room was warmed by a pleasant fire.*
snug	Comfortable, warm, and cozy:	*Our snug house keeps out the winter wind.*

common
adjective

| | Happening often; not special: | *Butterflies are common in summer, but not in winter. Wagons pulled by horses were once a common means of transportation.* |

   familiar — Often heard or seen: — *The moon is a familiar sight at night. I didn't know anyone at the party, but then I spotted a familiar face.*

   frequent — Happening often: — *We have frequent thunderstorms in spring.*

   well-known — Known to many people: — *We saw a well-known movie star in the department store.*

For more choices see the entries for NORMAL, REGULAR, and USUAL.
Antonyms: See the entries for ODD and UNUSUAL.

---

communicate
verb

| | To exchange or pass along feelings, thoughts, or information: | *People communicate by speaking or writing. Herb communicates with his friends by e-mail.* |

   contact — To get in touch with; communicate with: — *We contacted everyone we know with the good news.*

   get in touch with — To communicate with; contact: — *I got in touch with my friends as soon as I got back from our trip.*

   reach — To get in touch with someone: — *Samantha tried to reach Alyssa on the phone.*

   speak to or speak with — To communicate by talking: — *I spoke to my teacher about our assignment. I will speak with my parents about it tonight.*

For more choices see the entry for TALK.

---

compare *verb*

| | To study persons or things to discover how they are alike or different: | *Each day they would compare their lunches to decide what to trade. A horse seems small compared to an elephant.* |

   contrast — To show differences that are based on comparing: — *The movie contrasted life today with life a hundred years ago.*

   distinguish — To show a difference between certain things: — *We finally learned to distinguish genuine leather from fake.*

---

complain *verb*

| | To say something is wrong: | *Austin complained about being late. You can complain if you want to, but it won't do any good.* |

   gripe — To complain: — *The players griped about the umpire's call.*

   grumble — To complain in a low voice: — *The students were always grumbling about the bad food in the cafeteria.*

   protest — To object to something: — *A crowd protested the closing of the library.*

complete
adjective

Having all its parts:

They found a **complete** deck of cards and played hearts.
Emma wants to read the **complete** works of Shakespeare.

   entire

Having all its parts; nothing left out:

We ate the *entire* bowl of spaghetti.
The *entire* class passed the spelling test.

   full

Complete; entire:

We get a *full* two weeks of vacation.

   total

Complete; utter:

Their play was a *total* success.

   whole

Having all its parts:

Garret finished the *whole* book in a few hours.

Antonyms: See the entries for EMPTY and INCOMPLETE.

---

complicated
adjective

Hard to understand or do:

The directions for fixing the computer were too **complicated** to follow.
The gymnast made **complicated** exercises look easy.

   complex

Hard to understand or do:

The test included several *complex* math problems.

   difficult

Needing much effort; not easy:

Learning a new language can be *difficult*.

   intricate

Very involved and complicated:

It was hard to untie the *intricate* knot.

For more choices see the entry for HARD.
Antonyms: See the entry for EASY.

---

conceal *verb*

To keep out of sight; hide:

Melissa **concealed** her diary in a drawer.
Jose was so pleased he couldn't **conceal** his smile.

   camouflage

To change the appearance of something in order to hide it:

A chameleon *camouflages* itself by changing its skin color to match its surroundings.

   cloak

To conceal or cover up:

He *cloaked* his jealousy in a smile of friendship.

   obscure

To conceal; hide:

Thick clouds *obscured* the moon last night.

   veil

To cover or hide with a veil or something like a veil:

He *veiled* his snide insults with the claim that he was just trying to be helpful.
In many places women *veil* their faces when they go outside of their homes.

For more choices see the entry for HIDE.
Antonyms: See the entries for SHOW and REVEAL.

---

confuse *verb*

To mix up or cause someone to misunderstand:

People often **confuse** Morgan for Julia, even though they aren't related.
Kyle was **confused** by the instructions for the test.

   bewilder

To confuse or mix up:

The math problem *bewildered* me.

   mystify

To confuse or puzzle:

We were all *mystified* by the magician's tricks.

   puzzle

To confuse or be hard to understand:

How the cat got out *puzzled* us.

conserve *verb* — To keep and protect from harm, loss, or change:
We try to **conserve** energy by shutting off lights when no one is in the room.
Many people are concerned about **conserving** natural resources.

maintain — To take care of:
It takes a large number of gardeners to maintain our parks.

preserve — To keep from being lost or damaged:
The dry desert air of Egypt has preserved mummies for thousands of years.
Creating National Parks is one way to preserve natural places.
We have laws that preserve our rights.

For more choices see the entries for DEFEND and PROTECT.

consider *verb* — To think carefully about before deciding:
You need to **consider** what is best for you.
Beth **considered** going outside but decided it was too cold.

contemplate — To think about for a long time:
Jackson contemplated the painting carefully before deciding what he thought of it.

evaluate — To judge or discover the value of:
A test will be given each year to evaluate how well each student is performing.

weigh — To think about and examine carefully:
We weighed our chances of winning the game.

For more choices see the entry for THINK.

contain *verb* — To have within itself:
A dictionary **contains** words and their meanings.
Courtney couldn't **contain** her laughter.

have — To consist of; contain:
A week has seven days.

hold — To contain:
This bottle holds two liters.

include — To have as part of the whole; contain:
No batteries were included with the toy.
The show included an intermission.

contest *noun* — A game or race that people try to win:
Our team won the soccer **contest**.
Jerry won the spelling **contest**.

competition — A contest:
Pat took first place in the diving competition.

meet — A meeting or contest:
Our whole school is excited about our team's chances for winning the track meet.

tournament — A series of contests between two or more people or teams:
The tennis tournament will last three days.

For more choices see the entry for GAME.

continual
adjective

Happening again and again; never stopping:

*The **continual** banging from upstairs kept her awake.*
*The **continual** movement of the waves carried the sand out to sea.*

constant

Not changing; continuing:

*Nobody in the room could talk with the **constant** sound of drilling coming from outside.*

continuous

Going on without stopping:

*The **continuous** ticking of the clock began to bother me.*

incessant

Going on without stopping:

*The **incessant** buzz of crickets kept us up all night.*

perpetual

Continuing without stopping:

*The **perpetual** flow of the ocean tides is controlled by the gravity of the sun and moon.*

---

continue *verb*

To keep happening, being, doing; to go on without stopping:

*The game **continued** until the tie was broken.*
*Please **continue** with your story.*

endure

To continue; last:

*The great ideal of freedom will **endure** forever.*

go on

To continue; proceed:

*The road seemed to **go on** forever.*
*The meeting **went on** until late at night.*

last

To go on; continue:

*The class will **last** two hours.*

For more choices see the entry for WAIT.

---

contradict *verb*

To say the opposite; to disagree:

*Sierra's version of the accident **contradicted** what I had heard from Jenny.*
*Although they seem to **contradict** each other, both stories are true.*

deny

To say something is not true:

*The suspect **denied** being in the neighborhood at the time of the crime.*

dispute

To argue against; disagree:

*The coach **disputed** the referee's decision.*

refute

To show an argument is false:

*The facts **refuted** every point he made.*

For more choices see the entries for ARGUE, DISAGREE, and DISCUSS.

---

control *verb*

To command or regulate by using power or authority:

*She **controlled** the kite by jerking the string.*
*Nobody can **control** the weather.*

command

To have power over:

*An admiral **commands** ships in the navy.*

direct

To manage or control:

*A police officer **directs** traffic by our school.*
*A conductor **directed** the orchestra.*

manage

To direct or control:

*The foreman **manages** the workers at the plant.*

supervise

To watch over and direct:

*Some parents **supervised** the decorating of the gym for the dance.*

correct *verb* | To mark mistakes in; change to make right: | *Our teacher **corrected** our tests.*

adjust | To change to correct or improve: | *My father had a mechanic **adjust** the brakes on our car.*
*My grade was **adjusted** after I earned extra credit.*

revise | To correct or make better: | *Thomas **revised** a confusing paragraph in his story.*
*I **revised** my opinion when more facts came to light.*

For more choices see the entries for CHANGE and FIX.

---

country *noun* | An area of land with its own borders and government: | *Canada, Mexico, and the United States are **countries** in North America.*
*You often need a passport to travel from one **country** to another.*

nation | A group of people living together under one government: | *The leaders of all the **nations** gathered for a meeting on the environment.*

province | An area of a country that has its own government: | *A **province** is similar to a state.*
*Canada has ten **provinces**.*

state | A group of people living under one government: | *A **state** is often part of a nation.*
*The United States has fifty **states**.*

WORD BANK

COUNTRIES are often defined by the kind of government they have. Some kinds of **countries** are:

colony	dictatorship	federation	realm
commonwealth	dominion	kingdom	republic
democracy	empire	monarchy	territory

---

courage *noun* | The strength to overcome fear and face danger: | *The police officer was decorated for her **courage**.*
*Matthew had to summon up his **courage** to make a speech in front of the whole school.*

bravery | The ability to face danger or pain without being overcome by fear: | *The survivors owed their lives to the **bravery** of the firefighters.*

heroism | Great bravery; daring: | *The stories of King Arthur and his knights include many tales of **heroism**.*

valor | Bravery; courage: | *Medals are awarded to soldiers for acts of great **valor**.*

crash ◆◆ crime

crash *verb*	To make a sudden loud noise or to collide violently:	*The musician **crashed** the cymbals together.* *I don't want to **crash** my scooter into a tree.*
bump	To strike or knock suddenly:	*My bicycle **bumped** against a tree, but luckily it wasn't damaged.*
collide	To crash against each other:	*Two planes almost **collided** in mid-air.*
smash	To hit with a hard blow:	*A big truck **smashed** into a billboard next to the highway and knocked it down.*

For more choices see the entries for HIT and KNOCK.

---

crawl *verb*	To move very slowly:	*Babies **crawl** on their hands and knees before they begin to walk.* *The cars **crawled** along in heavy traffic.* *Worms were **crawling** through the rich soil.*
creep	To move slowly and quietly:	*The cat **crept** toward the robin's nest.* *Don't **creep** up behind me like that!*
inch	To move very slowly:	*We **inched** our way through the narrow passage.*

---

crazy *adjective*	Foolish; insane:	*The boys were acting **crazy** and put pepper on our ice cream.* *They had the **crazy** idea that we thought they were funny.*
fanatic	Too devoted or enthusiastic:	*He is a **fanatic** video game player and can't seem to talk about anything else.*
insane	Very foolish; crazy; not sane:	*She had an **insane** idea that she could wait until the last minute to start and still get her term paper done.* *Doctors said he was legally **insane**.*
mad	Crazy; insane:	*The story is about a **mad** scientist who turned out to be right.*

---

crime *noun*	Anything against the law:	*Robbery is a **crime**.* *The detective solved the **crime** after examining the clues.*
offense	The act of breaking the law or a rule:	*The robbers will be punished for their **offense**.*
violation	Failure to obey a law:	*Jaywalking is considered a **violation** of the law in many places.*

crowd *noun* — A large number of people gathered together: *There was a big **crowd** at the opening of the movie. The **crowd** cheered the home team.*

horde — A very large group that is close together: *A **horde** of ants ruined our picnic.*

mob — A large number of people: *Sometimes the people in a **mob** are so angry that they break the law or cause damage.*

multitude — A great number of people or things: *A **multitude** gathered for an outdoor music festival.*

swarm — A large group of people or animals: *A **swarm** of bees left their hive to form a new colony. A **swarm** of tourists went to the beach last weekend.*

throng — A large number of people: *A **throng** of people watched the parade.*

cruel *adjective* — Willing to cause pain or suffering: *The old man was **cruel** to his dog. She said **cruel** things about my clothing.*

heartless — Unkind and cruel; without kindness or sympathy: *Your **heartless** remarks made her cry.*

malicious — Feeling or showing a desire to cause harm or pain: *That gossip is nothing more than a **malicious** lie.*

ruthless — Not having pity or mercy: *The **ruthless** dictator forced his people to work until they dropped.*

unfeeling — Hardhearted; cruel: *He was a cold, **unfeeling** person.*

unkind — Not kind; cruel: *I resent your **unkind** remarks about my friends.*

For more choices see the entries for FIERCE, MEAN, and VICIOUS.

cry *verb* — To shed tears when sad: *The movie made Julia **cry**. I **cried** after I fell and hit my elbow.*

howl — To make a loud, wailing cry: *We **howled** like wolves at the moon, and the neighbor's dog joined in.*

sob — To cry with short gasps: *Tina **sobbed** as she told us about the accident.*

wail — To cry loudly for a long time: *The sick child **wailed**.*

weep — To show grief, joy, or other strong emotions by crying: *James began to **weep** every time he thought of his grandmother.*

Antonyms: See the entry for LAUGH.

curious *adjective* — Eager to learn new or strange things: *Ethan was **curious** about the old house.*

inquisitive — Eager to know: *An **inquisitive** student asks many questions.*

interested — Having a desire to learn about something: *Kim is **interested** in the life of Queen Elizabeth.*

 **cut**

cut *verb*	To divide, pierce, open, or take away a part with something sharp:	*She cut the birthday cake into equal pieces.* *They cut the rope and let the horse go.*
carve	To cut something into a shape:	*He carved an eagle out of a tree stump.*
chop	To cut with a quick blow:	*She used an ax to chop down the tree and then chopped off the branches with a hatchet.*
slice	To cut into thin, flat pieces:	*I sliced the bread.*

WORDS from Words

CUT is often combined with other words to form expressions that have special meanings. These expressions also have synonyms. *For example:*

to cut back means to shorten: *We cut back the trees so the grass could grow.* A useful synonym is **prune**.

to cut down means to remove extra material: *My mother cut down the draperies to make curtains.* Useful synonyms are **reduce** and **decrease**.

to cut off means to separate from others: *The mountain climber was cut off from his base camp by an avalanche.* Useful synonyms are **detach** and **separate**. As a noun, **cut off** can also mean a shortcut: *We took the cut off and saved ten minutes of traveling time.*

to cut out means to remove or shape by cutting: *They cut out decorations for the party.* Useful synonyms are **clip**, **crop**, and **trim**.

to cut up means to cut into pieces: *Rachel cut up the meat and vegetables for the stew.* Useful synonyms are **chop** and **dice**. **To cut up** also means to behave in a playful, silly, or comic way: *The boys cut up during recess.* Useful synonyms are **clown around**, **fool around**, and **joke**.

damp *adjective*   A little wet: *The weather in November was **damp** and chilly.*
*Jordan wiped mud off his bicycle with a **damp** cloth.*

   clammy   Cold and damp: *The rocks in the cave were clammy with ocean spray.*
His hands were clammy with nervous sweat.

   moist   Slightly wet; damp: *You can wipe up the spilled syrup with a moist cloth.*

   wet   Covered, soaked, or moist with water or other liquid: *The sun will dry our wet bathing suits.*
The ground was wet from the rain.
There was a wet spot on the rug where I spilled soda.

For more choices see the entry for WET.
Antonyms: See the entry for DRY.

---

danger *noun*   The chance that something might cause harm or injury: *Heavy rains can create a **danger** of flooding.*
*Signs warned of **danger** near the icy pond.*

   hazard   Something that can cause harm: *Mountain lions and grizzly bears were among the hazards faced by the pioneers in the West.*

   peril   Something dangerous: *Drive on icy roads at your own peril.*

   threat   A person or thing that may cause harm: *Pollution is a threat to our health.*

---

dangerous *adjective*   Likely to cause something bad to happen: *The steep mountain road had several **dangerous** curves.*
*Crossing a street without looking both ways is **dangerous**.*

   hazardous   Likely to cause injury: *Smoking is hazardous to your health.*

   risky   Harmful or dangerous: *Skydiving is a risky sport.*

   unsafe   Dangerous: *It is unsafe to skate on thin ice.*

For more choices see the entry for DEADLY.
Antonyms: See the entry for SAFE.

D dare ◦◦ data

dare *verb*	To challenge somebody to do something as a test of courage or ability:	*Danielle **dared** Olivia to play checkers with her.* *I didn't **dare** ask my mother to let me go out until I cleaned my room.*
challenge	To ask to take part in a contest or fight:	*We **challenged** the other team to a tug-of-war.*
defy	To challenge someone to something difficult:	*I **defy** you to swim across the lake.*
provoke	To stir up; excite:	*Don't let her insults **provoke** you.* *The speaker **provoked** the crowd to march on city hall.*

daring *adjective*	Courage or boldness:	*The explorer told us about her **daring** exploits in the Amazon jungle.* *The lifeguards made a **daring** rescue in the rough surf.*
adventurous	Willing to take risks to have unusual experiences:	*The first people to fly airplanes were **adventurous**.* *The **adventurous** hikers took a new trail.*
fearless	Feeling or showing no fear:	*The **fearless** woman rode a killer whale in the show.*
gallant	Good and brave:	*The **gallant** knight rescued the damsel from the dragon.*

For more choices see the entry for BRAVE.
Antonyms: See the entries for AFRAID and SHY.

dark *adjective*	Having little or no light:	*The night was so **dark** I couldn't see where to step.* *Zachary used his flashlight to light up the **dark** room.*
gloomy	In shadow or dark:	*The deep forest is **gloomy** even on a sunny day.*
murky	Dark and gloomy:	*Jesse couldn't see any fish in the **murky** water.*
unlit	Having little or no light:	*The **unlit** room was nearly dark after sunset.*

For more choices see the entry for DIM.
Antonyms: See the entry for BRIGHT.

data *noun*	Individual facts or figures:	*The government collects **data** on the weather.* *The **data** Alyssa found on the Web seem to be wrong.*
facts	Things that are known to be true or real:	*The **facts** tell us that the earth travels around the sun.*
figures	An amount given in numbers:	*New **figures** for the size of the population are announced every ten years.*

For more choices see the entries for INFORMATION and KNOWLEDGE.

Word Alert

DATA is always a plural when describing facts and figures. The rarely used singular of **data** is datum.

dead *adjective* — No longer living or active: *The plant was **dead** because I forgot to water it. Our phone went **dead** during the thunderstorm. When our opponents scored a last-minute goal, our hopes for a win were **dead**.*

    deceased — Dead: *The high school is named after a deceased president.*

    expired — Coming to an end: *You need to renew your expired magazine subscription.*

    lifeless — Not having life: *Mercury is a lifeless planet. The celebration was dull and lifeless.*

deadly *adjective* — Likely to cause death: *Some mushrooms contain **deadly** poison. A rattlesnake's bite can be **deadly**.*

    fatal — Causing death: *There was a fatal accident last night. Taking the wrong medicine can be fatal.*

    mortal — Causing death: *King Arthur suffered a mortal wound during his last battle.*

    toxic — Poisonous and likely to cause sickness or death: *Those factories no longer dump toxic chemicals into the river.*

For more choices see the entry for DANGEROUS.
Antonyms: See the entry for SAFE.

deceive *verb* — To make someone believe something that is not true: *The magician **deceived** us into thinking he could read our thoughts. We were **deceived** by the false advertising.*

    cheat — To act dishonestly or get something dishonestly: *He tried to cheat on the exam but got caught. When you cheat, you don't learn.*

    fool — To trick: *The teacher tried to fool us with a trick question. Their story about buried gold didn't fool us for a minute.*

    mislead — To lead in the wrong direction: *The instructions misled us on how long the project would take.*

    trick — To fool or cheat with a trick: *The child tried to trick us into believing his dog was vicious even though it was wagging its tail.*

decide *verb* — To make up one's mind or settle a question: *You must **decide** which movie you want to see. The teacher **decided** which answer was right.*

    conclude — To decide after thinking: *The judge concluded that no crime had been committed.*

    determine — To decide or settle definitely: *Shelby determined the name of the butterfly by looking it up in a nature guide.*

    resolve — To make up one's mind: *Jonathan resolved to exercise more. The problem was resolved by holding a vote.*

    settle — To agree about something; decide: *They settled their argument by flipping a coin.*

declare *verb* | To say strongly and firmly: | Megan **declared** she was running for class president.
The judge **declared** the accused innocent.

   assert | To state in a positive way: | Christina asserted that her answer was correct.

   claim | To say that something is true: | People once claimed that the world is flat.

   state | To show or explain in words: | We were asked to state the reasons for the Revolutionary War on the test.

---

decorate *verb* | To make something beautiful: | They **decorate** their house every year for the holidays.
My room is **decorated** with pictures of my favorite singers.

   adorn | To add something beautiful to; decorate: | The ballroom was adorned with flowers.

   ornament | To decorate with ornaments: | The tree was ornamented with oranges and cranberries.

   trim | To add decorations to: | Her party dress was trimmed with white lace.

---

decrease *verb* | To make or become less: | The number of birds **decreased** when a cat appeared in the neighborhood.
The temperature **decreases** after the sun sets.

   diminish | To become or make smaller: | Our water supply diminishes during summer.

   lessen | To make or become less: | The pain in my legs lessened as I exercised.

   reduce | To make or become smaller or less: | The store reduced prices.

---

defeat *verb* | To win a victory over: | Our team **defeated** our biggest rival.
Sarah always **defeats** me in spelling bees.

   beat | To do better than; defeat: | Michael beat all the other swimmers and won a trophy.

   conquer | To overcome; defeat: | The Greeks conquered the Trojans by tricking them.
We conquered our fears.

   subdue | To defeat; conquer; bring under control: | The soldiers subdued the enemy.

---

defend *verb* | To protect against attack or danger: | The military **defends** the country.
We **defended** our goal and the other team never scored.

   guard | To keep safe from harm or danger: | A watchdog guards the store at night.
Toothpaste helps guard against tooth decay.

   safeguard | To protect or guard: | Vaccines safeguard against disease.
Laws safeguard our rights.

   shield | To defend and protect: | Carol used sunglasses to shield her eyes from the glare.
I shielded my eyes with my hand.

For more choices see the entry for PROTECT.
Antonyms: See the entry for ATTACK.

delay *verb*   To put off to a later time: *The game was **delayed** because of rain.*
*If I **delay**, I'll miss my ride.*

    put off   To delay or postpone: *Don't put off going to the dentist.*

    suspend   To stop for a time: *We suspended our mail delivery while we were away.*

    tarry   To wait; delay: *They tarried too long at the bookstore
and almost missed their bus.*

For more choices see the entries for HESITATE and PAUSE.

---

delicate *adjective*   Easily damaged; finely made: *Be careful when you handle **delicate** objects.*
*A **delicate** spider's web glistened with raindrops.*

    dainty   Small and easily harmed: *The dainty flower buds broke off in the wind.*

    flimsy   Without strength; light and thin; frail: *The winter wind blew right through my flimsy jacket.*

    frail   Lacking in strength: *When I had the flu, I was too frail to play.*

For more choices see the entries for FRAGILE and WEAK.
Antonyms: See the entry for TOUGH.

---

delicious *adjective*   Pleasing to taste or smell: *A **delicious** aroma came from the kitchen.*

    appetizing   Pleasing or stimulating: *The cake looked very appetizing.*

    good   Nice and pleasant: *That was a good dinner.*

    tasty   Pleasing to the sense of taste: *We ended our meal with a tasty dessert.*

---

delight *noun*   Great pleasure or joy: *Gerald beamed with **delight** at the surprise gift.*
*Cole took great **delight** in his coin collection.*

    glee   Joy or delight: *We all laughed with glee when the class party
was announced.*

    happiness   The condition of being glad or content: *The children were filled with happiness
when the clowns appeared.*

    joy   A strong feeling of happiness or delight: *There was great joy in the house when our guests arrived.*
Our puppy jumps for joy when we take him outdoors.

    thrill   A sudden feeling of pleasure or excitement: *It was a thrill for Mark to see his favorite
football star in person.*

For more choices see the entry for PLEASURE.
Antonyms: See the entries for SADNESS and SUFFERING.

dense *adjective* | Packed closely together: | The woods were so **dense** we lost the trail.
A **dense** fog kept the planes from landing.

solid | Very strong, hard, and dense: | There is a solid concrete wall in back of our school.

thick | Growing or being close together: | It was difficult to make our way through the thick forest.

tight | Packed or put together firmly: | Getting all those clothes into one suitcase will be a tight fit.

For more choices see the entry for THICK.
Antonyms: See the entries for NARROW and THIN.

---

descend *verb* | To come from an earlier source or ancestor: | Our Chihuahua **descended** from a champion in Mexico.
Her family **descends** from Dutch settlers in New York.

come from | To originate from a source: | Where did you come from?
Seth came from Arizona.

derive | To come from a source: | Sugar is derived from sugar cane.
Paul derives much pleasure from reading.

originate | To come into being; start: | This television show originated in New York.

Word Alert

DESCEND also means to move from a higher place to a lower one: *The climbers descended the mountain more quickly than they climbed it.* Synonyms for this meaning of **descend** can be found at the entries for **DIVE** and **DROP**.

---

describe *verb* | To picture something in words: | She **described** her victory in vivid detail.
Sometimes it is difficult to **describe** a painting.

depict | To describe in words or pictures: | This story depicts the lives of the early pioneers.
The artist depicted the ocean waves in his painting.

narrate | To tell or relate in detail; to provide commentary: | Joseph narrated the story while Frank acted it out.
The reporter narrated a nature program about walruses.

picture | To give a description of: | The author pictured life in the distant future.

For more choices see the entries for REPORT and TELL.

deserve *verb* | To have a right to; to be worthy of: | *He **deserved** everything he got.* *The whole class **deserves** congratulations for their excellent performance.*

earn | To deserve or win because of hard work and good behavior: | *Mariah earned a place on the team by practicing hard.*

merit | To deserve; be worthy of: | *Your work this year merits a good grade.*

rate | To consider; regard: | *This school is rated one of the best in the state.*

---

desire *noun* | A longing; wish: | *I have a **desire** to see new places.* *Jane's **desire** is to have a big birthday party.*

longing | A feeling of strong desire; yearning: | *The child had a longing to ride a pony.* *I had a strong longing for home when I was away at camp.*

yen | A strong desire; longing: | *I have a yen for lemonade on hot days.* *She had a yen to travel.*

For more choices see the entry for WISH.

---

destroy *verb* | To damage or smash beyond repair: | *I **destroyed** my running shoes training for the race.* *In the movie, the aliens **destroyed** a whole city with powerful rays.*

demolish | To tear down or destroy: | *They plan to demolish some old buildings to make way for a new stadium.*

ruin | To harm or damage greatly: | *An earthquake ruined this town, but it was rebuilt.*

wreck | To destroy or ruin: | *A steel ball was used to wreck the brick buildings.* *The owner's mistakes wrecked his business.*

For more choices see the entry for BREAK.
Antonyms: See the entries for BUILD and MAKE[1].

---

determined *adjective* | Sticking firmly to a purpose: | *The **determined** boy was going to finish the job, no matter how long it took.* *The **determined** look on her face showed that she had made up her mind.*

firm | Not changing; staying the same: | *They had a firm belief that they were doing the right thing.*

intent | Having the mind firmly fixed on something: | *They were intent on reaching home.*

purposeful | Having determination: | *Tristan hurried about in a purposeful way.*

D die ◗ dim

die *verb*	To stop living; to come to an end:	Many plants may **die** because of the drought. Several animals **died** in the flood. The fire **died**, and the room was dark.
expire	To come to the end; die:	Your subscription to your favorite magazine *expires* next month. A fish will *expire* if it is left out of water for any length of time.
pass away **or** pass on	To die:	My grandparents *passed away* several years ago. The famous artist *passed on* at the end of last month.
perish	To be destroyed:	The dinosaurs *perished* millions of years ago.

Antonyms: See the entry for LIVE.

different *adjective*	Not alike, not the same:	The two boys had **different** interests but were still friends. A house is **different** from an apartment.
distinct	Not the same:	The votes were sorted into three *distinct* piles.
diverse	Not all the same:	Students in our school come from *diverse* backgrounds.
special	Different from others, not ordinary:	You need *special* training to become a doctor. Birthdays are *special* occasions.
unlike	Not the same:	Her bicycle is *unlike* any that I have seen.
various	Different from one another:	There are *various* art classes available at our school.

For more choices see the entry for UNUSUAL.
Antonyms: See the entries for COMMON, NORMAL, and USUAL.

dim *adjective*	Having or giving little light:	Trying to read in **dim** light might strain your eyes. Michelle could only see a **dim** outline of a building in the thick fog. Only a single **dim** lightbulb lit the dark hallway.
faint	Not clear or strong:	We saw a *faint* light in the woods. The kitten gave a *faint* cry.
hazy	Not clear:	Without the map they had only a *hazy* idea of where they were. The sky was *hazy* because of smog.
obscure	Not clearly seen, felt, or heard:	There was an *obscure* shape in each of the photos that no one could identify.

For more choices see the entry for DARK.

dirt *noun*   Loose earth or soil: *They piled **dirt** next to the construction site.*
*My dog loves to dig in the **dirt**.*

    dust   Tiny pieces of earth, dirt, or other matter: *A cloud of dust rose up behind our car as we traveled down the dirt road.*
The dust in the air made me sneeze.

    earth   Soil; dirt: *We planted seeds in the earth.*

    ground   The part of the earth that is solid; soil; land: *Scientists dug into the ground looking for dinosaur bones.*

    mud   Soft, wet, sticky earth or dirt: *There was a lot of mud in the streets after the heavy rain.*
We were careful not to track mud into the house.

    soil   The top part of the ground in which plants grow; dirt: *The soil is sandy where we live.*
We put soil in pots for planting flowers.

---

dirty *adjective*   Not clean; covered with dirt: *After lunch, they washed their **dirty** dishes.*
*The puppy rolled in the mud and got **dirty**.*

    dingy   Having a dirty and dull appearance: *The dingy curtains made the room dark.*

    filthy   Extremely dirty; foul: *The water was so filthy no one wanted to swim.*

    grimy   Covered with dirt: *My dog was grimy after digging in the woods.*

    soiled   Dirty: *My gym clothes were soiled after practice.*

For more choices see the entries for MESSY **and** UNTIDY.
Antonyms: See the entry for CLEAN.

---

dirty *verb*   To soil or make dirty: *Be careful not to **dirty** your white shirt.*
*Stirring up the river bottom **dirtied** the water.*

    contaminate   To make dirty; pollute: *Last summer, dangerous bacteria contaminated our beaches and we couldn't go swimming.*

    foul   To make dirty: *The factory fouled the lake by pumping waste into it.*

    pollute   To make dirty or impure: *Garbage from a nearby dump polluted the beach.*

    soil   To make or become dirty: *I soiled my uniform when I played soccer.*

disadvantage
noun
Something that makes it harder to succeed:
You may find not knowing how to use a computer a **disadvantage**.
One **disadvantage** of living in the city is the noise.

drawback
A thing that makes something more difficult or unpleasant:
The major drawback of the new library is how much farther it is from school than the old one.

handicap
Anything that makes it harder for a person to do well or get ahead:
Her major handicap was not being able to read the instructions without her glasses.

shortcoming
A fault, defect, or weakness, often in behavior or character:
His rudeness is a serious shortcoming.

weakness
A weak point; flaw:
One of my weaknesses is poor handwriting.

For more choices see the entries for FAULT and MISTAKE.

---

disagree *verb*
To differ in opinion:
The police were confused because the two witnesses **disagreed** about what happened.
She **disagrees** with me about sports, but we like the same movies.

differ
To have a different opinion:
My sisters and I differ about where to go for vacation.

dissent
To differ in opinion; disagree:
The majority of the court agreed to a decision, but two judges dissented.

oppose
To be against; resist:
Most voters opposed raising taxes.

For more choices see the entries for ARGUE, CONTRADICT, and DISCUSS.

---

disapprove *verb*
To have a strong feeling against:
People who want to stay healthy **disapprove** of smoking.
The neighbors **disapproved** of the noise.

condemn
To express strong opposition to:
Most people condemn cruelty to animals.

denounce
To speak against:
The candidate denounced high taxes.

object to
To oppose:
Our neighbors object to loud music after midnight.

For more choices see the entries for BLAME and OBJECT.

disaster *noun* — An event that causes much suffering or loss: *The **disaster** that devastated the city was caused by an earthquake.* *The party was a **disaster** because the band didn't show up.*

    accident — A sad event in which people are hurt or property is damaged: *The sudden thunderstorm caused several traffic **accidents**.*

    calamity — A disaster causing great pain and sorrow: *The epidemic was a great **calamity**.*

    catastrophe — A great disaster: *The eruption of the volcano was the worst **catastrophe** of the decade.*

    misfortune — An unlucky event: *Losing their car in the flood was a great **misfortune**.*

---

discourage *verb* — To cause one to lose courage, hope, or confidence: *Losing the first two games **discouraged** our team.* *The staff **discourages** talking in the library.*

    deter — To discourage from doing something: *The heavy snow **deterred** us from going outside.*

Antonyms: See the entries for ENCOURAGE, PERSUADE, and URGE.

---

discover *verb* — To see or find for the first time: *Astronomers have **discovered** several planets beyond our solar system.* *Erin **discovered** several errors in my math homework.*

    detect — To find out or notice: *Brendan **detected** something suspicious in the bushes.* *If you **detect** smoke, call the fire department.*

    identify — To find out what a thing is: *They **identified** the thief by his fingerprints.* *Can you **identify** the use for this strange object?*

    unearth — To search for or find: *My brother **unearthed** some old photos in a trunk.*

For more choices see the entries for FIND and NOTICE.

---

discuss *verb* — To talk over; speak about: *The whole class **discussed** the upcoming election.* *After **discussing** what to do next with several friends, Andrea still couldn't make up her mind.*

    confer — To meet and talk together: *The judges **conferred** before voting on the winner.*

    debate — To argue or discuss at a meeting: *The class **debated** what our mascot should be.*

    talk about — To discuss: *They **talked about** the problem and finally came up with a solution.*

For more choices see the entries for ARGUE, CONTRADICT, and DISAGREE.

D dishonest ◆ dive

dishonest
adjective | Not fair or honest: | *It is **dishonest** to lie or cheat.*
*The **dishonest** advertisement made the boring movie sound exciting.*

deceitful	Lying or cheating:	*The deceitful boy was caught cheating on a test.*
devious	Sneaky; untrustworthy:	*The criminal came up with a devious plan to cheat the bank.*
untruthful	Not telling the truth:	*Her untruthful answers only got her into more trouble.*

disobey *verb* | To refuse or fail to obey: | *The driver **disobeyed** the stop sign and almost caused an accident.*
*If you **disobey** the teacher, you will have to stay after school.*

break	To fail to obey or fulfill:	*Don't break the rules.*
ignore	To not pay attention to:	*She ignored the rumors about her friend.*
violate	To fail to obey or keep:	*The driver violated the law by going through a red light.*

disorder *noun* | Lack of order; confusion: | *Our classroom was in complete **disorder** after the party.*
*A **disorder** broke out after a soccer game.*

chaos	Complete confusion; great disorder:	*The flood left the roads in chaos.*
confusion	The condition of being mixed up:	*In my confusion I turned the wrong way.*
turmoil	Great confusion or disorder:	*My shoes were misplaced in the turmoil of our move.*

disrupt *verb* | To break up or break apart: | *The storm **disrupted** the electricity, and the lights went out.*
*The crowd **disrupted** the speech with loud applause.*

| **disturb** | To break in on: | *The loud noise disturbed the class.* |
| **interrupt** | To break in upon conversation, rest, or work, or stop a person who is speaking or acting: | *Our discussion was interrupted by a loud noise from the street.*
The announcer interrupted the program with a news bulletin. |
| **upset** | To interfere with: | *The sudden rainstorm upset our plans for a picnic.* |

dive *verb* | To plunge downward at a steep angle: | *They **dove** into the water and swam for shore.*
*The children watched the acrobats **dive** through the air.*

| **leap** | To jump: | *The skydiver was ready to leap from the plane.*
The crowd leaped to its feet. |
| **plunge** | To dive or fall suddenly: | *When the string broke, my kite plunged to the ground.* |
| **swoop** | To rush down suddenly: | *A bird swooped down out of nowhere.* |

For more choices see the entries for DROP and JUMP.

divide *verb* | To separate into parts, pieces, or groups: | *The class was **divided** into groups for the history project.*
*My mother **divided** my birthday cake equally among our guests.*

separate | To place or keep apart; divide: | *We separated the jelly beans by color.*
A fence separates the school playground from the street.

split | To break apart or divide into parts or layers: | *We split a sandwich because neither of us was very hungry.*
The seam of my jacket split.

Antonyms: See the entries for JOIN and MIX.

---

do *verb* | To carry out an action: | *When you are **done** with your homework, let's **do** something fun.*
*Richard **does** everything carefully.*

accomplish | To do something successfully: | *We accomplished more work than we expected.*

achieve | To do or carry out successfully: | *We achieved our goal.*

carry out | To do; complete: | *We carried out our plan perfectly.*

execute | To do what has been ordered: | *The soldier executed the command.*

For more choices see the entries for ACT and FINISH.

WORDS from Words

DO is often combined with other words to form expressions that have special meanings. These expressions also have synonyms. *For example:*

to do away with means to put an end to: *The Thirteenth Amendment to the Constitution **did away with** slavery. The new principal plans **to do away with** holding weekly assemblies.* Useful synonyms are **abolish**, **eliminate**, and **end**.

to make do means to manage, get along: *We can **make do** with what we have. The pioneers **made do** with what they could carry in a wagon.* Useful synonyms are **continue**, **get by**, and **survive**.

to overdo means to do or use too much; carry too far: *The actor's makeup was so **overdone** it looked silly instead of frightening. I'm tired today because I **overdid** it yesterday.* Useful synonyms are **exaggerate** and **overwork**. **To overdo** can also mean to cook too much: *My steak was **overdone**.*

dog *noun* — An animal with four legs that makes a barking sound: — *My dog sleeps all day, unless there is a cat around. Dogs are related to wolves and coyotes.*

canine — A member of the dog family: — *Retrievers and Labradors are canines often trained to assist the blind.*

hound — A dog trained to hunt: — *Beagles and Dalmatians are hounds.*

mutt — A dog that is a mixture of breeds: — *We were excited when we picked out a mutt at the shelter.*

puppy — A young dog: — *Our puppy is clumsy but lovable. Our dog had five puppies.*

WORD BANK

Sometimes you can make things clearer or more interesting for your reader by naming the particular **DOG** you mean. There are over a hundred breeds of **dogs**, but some common ones are:

bloodhound	dachshund	greyhound	poodle
bulldog	dingo	husky	pug
Chihuahua	Doberman pinscher	Irish setter	Shetland sheepdog
cocker spaniel	fox terrier	Labrador retriever	St. Bernard
collie	German shepherd	Pekingese	terrier
corgi	Great Dane	pointer	wolfhound

door *noun* — A movable barrier used to open or close an entrance to something: — *The open door let in the cold wind. Henry slipped a note under the closed door.*

entrance — The place where one enters: — *They took our tickets at the entrance to the theater. The entrance was marked with a large arrow.*

entry — A place through which one enters: — *The entry led through a door to a long hallway.*

exit — The way out: — *We left by the side exit.*

gateway — The way to get somewhere or do something: — *Education is the gateway to success.*

doubt *verb* — To be uncertain about something; not to trust fully: — Casey **doubted** she could finish the work, but she kept on anyway.
The weatherman **doubted** that the storm would hit our town.

   distrust — To not trust someone or something: — I *distrust* her motives for being unusually nice.

   question — To ask questions about: — The police *questioned* the witnesses about the accident.

   suspect — To think that something is possible or true: — We *suspected* that the rain had delayed our friends.

---

doubtful *adjective* — Not sure or certain: — The outcome of the game was **doubtful** because the teams were so evenly matched.
It's **doubtful** that the project can be finished on time.

   impossible — Not able to happen: — Building a new house seemed like an *impossible* dream.

   questionable — Open to question: — It is *questionable* whether it will rain tomorrow.

   unlikely — Not likely: — Winning a sweepstakes is an *unlikely* event.

For more choices see the entries for UNBELIEVABLE **and** UNCERTAIN.
Antonyms: See the entry for TRUE.

---

down *adverb* — From a higher to a lower place or degree; in a lower place or condition: — We climbed **down** from the roof.
Prices went **down** for the sale.
I tripped and fell **down**.

   below — In or to a lower place: — Satellites watch the weather *below*.

   beneath — In a lower place; below: — Apples from the tree lay on the grass *beneath*.

   downward — From a higher to a lower place: — The road ran *downward* to the valley.

   under — In or into a lower position: — I jumped into the waves and dove *under*.

Antonyms: See the entry for UP.

---

drink *verb* — To swallow a liquid: — I **drink** milk at every meal.
They **drank** soft drinks at the party.

   gulp — To swallow quickly, greedily, or in large amounts: — He *gulped* a glass of water and ran outside.

   sip — To drink little by little: — Elijah *sipped* the hot soup.

   swallow — To cause food or drink to pass from the mouth to the stomach: — I *swallowed* my drink too quickly.

drop *verb*	To fall to a lower position:	*I **dropped** a letter into the mailbox.* *The temperature may **drop** below freezing.*
descend	To move or cause to move from a higher place to a lower one:	*The stairs **descend** into the basement.* *The airplane **descended** from the sky.*
plummet	To drop suddenly:	*The skydiver **plummeted** toward the ground until he opened his parachute and floated safely to earth.*
sink	To go down or cause to go down below the surface:	*The canoe will **sink** if we don't repair it.* *The sun **sank** below the horizon.*

For more choices see the entries for DIVE and FALL.

WORDS from Words

DROP is often combined with other words to form expressions that have special meanings. These expressions also have synonyms. *For example:*

to drop in means to make an informal or unplanned visit: *Our neighbor **dropped in** just as we were sitting down to dinner. While we are running errands we can **drop in** on your aunt and see how she is doing.* Useful synonyms are **call** and **visit.**

to drop off means to deliver: *Please **drop off** this package at the post office. They **dropped** me **off** at my house.* Useful synonyms are **deliver, give,** and **transfer.**

dry *adjective*	Not wet or damp; free of moisture:	*Please bring me a **dry** towel.* *A desert has a very **dry** climate.*
arid	Dry as a result of having little rainfall:	*The Gobi Desert is an **arid** place.*
parched	Dried out by heat:	*It was so hot that my throat was **parched**.*
waterless	Having no water:	*The **waterless** desert stretched before us.*

Antonyms: See the entries for DAMP and WET.

dull *adjective*	Not interesting or exciting:	*The speech was so **dull**, I almost fell asleep.* *The **dull** book was made into an even **duller** movie.*
boring	Something that makes one tired or restless by being dull:	*The **boring** speech seemed to go on for hours.*
monotonous	Tiring or uninteresting because it does not change:	*The **monotonous** music put us to sleep.*
tiring	Something that makes one tired or weary:	*Sitting in the car during the long trip was very **tiring**.*
uninteresting	Not interesting:	*The **uninteresting** presentation made us restless.*

Antonyms: See the entry for INTERESTING.

dumb *adjective*   Not intelligent; stupid or unwise: *I made a really **dumb** mistake on my math test. It's **dumb** to speak before you think.*

    crazy   Foolish: *Jumping into the icy water was a crazy idea.*

    foolish   Without good sense; unwise: *We made foolish mistakes because we didn't listen carefully.*

    ridiculous   Very silly or foolish: *Kelly felt ridiculous when she couldn't remember the boy's name.*

For more choices see the entries for SILLY and STUPID.
Antonyms: See the entries for SMART and WISE.

---

duty *noun*   Something a person is supposed to do: *The **duties** of a nurse include checking the patient's blood pressure. It is your **duty** to take out the trash on Tuesday.*

    assignment   Something given out as a task: *Your history assignment is due tomorrow.*

    responsibility   A job or duty for which you are responsible: *Jade takes complete responsibility for caring for her cat.*

    task   A piece of work to be done: *Each student was assigned a different task for the project.*

For more choices see the entry for JOB.

---

dwindle *verb*   To become less or smaller: *The crowd **dwindled** away after the concert ended.*

    decrease   To make or become less: *He decreased the speed of his bicycle by dragging his feet. The amount of snow decreased as the day warmed up.*

    thin   To make or become smaller: *We have to thin the forest so young trees can grow.*

For more choices see the entry for SHRINK.
Antonyms: See the entries for EXPAND and GROW.

Ee

eager *adjective*   Wanting very much to do something: *The class was **eager** to go on a field trip.*
*Vanessa is **eager** to see her friends.*

   avid   Very eager or enthusiastic: *Colton is an **avid** baseball fan.*

   enthusiastic   Excited and interested in something; full of enthusiasm: *The **enthusiastic** fans cheered the team loudly.*

   keen   Full of enthusiasm; eager: *Angie is very **keen** on horses.*

---

early *adjective*   Before the usual time: *Patrick was **early** for his appointment.*
*It was **early** morning when they heard the news.*

   ahead   In front; in advance: *We planned our trip **ahead** of time.*

   before   In front of; ahead of: *We arrived at the theater **before** the movie started.*

   beforehand   Ahead of time: *We should have asked **beforehand** what time the show began.*

   in advance   Ahead of time: *We ordered our tickets in **advance**.*

---

earn *verb*   To gain through effort: *She **earned** all A's on her report card.*

   gain   To get or win: *You will **gain** experience working during the summer.*

   make   To earn: *He **made** millions on his invention.*

   win   To get by effort; gain: *A well-known writer is **winning** new fame as a photographer.*

For more choices see the entry for GET.

---

earth *noun*   The planet on which we live; dry land; ground: *The **earth** is the third planet from the sun.*
*Trees send their roots deep into the **earth**.*

   planet   A heavenly body that orbits a star such as our sun: *Earth is a **planet**.*

   world   The earth: *Bianca wants to sail around the **world**.*

Word Alert

EARTH sometimes means the ground or land: *My kite fell to* earth. Synonyms for this meaning can be found at the entry for **LAND**. **Earth** also means dirt or soil: *We planted flowers in the rich* earth. Synonyms for this meaning can be found at the entry for **DIRT**.

---

ease *verb*	To make free from trouble, pain, or hard work:	*The news that everyone was safe after the hurricane* **eased** *our worried minds.* *The soup* **eased** *my hunger pangs.*
calm	To make or become quiet or still:	*The music* calmed *my nerves.*
comfort	To ease the sorrow or pain of someone:	*My mother* comforted *me when I was worried about the dentist.*
soothe	To quiet, calm, or ease:	*The lotion* soothed *my sunburn.*

Antonyms: See the entry for INFURIATE.

WORDS from Words

EASE is often combined with other words to form expressions that have special meanings. These expressions also have synonyms. *For example:*

at ease means in a relaxed position: *We felt* **at ease** *at the party. I am always* **at ease** *with my parents.* Useful synonyms are **comfortable** and **relaxed**.

to ease into means to begin to do gradually: *I* **eased into** *my new schedule so I wouldn't make any mistakes.* A useful synonym is **begin slowly**.

to ease off means to relax or loosen up: *Joe* **eased off** *on the gas to slow the boat.* Useful synonyms are **loosen up**, **relax**, and **slacken**.

to ease up means to use, go, or stop slowly: *You better* **ease up** *on the potato chips or you'll spoil your dinner. Ease up on the gas pedal. We* **eased up** *to the parking space.* A useful synonym is **move slowly**.

---

easy *adjective*	Not hard to do:	*The spelling test was* **easy**. *Connor had an* **easy** *time with science.*
effortless	Not requiring hard work:	*He ran the race with* effortless *ease.* *Her graceful ice skating looked* effortless.
simple	Easy to understand or do:	*Learning to jump with a horse is not* simple.
uncomplicated	Not hard to understand or do:	*The directions for starting the computer were* uncomplicated.

Antonyms: See the entry for HARD.

eat *verb*	To chew on and swallow:	*I ate ice cream for dessert.* *Riley saw a robin eat a worm.*
consume	To eat up or destroy:	*The kids consumed all the snacks at the party.* *A large building was consumed by fire.*
devour	To eat; consume:	*I was so hungry I devoured two sandwiches.* *Lions sometimes devour zebras.*
feast	To have a feast; eat a great deal:	*The family feasted on hamburgers at the picnic.*
feed	To take in food; eat:	*Many birds feed on insects.*

edge *noun*	A line or place where something ends:	*The rock tumbled over the edge of a cliff.* *Sophia lives near the edge of the forest.* *The edge of a circle or a rectangle is called a perimeter.*
border	A strip along the edge of something:	*The garden path had a border of shrubs.*
boundary	A line that marks an edge:	*The Rio Grande forms part of the boundary between the United States and Mexico.*
fringe	A border of hanging threads or cords; the edge:	*The tablecloth has a fringe around the edge.* *Edwin lives on the fringe of town.*
side	A line or surface that encloses something:	*A rectangle has four sides.* *Our houses are on different sides of the street.*

WORDS from Words

EDGE can be combined with other words to form expressions that have special meanings.
These expressions also have synonyms. *For example:*

on edge means nervous or irritated: *I felt on edge before the big test.* Useful synonyms can be found at the entry
for **NERVOUS**.

education *noun*	The process of gaining knowledge:	*A good education will help you get a good job.*
comprehension	Understanding or the ability to understand:	*I know how to use the Web, but I do not comprehend how it works.*
knowledge	An understanding gained through experience or study:	*Although I have friends who live there, my knowledge of India is very limited.*
training	Education in a profession or trade:	*Diana had many years of training in ballet.*

For more choices see the entries for INFORMATION and KNOWLEDGE.

effect *noun* — Something that happens as the result of something else:

*The **effect** of heat on water is to turn it to steam.*
*My advice had no **effect** on Cassandra.*

consequence — The result of an action:

I got a poor grade on the spelling test as a consequence of not studying.

outcome — A result; end:

They waited to hear the outcome of the election.

result — Something that happens because of something else; the outcome:

Fran's high marks are the result of her hard work.
The results of the test will be posted on the bulletin board.

For more choices see the entries for END and PURPOSE.

---

embarrass *verb* — To make someone feel uncomfortable or ashamed:

*The outfielder was **embarrassed** when he missed an easy catch.*
*My parents try to be nice, but sometimes they **embarrass** me in front of my friends.*

fluster — To make embarrassed or nervous:

I became flustered when I couldn't remember my lines in the play.

humiliate — To make a person feel ashamed or foolish:

He was humiliated when the coach criticized him in front of his teammates.

shame — To cause or feel a painful feeling of having done something wrong or foolish:

He was shamed into admitting he played the prank.

---

emotion *noun* — A strong feeling:

*Love, hate, happiness, sorrow, and fear are **emotions**.*
*Sometimes it is best to let your **emotions** show.*

feeling — An emotion:

Bethany had a feeling of joy when she saw her high grades.
People expressed strong feelings about the election.

sentiment — Feeling or emotion:

There is strong sentiment in our neighborhood against canceling the annual street fair.

---

emphasize *verb* — To give special attention or importance to something:

*The teacher **emphasized** how important creativity is.*
*You should **emphasize** your strengths.*

feature — To have as the main attraction:

The concert features one of the world's greatest pop artists.

highlight — To emphasize the outstanding part:

The senator's speech highlighted the importance of oil to the world.

stress — To give special importance to:

Our teacher stressed the need for good study habits.

empty ↔ end

empty *adjective*   Having nothing in it: *When he had finished his drink, he threw the **empty** container into a recycling bin.*
*The theater was **empty** until people started arriving.*

    bare   Empty: *The shelves were bare.*

    blank   Without writing or printing: *There are many blank pages in my notebook.*

    unoccupied   Not lived in: *The apartment next to ours has been unoccupied for months.*

    vacant   Having nothing or no one in it: *A family is finally moving into the vacant house across the street.*
Please take any vacant seat so we can start.

For more choices see the entry for BARREN.
Antonyms: See the entry for COMPLETE.

---

encourage *verb*   To give courage or confidence to; to urge on: *The sound of applause **encouraged** us to try harder.*
*My teacher **encouraged** me to go out for the debate team.*

    inspire   To fill with strong, encouraging feeling: *Her success inspired hope for the future.*

    motivate   To give a reason for doing something: *The coach motivated me to study harder when he told me I could be on the team if I kept my grades up.*

    stimulate   To make active or excited: *My favorite author's novels always stimulate my imagination.*

For more choices see the entries for PERSUADE and URGE.
Antonyms: See the entry for DISCOURAGE.

---

end *noun*   The last part: *The **end** of the movie made Ian happy.*
*Kimberly tied knots at both **ends** of the rope.*

    close   End; finish: *At the close of the day, we all went home.*

    conclusion   The end of something: *Mike couldn't wait to read the conclusion of the mystery story and find out who committed the crime.*

    ending   The last or final part: *The story had a sad ending.*

    finale   The last part of something: *As a finale the acrobat did a triple somersault.*
The grand finale of the concert was a rousing march.

    finish   The last part of something; end: *Our relay team was way ahead at the finish of the race.*

For more choices see the entries for BACK, EFFECT, and PURPOSE.
Antonyms: See the entry for BEGINNING.

end *verb* — To bring or come to an end: *The movie **ends** at four o'clock.*
*The game **ended** in a tie.*
*I **ended** my paper with a quote from my favorite author.*

check — To bring to a sudden stop: *Our defense checked our opponent's advance and then scored.*

close — To bring or come to an end: *The movie closed with the hero being awarded a medal.*

discontinue — To put an end to; stop: *We discontinued our subscription to the local newspaper when we moved to another town.*

For more choices see the entries for FINISH, QUIT, and STOP.
Antonyms: See the entries for BEGIN and START.

---

enemy *noun* — Someone or something that hates or wishes harm to another: *The **enemy** threatened our border.*
*Snakes and birds are natural **enemies**.*

adversary — A person or group that fights another person or group: *The two countries were adversaries during the war.*

foe — An enemy: *The knight defeated many foes to rescue the princess.*
The guard asked the stranger, "Are you friend or foe?"

opponent — A person or group that is against another in a fight, contest, or discussion: *The candidate prepared to debate her opponent.*
Our strongest opponents are the teams from the two schools across town.

---

energy *noun* — The strength or eagerness to do things: *Caroline worked on her art project with great **energy**.*
*It takes a lot of **energy** to swim a mile.*

pep — A lively, vital quality: *Our puppy is always full of pep after eating.*

spirit — Enthusiasm and pep: *Dave was in good spirits after the team won.*

vigor — Active power or force: *Hannah argued with great vigor in favor of going to a movie.*

vitality — Energy or vigor of mind or body: *A proper diet and exercise helps maintain your vitality.*

---

enough *adjective* — As much as is needed: *There are **enough** players for two teams.*
*Have you had **enough** to eat?*

adequate — As much as needed: *You need an adequate supply of vitamins to grow properly.*

ample — More than enough: *We brought ample food for our picnic.*

sufficient — As much as needed: *We had sufficient gas to make it home.*

ensure ⇆ entertain

ensure *verb*	To make certain; guarantee:	*Careful planning ensures the trip will go well.* *They checked to ensure that nothing was left out in the rain.*
check	To test to find out if something is as it should be:	*We checked the tires on our car before we left on our trip.*
confirm	To show to be true or correct:	*News reports confirmed the rumor that he had won the election.*
make sure	To make certain; check:	*We made sure that everyone was on the bus before it left.*

enter *verb*	To go or come into or in:	*The ballet dancer entered the stage with a great leap.* *Our principal enters his office at the same time each morning.*
come in or come into	To enter:	*The dog came in out of the rain.* *The new student came into the classroom.*
go in or go into	To enter:	*I went in the front door.* *She wants to go into the video store to find a movie.*
penetrate	To go into or pass through:	*A nail penetrated the sole of my shoe.* *My flashlight couldn't penetrate the thick fog.*

Word Alert

ENTER can also means to enroll or join: *I entered our dog in a contest.* Synonyms for this meaning of **enter** can be found at the entry for *JOIN*. **Enter** also means to type information into a computer: *I entered several changes in my term paper and printed out a new version.* Useful synonyms are **input** and **typed in**.

entertain *verb*	To keep interested; amuse:	*Alexa was expected to entertain the guests until her sister arrived.* *We were entertained by the movie.*
amuse	To cause to laugh or smile:	*My uncle's funny stories amuse our whole family.*
delight	To give pleasure or joy:	*The clown delighted the children.*
divert	To amuse; entertain:	*The crowd was diverted by the juggler's tricks.*

entertainment *noun* — Something that interests or amuses: *The entertainment at the party was a puppet show. We often play video games for entertainment.*

  amusement — Something that amuses or entertains: *We go to the park sometimes for amusement.*

  diversion — Entertainment; amusement: *Reading is one of my favorite diversions.*

  recreation — Something done for amusement or relaxation: *Amber swims for recreation.*

  relaxation — Recreation; amusement: *I take walks and read for relaxation.*

Antonyms: See the entry for WORK[1].

enthusiasm *noun* — A strong feeling of excitement and interest about something: *They started the game with great enthusiasm. Mark's enthusiasm for hiking diminished as the day got hotter.*

  eagerness — A strong feeling of wanting to do something: *The students' excited whispers showed their eagerness to go on the class trip.*

  passion — A very strong liking: *Josh has a passion for baseball.*

  zeal — Great enthusiasm or commitment: *The team practiced for the big game with zeal.*

envy *noun* — A feeling of wishing you could have what another person has: *Ed envied Garret's new bicycle. I envy Marisa's ability to paint so well.*

  greed — A very great and selfish desire for more than one's share: *The boy's greed made him take all the candy.*

  jealousy — Envy of another person or his or her possessions: *I could not hide my jealousy over my friend's new computer game.*

  resentment — A feeling of anger or bitterness: *He was filled with resentment because he felt he was treated unfairly.*

equal *adjective* — The same in amount, size, value, or quality: *Even though Victor was a year younger, he was exactly Marsha's equal in height. They divided the cake into equal pieces.*

  equivalent — Equal: *Ten pennies are equivalent to two nickels or a dime.*

  even — The same or equal: *At the end of the first period the score was even.*

  interchangeable — Capable of being used in place of each other: *The ink cartridges for our printer are interchangeable.*

For more choices see the entry for SAME.
Antonyms: See the entry for UNEQUAL.

erase *verb*

To remove by rubbing, scratching, or wiping off:

*I made a mess of my homework when I tried to **erase** a wrong answer.*
*Seth accidentally **erased** several computer files when he pressed the wrong button.*

delete

To remove something:

*I **deleted** my homework from our computer by mistake.*
*The editor **deleted** several words from the text and made its meaning clearer.*

rub out

To apply pressure to clean something:

*I tried to **rub out** the wrong answer with my pencil eraser.*

For more choices see the entries for REMOVE and UNDO.

---

escape *verb*

To get free:

*The squirrel **escaped** every trap we set for it.*
*I need to **escape** the winter cold.*

elude

To escape by being clever or quick:

*The sly raccoon easily **eluded** the dogs.*

flee

To run away:

*If a severe storm comes this way, we may have to **flee**.*
*The family **fled** from the rising floodwaters.*

get away

To make a quick escape:

*We love to **get away** to someplace sunny during winter.*

For more choices see the entry for AVOID.

---

eternal *adjective*

Lasting forever:

*The mountains seem **eternal**, but erosion is slowly wearing them down.*
*Please stop that **eternal** racket!*

endless

Having no limit or end:

*The ride on the slow train seemed **endless**.*

everlasting

Lasting forever; eternal:

*They loved to hike and enjoy the **everlasting** beauty of nature.*

timeless

Ageless; lasting forever:

*A classic is a work of art that has **timeless** appeal.*

Antonyms: See the entry for TEMPORARY.

---

event *noun*

Anything that happens, especially if it is important:

*The relay was the main **event** at the track meet.*
*The teacher mentioned several important **events** that led to the Civil War.*

incident

Something that happens; an event:

*A funny **incident** happened on the way to school today.*

occasion

A time when something happens:

*We have met before on several **occasions**.*
*Morgan's graduation was an **occasion** for celebration.*
*I often send notes to people on special **occasions**.*

occurrence

Something that takes place or happens:

*Floods are an unusual **occurrence** in the desert.*

example *noun* — A thing used to show what other similar things are like: *A beetle is an **example** of an insect; a tiger is an **example** of a mammal.*

case — An example of something: *The police investigated several cases of vandalism.*

instance — An example; case: *A fair election is an instance of democracy at work.*

sample — A small piece that shows what the whole is like: *The salesclerk gave us samples of the new flavor of ice cream.*

---

excessive *adjective* — More than is necessary or usual: *He spent an **excessive** amount of money on candy. The price for the tickets to the concert was **excessive**.*

extravagant — Spending too much money: *His extravagant spending put him deep in debt.*

lavish — Costing or being a great amount; more than enough: *The cruise ship had a lavish banquet to welcome the passengers.*

undue — Beyond what is right or proper; too much: *They spent an undue amount on decorations for the party.*

For more choices see the entries for EXPENSIVE and LUXURIOUS.
Antonyms: See the entry for CHEAP².

---

expand *verb* — To make or become larger: *The heated air made the balloon **expand**. Water **expands** as it freezes.*

enlarge — To make or become larger: *We had several photos enlarged so they could be framed.*

increase — To make or become larger in number or size: *The membership of the chorus increased this year. The size of the balloon increased as I blew air into it.*

swell — To grow or increase in size: *Bread dough swells as it bakes. My sprained ankle was swollen.*

For more choices see the entry for GROW.
Antonyms: See the entry for SHRINK.

---

expensive *adjective* — Having a high price: *A jet airplane is very **expensive**. His parents gave Jerrod an **expensive** watch.*

costly — Costing a lot: *Diamonds and emeralds are costly jewels.*

high-priced — Expensive; costly: *She had a high-priced outfit that she only wore on special occasions.*

valuable — Worth much money: *The paintings in the museum are very valuable. Guards protected the valuable shipment of gold.*

For more choices see the entry for LUXURIOUS.
Antonyms: See the entry for CHEAP¹.

expert *noun*
A person who knows a great deal about some special thing:
Drew is an expert on repairing cars.
They called in several experts to fix the school's heating system.

ace
A person who is an expert at something:
Rick is an ace at bowling.

genius
Great ability to think, invent, or create things:
Leonardo da Vinci was a genius in many fields.

master
A person who has great skill or knowledge about something:
That basketball player is a master of the hook shot.

wizard
A person who is very clever and skillful:
He is a wizard at chess.

---

explain *verb*
To make something plain or clear:
The professor explained the science experiment.
I can't explain why I'm so tired.

clarify
To make something easier to understand:
Our teacher clarified the confusing instructions for us.

define
To give the meaning of:
A dictionary defines words.

describe
To give a picture of something in words:
He described the movie so well, we didn't bother to see it.

interpret
To explain the meaning of something:
We were asked to interpret a poem.

state
To express or explain fully in words:
Jackie stated her opinion during the meeting.

For more choices see the entries for SAY, TALK, and TELL.

---

extend *verb*
To make longer:
The elephant extended its trunk to take a peanut.
The new student extended his hand in greeting.
Our vacation was extended an extra week.

draw out
To make longer:
The speaker drew out his speech until the audience could barely sit still.

prolong
To make longer:
Improvements in medical care have prolonged people's lives.

stretch out
To make longer; extend:
I stretched out my arm to try to touch the ceiling.

For more choices see the entries for DELAY.

fail *verb*   To not succeed in doing or getting something:

*The bus **failed** to arrive on time.*
*I tried hard to learn to play the trumpet, but I **failed**.*

     fall short   To fail to achieve a goal or level:

Despite his efforts, the athlete fell short of setting a school record.
The movie fell short of our expectations.

     miss   To fail to do something attempted or planned:

The batter swung the bat but missed the ball.
I missed two days of class because I was sick.

Word Alert

FAIL also means to get too low a grade in a test or course of study: *He failed his driving test and didn't get a license. She always studies so hard that there is no chance that she will fail.* A synonym for this meaning of **fail** is **flunk**. Antonyms can be found at the entry for **PASS**.

---

fair *adjective*   Not in favor of one more than another:

*The judges were **fair** in awarding the prizes.*
*I try to be **fair** when sharing with my brothers.*

     impartial   Not favoring one more than others:

A referee must be impartial.

     just   Fair and right; honest:

Although our teacher is strict, her decisions are just.

     unbiased   Without strong feeling for or against someone; fair:

In my unbiased opinion, both of you are wrong.

Antonyms: See the entry for UNFAIR.

---

faithful *adjective*   Firm in keeping promises or fulfilling duties:

*Caroline is my **faithful** friend and never lets me down.*
*A dog can be a **faithful** companion.*

     devoted   Very loyal and faithful:

Cody is devoted to his family.

     loyal   Having strong and lasting affection or support:

She was always loyal to her country.

     true   Faithful to someone or something:

A true friend is true to his word.

fake *adjective* A person or thing that is not what it claims to be: *The fake painting looked almost as good as the real one. He didn't feel well, so his smile looked fake in the photo.*

   counterfeit A copy made to cheat someone: *The police showed us a counterfeit twenty-dollar bill that looked very real.*

   false Not real; artificial: *He wore a wig and a false beard for his part in the play.*

   imitation Something that is a copy of something else: *She wore earrings made with imitation diamonds.*

---

fall *verb* To come down from a high place: *I fell off a chair and hurt my knee. All the leaves have fallen off the trees.*

   decline To fall to a lower level: *The cost of computer memory has declined remarkably in the last few years.*

   topple To fall forward: *The bookcase toppled over with a loud crash.*

   tumble To fall in a helpless or clumsy way: *My skateboard hit a bump, and I tumbled to the ground.*

For more choices see the entries for DIVE and DROP.

WORDS from Words

FALL is often combined with other words to form expressions that have special meanings. These expressions also have synonyms. *For example:*

to fall back means to give ground or retreat: *The army **fall back** as the enemy advanced.* Useful synonyms are **retreat** and **withdraw**.

to fall back on means to turn to someone or something for help: *It's great to have friends you can **fall back on** in times of need.* Useful synonyms are **look to**, **resort to**, and **turn to**.

to fall behind means not to keep up: *Jeremy **fell behind** the others when he stopped to tie his shoe. While I was sick, I **fell behind** in my schoolwork.* Useful synonyms are **lag behind** and **trail**.

to fall short and **to fall through** mean to fail: *Our efforts **fell short** of our goal. Our plans for this weekend **fell through**.* Useful synonyms are **fail** and **miss**.

---

family *noun* A group of people who are related: *Luke's large family includes four brothers. My family got together for my cousin's wedding.*

   household All the people living in a home: *Our household was busy during the holidays.*

   kin A person's whole family: *All my father's kin are from Illinois.*

   relations A person in the same family as someone else: *Many of my relations live in another country.*

   relatives A person from the same family as someone else: *Among my relatives are two aunts, an uncle, and four cousins.*

famous *adjective* — Very well-known:
*The **famous** singer drew a large crowd.*
*The Mona Lisa is a **famous** painting.*

    celebrated — Well-known and honored: *The **celebrated** musician will give a concert tonight.*

    notable — Worthy of notice; important: *A **notable** scientist spoke to us in class.*

    noted — Noticed for a particular reason; well-known: *A **noted** author signed books at our bookstore.*

    prominent — Well-known; important: *The board of judges for the contest was made up of **prominent** citizens.*

---

far *adjective* — A long way:
*She travels **far** from home to go to a special school for artists.*
*The stars in the sky are **far** away.*

    distant — Far away in space or time: *Dinosaurs lived in the **distant** past.*

    faraway — A long way away; remote: *Lauren dreams of visiting **faraway** places.*

    remote — Not near: *The biologist explored a **remote** island.*

Antonyms: See the entry for NEAR.

---

fashion *noun* — The current custom or style of dress or behavior:
*It used to be the **fashion** to wear baseball caps backwards.*
***Fashions** change all the time.*

    craze — A temporary interest in doing one thing: *The **craze** for skateboards was replaced by a **craze** for scooters.*

    fad — Something that is popular for a very short time: *The hula hoop was once a **fad**.*

    rage — A temporary fashion; what everybody wants for a short time: *White leather boots were all the **rage** in the 1960s.*

    style — Fashion: *Models in magazines wear the latest **styles**.*

---

fast *adjective* — Acting, moving, or doing something in a short time:
*The **fast** rabbit lost the race to the slow tortoise.*
*A car is **fast**, but an airplane is **faster**.*

    fleet — Moving very quickly; swift: *A deer is a **fleet** animal.*

    rapid — With great speed: *She kept up a **rapid** pace for the whole race.*

    swift — Moving with great speed, often said of animals or people: *The **swift** horse galloped across the field.*

For more choices see the entry for QUICK.
Antonyms: See the entry for SLOW.

fasten *verb* — To attach firmly:

The sign was **fastened** to the wall with nails.
Kate's mother **fastened** a gold pin to her dress.

> **affix** — To attach or fasten:
>
> Faith **affixed** stamps to her party invitations and mailed them.

> **attach** — To fasten:
>
> We **attached** the notice to the bulletin board with thumbtacks.

> **bind** — To tie together; fasten:
>
> I plan to **bind** the pages of my report with staples.
> The package was **bound** with string.

---

fate *noun* — What finally happens to a person or thing:

It seems to be my **fate** to be last in line.
Many people don't believe in **fate**.

> **destiny** — What happens to a person or thing:
>
> Kim felt it was her **destiny** to become a television star.

> **doom** — A sad end or death:
>
> Global warming might mean **doom** for some animals.

> **fortune** — Something good or bad that will happen to a person:
>
> It was her good **fortune** to win the lottery.

For more choices see the entry for END.

---

fault *noun* — Something wrong that spoils something else:

Erica's biggest **fault** is her quick temper.
The computer crashed because of a **fault** in the program.

> **bug** — A fault or weakness:
>
> A **bug** in my computer made it crash.

> **defect** — A flaw or weakness:
>
> One of the tires had a **defect**, so we replaced it.

> **flaw** — A scratch, crack, or other defect:
>
> The crystal bowl had a slight **flaw** in it.
> Selfishness is a character **flaw**.

> **imperfection** — A mistake or fault:
>
> A slight **imperfection** in my new glasses bothered my eyes.

For more choices see the entries for DISADVANTAGE and MISTAKE.

---

fear *noun* — A strong feeling caused by believing or anticipating danger, pain, or evil:

Leo and Jane stayed out of the ocean because of their **fear** of sharks.
I have a **fear** of high places.

> **dread** — A feeling of great fear:
>
> My fear of flying filled me with **dread**.

> **fright** — A sudden fear or alarm:
>
> The thunder gave me a **fright**.

> **panic** — A strong feeling of fear that makes a person want to run away:
>
> I had a moment of **panic** before the test, but it turned out to be easy.

> **terror** — Great fear:
>
> The horror story filled me with **terror**.

For more choices see the entry for WORRY.

few *adjective* Not many: *Only a few movies make her laugh.*
I have only a few cents in my pocket.

limited Kept within boundaries; restricted: *Only a limited number of people can see each showing because there are so few seats.*

occasional Happening or appearing infrequently: *The weather report says there will be occasional showers tomorrow.*

scant Barely enough: *We have scant supplies for this trip.*

For more choices see the entries for RARE and UNUSUAL.
Antonyms: See the entry for MANY.

---

fierce *adjective* Likely to make violent attacks; dangerous; savage: *Lions, hawks, and sharks are all fierce predators.*
There was a fierce competition for the prize.

brutal Causing or allowing pain without caring; cruel: *The brutal treatment of children in the workplace led to child labor laws.*
Our team has a brutal training schedule.

ferocious Fierce; savage; very cruel: *Tyrannosaurus rex must have been a ferocious hunter.*

savage Fierce or cruel: *A savage tiger snarled at us from its cage.*

For more choices see the entry for CRUEL and WILD.
Antonyms: See the entry for GENTLE.

---

fight *noun* A struggle in which animals, persons, or groups try to hurt each other: *Sometimes my brother and I fight over silly things.*
The two elephants fought by pushing each other with their trunks.

battle A fight between armed groups: *The battle between the two armies lasted several days.*

combat Fighting: *Several soldiers were wounded in combat.*

conflict A long fight; war: *The conflict between the North and South lasted four years.*

war A long struggle or fight: *When they could not solve their differences peacefully, the countries went to war.*

Antonyms: See the entry for PEACE.

---

fill *verb* To make or become full: *We filled the buckets with water.*
Chris's mind was filled with ideas.

load To fill with a load: *Load the wood on the wagon.*

pack To fill up with things: *We packed so many things in the car there was no room for passengers.*

stuff To pack full: *I stuffed all my clothes into a suitcase.*

find *verb* — To discover by accident; happen upon: — *Scientists hope to **find** life on other planets.*
*I **found** the missing sock in the back of my closet.*

   come across — To find or meet by chance: — *Zack **came across** some old photos in the attic.*

   locate — To find the place or position of something: — *The librarian **located** the book I needed for my report.*

   spot — To see; recognize: — *Andy **spotted** Becky in the crowd.*

For more choices see the entries for DISCOVER and NOTICE.
Antonyms: See the entry for LOSE[1].

---

finish *verb* — To bring to an end: — ***Finish** your homework before you start reading.*
*When the play **finished**, everyone applauded.*

   accomplish — To do something successfully; complete: — *I **accomplished** more work than I expected.*

   complete — To bring to an end; finish: — *Joe **completed** the test just as the bell rang.*

   conclude — To finish: — *When the singing **concluded**, the game began.*

For more choices see the entry for DO and END.
Antonyms: See the entry for BEGIN.

---

firm *adjective* — Not giving or changing much when pressed: — *I like sleeping on a **firm** mattress.*
*He had **firm** ideas and he stuck by them.*
*They were such **firm** friends nothing could come between them.*

   hard — Solid and firm: — *An egg has a **hard** but brittle shell.*
*The pear was too **hard** to eat.*

   solid — Having shape and hardness: — *Water becomes **solid** when it freezes.*
*The door to the vault was **solid** steel.*

   steady — Firm in movement or position: — *Steve needed a **steady** ladder to reach the roof.*

For more choices see the entries for STEADY and STIFF.

---

fitting *adjective* — Right or proper: — *His background in chemistry made him a **fit** choice for the job in the lab.*
*Is this cloudy water **fit** to drink?*

   appropriate — Suitable, proper, correct: — *Warm clothing is **appropriate** for going out in the snow.*

   suitable — Meeting the needs; right or proper: — *They chose **suitable** music for the ceremony.*

For more choices see the entry for RIGHT.

fix *verb* | To repair something or bring it back to its right condition: | Madeline will **fix** the flat tire.
The plumber **fixed** the broken pipe.

mend | To put in good condition again; repair: | I **mended** the broken plate with glue.

patch | To repair with a patch: | Laurie **patched** the elbow in her uncle's favorite jacket.
We **patched** the bicycle tire.

remedy | To heal or improve: | Chris **remedied** his mistake by apologizing.

repair | To put into good condition: | The mechanic **repaired** our car.

For more choices see the entries for CHANGE and CORRECT.

---

flat *adjective* | Smooth and even: | Our house is built on a **flat** piece of land.
A slight breeze ruffled the **flat** surface of the lake.

horizontal | Flat and straight across; parallel to the horizon: | The carpenter measured carefully to make sure the roof was **horizontal**.

level | Having a flat, horizontal surface: | We had to find **level** ground so that we could put up our tent.
The floor wasn't **level**, so everything rolled to the edge.

For more choices see the entry for SMOOTH.
Antonyms: See the entries for JAGGED and ROUGH.

---

flow *verb* | To move steadily in a stream: | The river **flows** into the ocean.
Juice **flowed** over the table when the container broke.

flush | To flow or rush suddenly: | Water **flushed** through the pipes.

pour | To flow or cause to flow: | Rainwater **poured** off the roof.
Grace **poured** milk for her friends.

rush | To move or go quickly: | Water **rushed** out of the fire hose.

stream | To move steadily; flow: | Light **streamed** through the window.

For more choices see the entry for SPILL.

---

flower *noun* | The part of the plant that makes seeds: | The garden was full of beautiful **flowers**.
A rose **flower** smells sweet.

bloom | The flower of a plant: | Spring **blooms** appear on many trees.

blossom | The flower of a plant or tree: | Bees and hummingbirds are attracted to **blossoms**.

bud | The part of a plant that grows into a flower, leaf, or branch: | **Buds** began to appear as soon as the snow melted.

For more choices see the WORD BANK on the next page.

WORD BANK

Sometimes you can make things clearer for your reader by naming the particular **FLOWER** you mean. Some **flowers** are:

chrysanthemum	iris	pansy	snapdragon
daffodil	lily	petunia	sunflower
daisy	marigold	poppy	tulip
geranium	orchid	rose	violet

---

fly *verb* — To move through the air with wings: — People fly on airplanes all around the world.
A diving falcon flies at over 100 miles per hour.

  glide — To move smoothly along without any effort: — A hawk glided overhead.

  sail — To move smoothly without difficulty: — The hang glider sailed to a soft landing.
A boat sailed out to sea.

  soar — To fly high: — The birds soared upward until they were out of sight.
A jet soared high in the sky.
The crowd's spirits soared when their team took the lead.

---

fog *noun* — A cloud close to the ground that is made up of small drops of water: — The fog made the city seem very mysterious.
We could barely see through the thick fog.

  haze — Mist, smoke, or dust in the air: — The sunlight was dimmed by a thick haze.

  mist — A cloud of tiny droplets of water or other liquid in the air: — The mist rose over the mountain lake.

  smog — A combination of smoke and fog in the air: — Smog is caused by pollution and is a health problem in many cities.

---

follow[1] *verb* — To come after, behind, or in back of: — My dog follows me everywhere.
One day followed the next, and soon the week was over.

  pursue — To follow in order to catch up or capture: — The hunters pursued the mountain lion but it got away.

  succeed — To come after and take the place of: — If the president dies, the vice president succeeds to the office of president.

  trail — To follow behind: — The students trailed behind the teacher in a single file.

follow² *verb*   To act according to: *If you **follow** the instructions, the job will be easy.*
*We **followed** the trail to the cabin.*

    abide by   To accept and obey: *A good citizen abides by the law.*

    heed   To listen or mind: *Natalie heeded her parents' advice.*

    obey   To carry out the orders, wishes, or instructions of others: *Eric obeyed his parents and came straight home after school.*

    observe   To follow or obey: *The drivers on the highway observed the speed limit.*

Word Alert

FOLLOW also means to pay attention and understand: *We **followed** his story with great interest.* Synonyms for this meaning of **follow** can be found at the entry for **UNDERSTAND**.

---

forbid *verb*   To order not to do something: *I **forbid** you to go into the pool.*
*State law **forbids** killing endangered species.*
*They were **forbidden** to enter the old house.*
*The owner **forbade** them because it was dangerous.*

    ban   To forbid by law: *The town banned riding a bicycle without a safety helmet.*

    bar   To keep out; forbid from entering: *Dogs are barred from most restaurants.*

    exclude   To shut out; keep from entering: *He was excluded from the contest because he had already won too many times.*

    prohibit   To not allow; forbid: *Smoking is prohibited in many places.*

For more choices see the entry for PREVENT.
Antonyms: See the entry for LET.

---

force *verb*   To cause someone to do something against their wishes: *She **forced** herself to practice every day before the tournament.*
*He **forced** the door shut against the winter wind.*

    compel   To force: *The rainstorm compelled us to get under cover quickly.*
The police compelled the man to leave the burning building.

    make   To cause or force to do: *Nicole's funny stories always make me laugh.*

    require   To force, order, or demand: *The rules require that you arrive on time.*
Everyone requires sleep.

For more choices see the entries for INSIST and ORDER.

foreign *adjective* — From another country:

Chris spent the summer in a **foreign** country learning the language.
Foreign athletes are often brought in to play on our teams.

alien — Of or from another country; of or from a place other than Earth:

This state has a large alien population.
The movie was about an alien invasion.

exotic — Foreign; strange; unusual:

This exotic plant comes from Brazil.

imported — Brought from another country:

Tea is imported from Asia because it doesn't grow in North America.

---

forget *verb* — To fail to remember:

As soon as the music starts, I **forget** the words to the song.
Alex **forgot** his homework.
Craig had **forgotten** to go to his appointment.

neglect — To fail to pay proper attention to:

I neglected my houseplants, and they almost died.

omit — To leave out; not include:

Josh omitted the part of the story that was boring.

overlook — To not see or notice:

The detective almost overlooked the clue that solved the crime.

For more choices see the entry for LOSE¹.

---

forgive *verb* — To stop blaming or feeling anger toward:

I **forgive** you for playing that trick on me.
They **forgave** their teammate for dropping the fly ball.
You will be **forgiven** if you apologize.

excuse — To forgive; pardon:

Please excuse my messy desk.

pardon — To not want to blame or punish:

Pardon me for yawning.

---

form *noun* — The outline of something:

I saw the dim **form** of a man looming out of the darkness.
The wind shaped the clouds into different **forms**.

design — A drawing or outline made to serve as a guide or pattern:

We studied the design before we put the bookcase together.
Vanessa found the design for her costume in an old book.

outline — The shape of an object:

We drew outlines of our hands by tracing the outer edges with a pencil.

pattern — The way colors, shapes, or lines are arranged:

The rug repeated the same flower pattern over and over.

For more choices see the entry for SHAPE.

fragile *adjective* — Easily broken: — *Those antique drinking glasses are very **fragile**.*
*The **fragile** spider web broke in the wind.*

    breakable — Able to be broken: — *Be careful when you put away those **breakable** dishes.*

    brittle — Very easily broken: — *The **brittle** wood railing gave me a splinter.*

For more choices see the entries for DELICATE and WEAK.
Antonyms: See the entry for TOUGH.

---

free *adjective* — Having liberty; not being under anyone's control: — *They opened the cages and set the birds **free**.*
*Lily has a **free** period after lunch.*

    independent — Free from control or rule of others: — *Each **independent** country in the world has its own government.*

    liberated — Free: — *The **liberated** citizens marched through town.*

---

freedom *noun* — The condition of being free from control by others: — *The struggle for **freedom** continues in many parts of the world.*
*Alexa loves the **freedom** that comes with riding her bicycle.*

    independence — Freedom from the control or rule of others: — *The American colonists won their **independence** from Great Britain.*

    liberty — Freedom from the control of another: — *After the colonists won their **liberty**, they set up their own government.*

---

fresh *adjective* — Newly done, made, or gathered; not spoiled by use: — *The farm stand sells **fresh** fruit.*
*I needed a **fresh** piece of paper to start my work.*
*The newly washed sheets smelled **fresh**.*

    unspoiled — Not spoiled or damaged: — *Jaime found boxes of **unspoiled** raspberries in the grocery store.*

    pure — Not dirty or polluted: — *They drank **pure** water from the spring.*

For more choices see the entry for NEW.
Antonyms: See the entry for OLD.

friend *noun* | A person you like or who likes you: | *I like to spend time with my friends.* |
		My best friend lives right down the street.
		After we went to camp together, Nadine and I became friends.
associate	A partner or companion, particularly in business:	*She just became an associate at a law firm.*
buddy	A close friend; pal:	*Jenny is Sarah's buddy.*
		I like to hang out with my buddies.
companion	A person or animal who keeps one company:	*Lucy's aunt was her companion on a trip to Italy.*
		Dogs make fine companions.
comrade	Someone who shares the same interests or profession:	*My comrades and I have just finished our project.*
pal	A close friend or buddy:	*I want to play soccer with my pals tomorrow.*

Word Alert

When the word **FRIEND** is combined with girl or boy, the resulting words have two different meanings. A **girlfriend** is a **friend** who is a girl or a woman, and a **boyfriend** means a **friend** who is a boy or a man. Both words can also mean that the friendship is romantic in nature.

---

friendly *adjective* | Wanting to be a friend; warm and pleasant: | *She gave us a friendly smile.* |
		Everyone was friendly and made Penny feel welcome.
amiable	Friendly and kind; good-natured:	*The amiable librarian helped me find information for my report.*
		The amiable kitten rubbed against Laura's leg.
cordial	Warm and friendly:	*My pals gave me a cordial greeting.*
neighborly	Showing the kindness of a good neighbor:	*Lending his shovel to me was a neighborly thing to do.*
sociable	Friendly:	*They are very sociable and love to go to parties.*

For more choices see the entries for KIND and NICE.
Antonyms: See the entry for MEAN.

---

frightening *adjective* | Causing sudden fear or alarm: | *The fire was a frightening experience for all of us.* |
		The haunted house at the fair was not very frightening.
eerie	Strange in a way that makes people frightened or nervous:	*An owl has an eerie call.*
scary	Causing fear or fright:	*We had a scary ride on the roller coaster.*
spooky	Strange and frightening:	*The deserted house looked spooky in the pale moonlight.*

For more choices see the entry for STRANGE.

front *noun* — The part that faces forward or comes first: *Our school band marched at the front of the parade. The introduction comes at the front of the book.*

    bow — The front end of a boat or ship: *I like to sit near the bow so I can see the waves the boat makes.*

    head — The top or front part of something: *He hit the nail on its head. She is at the head of her class.*

    start — The beginning or front: *He tried to cut in at the start of the line but had to go to the end.*

For more choices see the entry for BEGINNING.

---

frown *verb* — To wrinkle the forehead in thought, anger, or worry: *The coach frowned when the other team scored. Larry frowned as he concentrated on solving the puzzle.*

    glare — To give an angry look: *She glared at the girl who cut in line in front of her.*

    grimace — To twist the face when uncomfortable, unhappy, or displeased: *The child grimaced with pain when the doctor examined his broken arm.*

    scowl — To frown in an angry way: *He scowled when someone giggled during his speech.*

Antonyms: See the entry for SMILE.

---

funny *adjective* — Causing laughter: *Gary told a funny story that made us all laugh. Sometimes Seth's jokes aren't very funny.*

    amusing — Causing smiles or enjoyment: *The book I was reading was so amusing, I laughed out loud.*

    comical — Causing laughter through actions: *The clowns were comical.*

    hilarious — Very funny; causing noisy laughter: *The movie was so hilarious, we are still chuckling about it.*

    humorous — Funny or joking: *Jessica told a humorous story.*

    witty — Clever and amusing: *We all laughed at her witty remark.*

Antonyms: See the entry for SERIOUS.

game *noun*   Something done for fun or pleasure; a contest with rules: *At the party we played my favorite games.*
Our team lost the championship by one game.

sport   A game in which a person is active and often competing with someone else: *Soccer, bowling, and baseball are sports.*
We play indoor sports like volleyball during winter.

For more choices see the entry for CONTEST.

WORD BANK

Sometimes you can make things clearer and more interesting for your reader by naming the particular **GAME** or sport you mean. Some **games** are:

backgammon	cops and robbers	kick the can	relay race
bingo	gin rummy	Mother, may I	Simon says
capture the flag	go fish	musical chairs	snakes and ladders
cards	hangman	old maid	solitaire
cat's cradle	hide-and-seek	pantomime	spin the bottle
charades	hopscotch	piñata	tag
checkers	jacks	poker	telephone
chess	jump rope	red rover	tug of war

Some **sports** are:

automobile racing	diving	ice hockey	roller hockey
badminton	field hockey	ice skating	skiing
baseball	fishing	karate	soccer
basketball	football	kickball	softball
billiards	golf	lacrosse	swimming
boating	gymnastics	polo	tennis
bowling	handball	pool	track and field

gasp *verb* — To draw in air suddenly; to speak while breathing hard: *The audience **gasped** when Angela dove off the high board. "Water!" the man **gasped** when he reached the camp in the desert.*

pant — To breathe quickly and hard: *After the race, the runners stood panting at the finish line.*

puff — To blow or breathe in short bursts: *The old train engine puffed smoke. We puffed from carrying the heavy load up the stairs.*

wheeze — To breathe with a hoarse, whistling sound: *My bad cold made me wheeze.*

---

gather *verb* — To come or bring together; to increase bit by bit: *Bill **gathered** berries for dessert. My bike **gathered** speed going down the hill.*

accumulate — To gather or pile up: *The squirrel accumulated a huge pile of nuts.*

assemble — To come or bring together: *Over the years Jeremy assembled a large collection of foreign coins.*

collect — To gather together: *We collected cans for recycling.*

---

gentle *adjective* — Kind and mild; easy to handle: *A **gentle** breeze cooled the summer day. I picked that horse to ride because it is **gentle**.*

soft — Gentle or light: *The soft music was soothing.*

tame — Taken from a wild state and made obedient: *You can pet the tame elephant at the zoo.*

tender — Not tough or hard: *We had a tender steak for dinner.*

Antonyms: See the entry for FIERCE.

---

get *verb* — To come to have; to gain a possession: *We need to **get** some milk for dinner. Ken **got** a video game for his birthday.*

acquire — To come into possession of something through effort or merit: *He acquired a new house.*

obtain — To get as one's own, often with some difficulty: *Lily worked hard to obtain her job.*

receive — To take or get: *I received a watch on my birthday.*

For more choices see the entry for EARN.
Antonyms: See the entries for FORGET and LOSE[1].

Word Alert

GET also means to understand: *Did you get the joke?* Synonyms for this meaning of **get** can be found at the entry for **UNDERSTAND**.

 giant

WORDS from Words

GET is often combined with other words to form expressions that have special meanings. These expressions also have synonyms. *For example:*

to get along means to be friendly: *Jim gets along with everyone. We have always gotten along with our neighbors.* Useful synonyms are **to be friendly with** and **to be cordial**. **Get along** can also mean to survive: *A camel gets along with very little water. It's tough to get along on so little money.* Useful synonyms are **endure**, **manage**, and **persist**.

to get away with means to do something without being noticed, caught, or punished: *You can't get away with telling lies. He almost got away with it, but he was caught.* Useful synonyms are **avoid** and **evade**.

to get back means to come back: *We got back to our home about six o'clock. Let's get back to the point of our discussion.* A useful synonym is **return**.

to get in means to go in: *The movie was so crowded we couldn't get in.* Useful synonyms are **enter** and **gain entry**. **Get in** also means to reach a destination: *The plane got in on time.* A useful synonym is **arrive**.

to get out means to go to a social event: *Our whole family goes out to dinner on Saturday nights.* Useful synonyms are **attend** and **observe**.

to get together means to meet: *Our club gets together once a week.* Useful synonyms are **assemble** and **gather**.

to get through means to arrive at the end of something: *I got through the test in less than an hour.* Useful synonyms are **complete** and **finish**.

to get up means to rise from bed: *I get up at seven every morning.* Useful synonyms are **get out of bed** and **wake up**. **Get up** also means to sit up or stand up: *Nora got up from her desk and went to the kitchen for a snack.* Useful synonyms are **get to one's feet**, **rise**, and **stand up**.

giant *adjective*	Much larger or more important than ordinary:	*The company built a giant factory near town.* *Up to now, no one has seen a live giant squid.*
colossal	Huge; gigantic:	*A blue whale is a colossal animal.*
mighty	Great in power, size, or amount:	*The Mississippi is a mighty river.*
monstrous	Very large:	*A monstrous tree fell over in the storm.*

For more choices see the entries for BIG and LARGE.
Antonyms: See the entries for LITTLE, SMALL, and TINY.

gift *noun* | Something given: | The **gift** Shannon gave Bianca was small but very precious. The museum was supported by **gifts** from many people.

contribution | Something contributed or given: | The contributions will pay for the team's trip.

donation | A gift; contribution: | The hospital fund received many generous donations.

present | Something given: | My brother and I made presents for our parents.

Word Alert

GIFT also means an ability or talent: *She has a gift for dancing.* Synonyms for this meaning of **gift** can be found at the entries for **ABILITY** and **TALENT**.

---

give *verb* | To hand, deliver, or pass: | I **give** help to anyone who needs it. Bethany **gave** Andrew a new baseball glove.

bestow | To give: | The queen bestowed a knighthood on the actor.

endow | To give money or property to: | Many people show their gratitude to their schools or colleges by endowing them.

furnish | To supply or provide: | The church furnished a meeting place for our club.

grant | To give or allow: | The teacher granted us extra time to study for the test.

present | To give in a formal way: | The mayor presented medals to the firefighters.

For more choices see the entry for VOLUNTEER.

WORDS from Words

GIVE is often combined with other words to form expressions that have special meanings. These expressions also have synonyms. *For example:*

to give away means to cause to become known: *It will ruin their fun if you give away the end of the story.* Useful synonyms are **reveal** and **tell**.

to give back means to return: *I had to give back the library book when it became due.* Useful synonyms can be found at the entry for **RETURN**[2].

to give in means to stop being against something: *My mother gave in and let me stay up late.* Useful synonyms are **submit**, **surrender**, and **yield**.

to give out means to distribute: *The store is giving out free candy for the holiday.* Useful synonyms are **distribute**, **hand out**, and **issue**.

to give up means to surrender: *The army gave up after being surrounded. Our team has given up too many points to win.* Useful synonyms are **submit**, **surrender**, and **yield**. **To give up** also means to stop or stop trying: *I gave up tennis because I didn't have time to practice.* Useful synonyms are **abandon** and **stop**.

go *verb*	To move from one place to another:	*That road **goes** to the park.* *They had **gone** when we got there.* *We **went** to the beach.*
move	To change the direction or place of something:	*We **moved** to new seats so we could see the movie better.*
pass	To go past; go by:	*I **pass** the library on my way to school.* *Many cars **passed** me as I rode my bike.*
proceed	To move on or continue:	*The train **proceeded** to its final destination after a stop at our station.*
progress	To move forward:	*The building of our new school **progressed** quickly.*

For more choices see the entry for TRAVEL.
Antonyms: See the entry for WAIT.

WORDS from Words

GO is often combined with other words to form expressions that have special meanings. These expressions also have synonyms. *For example:*

to go after means to move toward someone or something: *If you throw the ball, my dog will **go after** it.* Useful synonyms are **chase**, **follow**, and **tail**.

to go along means to move together with someone: *You can **go along** if you want to. We **went along** for the ride.* Useful synonyms are **accompany** and **escort**.

to go back means to return: *We **go back** to the same place every summer.* Useful synonyms can be found at the entry for **RETURN**[1].

to go around means to move from place to place: *The three friends **go around** together.* Useful synonyms are **roam**, **stray**, and **wander**.

to go in or **to go into** means to enter: *I'll **go in** and save some seats while you wait for Sally. We **went into** the library to the meeting.* Useful synonyms can be found at the entry for **ENTER**.

to go on means to take place: *Is there something **going on** here?* Useful synonyms are **happen** and **occur**.

to go out means to go to a social event: *Our family **goes out** to dinner on Saturday nights.* Useful synonyms are **attend** and **observe**.

to go through means to look at something carefully: *I **went through** my desk looking for my pencil.* Useful synonyms are **examine** and **search**.

good *adjective* | Of high quality; not bad or poor: | *Faith had a **good** time at the party.* *I learned from my doctor that I am in **good** health.*

    admirable | Deserving respect: | *You did an admirable job.*

    excellent | Extremely good: | *Karl always does excellent work.*

    fine | Of high quality; very good: | *My mother made a fine dinner for the family.*

    nice | Pleasant and agreeable: | *We had a nice time at the party.* *The weather will be nice tomorrow.*

For more choices see the entries for GREAT and MORAL.
Antonyms: See the entries for BAD and AWFUL.

WORDS from Words

GOOD is often combined with other words to form expressions that have special meanings. These expressions also have synonyms. *For example:*

as good as means just about: *With a score of ten to nothing, the game is **as good as** lost.* Useful synonyms are ***almost**, **nearly**,* and ***practically**.*

for good means for all time: *The old movie theater is closing **for good**.* Useful synonyms are ***forever**, **once and for all**,* and ***permanently**.*

no good means having no value: *It's **no good** trying to please them.* Useful synonyms are ***useless*** and ***worthless**.*

---

govern *verb* | To control or manage: | *His actions were **governed** by envy.* *A mayor **governs** a city.*

    direct | To manage or control: | *The president directed that several new national parks be created.*

    rule | To have power or control over: | *The queen ruled her subjects well.*

    run | To be in charge of: | *My friend's mother runs an advertising business.*

For more choices see the entry at LEAD.

---

graceful *adjective* | Beautiful or pleasing in design, movement, or style: | *The **graceful** ballet dancers put on a wonderful show.* *We were surprised at how **graceful** the pole-vaulter was.*

    elegant | Fine in quality: | *The bride looked very elegant in her wedding gown.*

    lovely | Having a beautiful appearance: | *These lovely flowers were a gift.* *The new boy in my class has lovely manners.*

For more choices see the entries for HANDSOME and PRETTY.
Antonyms: See the entry for AWKWARD.

gracious *adjective*   Full of grace and charm: *The **gracious** hostess made her guests feel welcome.*
*The tennis player was very **gracious** about losing.*

    courtly   Having manners fit for a royal court; very polite: *The courtly gentleman kissed the woman's hand.*

    kindly   Having or showing kindness: *The kindly woman fed the birds in the park everyday.*

For more choices see the entries for FRIENDLY and POLITE.
Antonyms: See the entry for RUDE.

---

grateful *adjective*   Full of thanks for a favor: *Nina was **grateful** for the help we gave her.*
*We were **grateful** to be inside our house on such a stormy night.*

    appreciative   Showing thankfulness: *The appreciative audience gave a standing ovation.*

    thankful   Feeling or expressing thanks: *She was thankful for the help she received while she was ill.*

---

great *adjective*   Very large size or amount; more than usual; very important: *A **great** crowd gathered to see the president.*
*We had a **great** time at the parade.*
*The scientists made a **great** discovery.*

    excellent   Very good; outstanding: *Your record at school is excellent.*

    notable   Worthy of notice; important: *Climbing Mount Everest is a notable achievement.*

    outstanding   So good it stands out from the rest: *Kelly wrote an outstanding book report.*

    remarkable   Worthy of being noticed: *Your dog can do some remarkable tricks.*

For more choices see the entry for GOOD.
Antonyms: See the entries for BAD and AWFUL.

Word Alert

GREAT is often used in casual conversation to express approval, as in *"That's great!"*

---

greatest *adjective*   The largest in size, number, or amount: *The team that scores the **greatest** number of points wins.*
*China has the **greatest** population of any country.*

    highest   Greater that any other: *Mount Everest is the highest mountain in the world.*

    maximum   The greatest possible: *The maximum number the bus can hold is thirty.*

    supreme   Highest; utmost: *My supreme achievement was winning the state finals.*

    ultimate   Highest: *The ultimate achievement of the space program was the walk on the moon.*

    utmost   Greatest or highest: *The students have the utmost respect for the principal.*

greed *noun* — A selfish desire for more than one's share: — *His **greed** made him steal the money.*

craving — A feeling of longing for something: — *Nelson and Mark had a strong **craving** for lemonade on that hot summer day.*

desire — A longing or wish: — *Laura had a strong **desire** to travel.*

hunger — A strong wish or need for something: — *The corrupt politician would do anything to satisfy his **hunger** for power.*

longing — To want very much: — *She had a **longing** to see her old home again.*

---

group *noun* — A number of persons or things: — *A **group** of boys went to the football game together. The **group** decided not to attend the concert.*

band — A group of people or animals: — *The police caught a **band** of jewel thieves. A **band** of monkeys scampered through the jungle.*

bunch — A group of people or things: — *A **bunch** of us went to the movies. I bought a **bunch** of bananas.*

crowd — A lot of people gathered together: — *A huge **crowd** waited for the store to open on the day of the sale.*

gang — A group of people who do things together: — *Our **gang** gets together on Saturday and collects trash for recycling.*

set — A group of things or persons: — *We have a new **set** of dishes.*

troop — A group of people doing something together: — *A **troop** of children waited for the library to open.*

WORD BANK

GROUPS of animals often have special names. Sometimes you can make things clearer for your reader by naming the particular **group** of animals you mean. Some **groups** are:

brace — ducks
colony — ants, termites, frogs
covey — quail, pheasants
flock — birds, sheep
gaggle — geese
gang — elk

herd — cattle, deer, horses
litter — kittens, puppies
mob — kangaroos
nest — rabbits, wasps, vipers
pack — dogs, wolves
pod — seals, whales

pride — lions
school — fish
shoal — fish
swarm — bees, wasps, ants
troop — baboons, monkeys
yoke — oxen

grow *verb* — To become bigger: — *Flowers **grow** in the sunshine.*
*Veronica **grew** two inches over the summer.*

    develop — To grow or cause to grow: — *You can **develop** your muscles by exercising.*

    mature — To become fully grown or developed: — *An elephant takes years to **mature**; a mouse takes days.*

For more choices see the entry for EXPAND.
Antonyms: See the entry for DWINDLE.

---

guess *verb* — To give an answer you are not sure about: — *He **guessed** the time.*
*Can you **guess** how much farther we have to go?*

    estimate — To form an opinion by reasoning: — *We **estimated** that at this rate we had another hour to travel before we reached home.*

    imagine — To suppose; guess: — *I don't **imagine** the ball game will be played if it rains.*

    judge — To form an opinion: — *Jack **judged** the distance to the other side of the river to be about fifty feet.*

    reckon — To count or calculate: — *We **reckoned** that the boat could comfortably hold about a dozen people.*

---

guide *verb* — To show the way: — *The ranger **guided** us through the forest.*
*Evan will **guide** you to the library.*

    shepherd — To take care of in the way a shepherd takes care of sheep: — *The teacher **shepherded** the class through the museum.*

    show the way — To guide or lead: — *The conductor **showed the way** to our seats on the train.*

    steer — To follow or direct one's course: — *Caroline **steered** the sailboat into the harbor.*

    usher — To lead: — *The waiter **ushered** us to our table.*

For more choices see the entry for LEAD.

habit *noun* — An action you repeat without thinking: *Dalton has a **habit** of shutting his eyes when he is nervous.*

    custom — The usual way of doing something; habit: *It is my **custom** to walk the same way to school every morning.*

    practice — The usual way of doing something: *My usual **practice** is to eat lunch in the cafeteria.*

    routine — A regular way of doing something: *Doing my homework before I watch television is part of my daily **routine**.*

---

hand *verb* — To give or pass with the hand: *I **handed** a hammer to my dad. **Hand** me the telephone, please.*

    deliver — To take to the proper place or person: *The pizzas were **delivered** only a few minutes after we ordered them.*

    pass — To hand or move from one person to another: *Please take one paper and **pass** the rest to the person seated behind you. Courtney **passed** the salt to Doug.*

    transfer — To move from one person or place to another: *I **transferred** from French class to Spanish.*

WORDS from Words

HAND is often combined with other words to form expressions that have special meanings. These expressions also have synonyms. *For example:*

on hand means ready or available for use: *We always keep a first aid kit **on hand** in case of emergency.* Useful synonyms are ***available*** and ***ready***.

to hand down means to pass along, usually from one generation to another: *This pocket watch was **handed down** from my grandfather to my father, and now I am **handing** it **down** to you.* Useful synonyms are ***give*** and ***pass on***.

to hand in and **hand over** mean to give or deliver: *I **handed in** my book report on time. The train passengers **handed over** their tickets to the conductor.* Useful synonyms are ***give***, ***submit***, and ***transfer***.

to hand out means to give out: *The teacher **handed out** the tests.* Useful synonyms are ***deliver***, ***distribute***, and ***pass out***.

handsome
adjective

Having a pleasing appearance:

She purchased a **handsome** bookcase at the antique shop.
He wore a **handsome** suit for the meeting.
The leading man in the movie was very **handsome**.

attractive

Appealing; pleasing:

Leslie is wearing an attractive outfit today.

good-looking

Handsome; having a pleasing appearance:

The star drove a good-looking car in the movie.

For more choices see the entries for BEAUTIFUL, MAGNIFICENT, **and** PRETTY.

---

happen *verb*

To take place:

The meeting **happened** last week.
What **happened** while I was away?

develop

To gradually come into being:

As he moved his pieces on the board, his plan for the chess game slowly developed.

occur

To take place:

The fire drill occurred last week.

take place

To happen; occur:

The game will take place on Saturday.
The party took place last weekend.

---

happy *adjective*

Feeling or showing pleasure or gladness:

They were **happy** when their team won.
The **happy** puppy wagged its tail.

cheerful

Showing or feeling happiness:

Adrian gave everyone a cheerful grin.

glad

Happy; pleased:

We were glad to meet the new student.

pleasing

Agreeable or giving pleasure:

Chelsea had a very pleasing smile.

For more choices see the entry for JOLLY.
Antonyms: See the entries for SAD, SULLEN, and UNHAPPY.

---

hard *adjective*

Needing or using much effort; not easy to do or deal with:

Mowing the lawn is **hard** work.
The old car had a **hard** time getting up the steep hill.

demanding

Requiring great skill, attention, or effort:

Being a teacher is a demanding job.

difficult

Hard to do; requiring effort:

Steering the ship through the storm was a difficult task.

tough

Difficult to do, often in a physical sense:

Catching wild horses is tough work.

Antonyms: See the entry for EASY.

hate *verb* — To have very strong feelings against: — *I **hated** broccoli until my grandmother cooked it for me. If your cat **hates** my dog, why are they playing together?*

    despise — To look down on as worthless; scorn: — *My teacher **despises** cheating.*

    detest — To dislike very much; hate: — *Alex **detests** winter weather.*

    dislike — To have a feeling of not liking something: — *Jason **dislikes** football but loves soccer.*

    loathe — To dislike strongly; to feel disgust toward: — *I **loathed** bugs until I learned how interesting they are.*

    scorn — To have a feeling of hatred for someone or something thought of as low or bad: — *Most of us would **scorn** a person who lies all the time. She looked at the rat with **scorn**.*

Antonyms: See the entry for LOVE.

---

heal *verb* — To make or become healthy again: — *The doctor **healed** her sore knee in a few days. The cut **healed** without leaving a scar.*

    cure — To make a person or animal healthy again: — *My doctor **cured** my infection with medicine.*

    mend — To heal; improve: — *It took weeks for my broken arm to **mend**.*

    recover — To return to a normal condition: — *My friend is **recovering** from the flu.*

    restore — To bring back to a former condition: — *A week at home **restored** my health.*

---

heavy *adjective* — Having great weight; hard to move: — *Ellen carried a **heavy** load of books in her backpack. The sofa was too **heavy** for us to lift.*

    massive — Of great size or extent: — *The **massive** cabinet weighed a ton.*

    stout — Thick and heavy: — *Our cat is so **stout** it can barely climb the stairs.*

    weighty — Having great weight or significance: — *I couldn't lift his **weighty** suitcase. Controlling pollution is a **weighty** problem.*

---

height *noun* — The distance from bottom to top: — *The building had a **height** of 60 feet. They measured the **height** of the tree.*

    altitude — The height something is above ground or above sea level: — *Jet airliners fly at an **altitude** of more than 30,000 feet.*

    elevation — The height above the earth's surface or above sea level: — *The **elevation** of our town is 240 feet above sea level.*

help *verb*

To give something useful or needed:

Sharon **helped** me with my homework.
I will **help** clean out the garage.

aid
To give help or support:
The lifeguard aided a swimmer who was floundering in the rough waves.

assist
To help; aid:
We assisted our teacher by passing out pencils and paper.

back
To help or support:
My friends backed me in the election for secretary.

For more choices see the entry for SUPPORT.
Antonyms: See the entry for HURT.

---

hesitant *adjective*

Showing hesitation; not quite willing:

Jake was **hesitant** about jumping into the lake for a swim.
I was **hesitant** about working with her until I knew the whole plan.

doubtful
Feeling, showing, or causing doubt; not sure or certain:
The outcome of the contest was doubtful until the last moment.

reluctant
Unwilling:
She was reluctant to lend her sweater because she didn't want it to get dirty.

uncertain
Not dependable; changing:
It is best to wear a jacket in uncertain weather.

wavering
Undecided; hesitant:
The wavering support for our team didn't help their confidence.

Antonyms: See the entry for SURE.

---

hesitate *verb*

To wait or stop for a moment, especially because of feeling unsure; to be unwilling:

I **hesitated** before entering my new school for the first time.
The horse **hesitated** and refused to jump the fence.

falter
To act or move in an unsteady or hesitant way:
The child faltered while trying to take a step.

lag
To move less quickly and follow:
My little sister always lags behind the rest of us.
After lagging behind the pack, the runner sprinted to the finish line and won the race.

waver
To be undecided; hesitate:
Public opinion wavered during the long campaign.

For more choices see the entries for DELAY and PAUSE.

---

hesitation *noun*

A delay or pause because of fear, uncertainty, or forgetting:

Becky stepped up to the podium without **hesitation** and delivered her speech.
After a moment's **hesitation**, I decided to go ahead.

delay
The act of putting off to another time or being put off:
There will be an hour's delay before the plane takes off.

pause
A short stop or rest:
We took a pause while we decided what to do next.
There was a pause while the computer started.

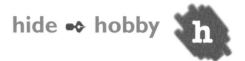
hide *verb*   To put or keep out of sight: The class tried to **hide** the surprise gift from the teacher.
We **hid** behind a tree.
The ball was **hidden** in the deep grass.

    cover   To hide: Grass covered the old path.

    cover up   To hide: She tried to cover up her embarrassment by smiling.

    disguise   To hide: We disguised our hiding place with branches and leaves.

    mask   To hide or cover up: A row of trees masks the view of the house from the road.
Guy tried to mask his disappointment with a joke.

For more choices see the entry for CONCEAL.
Antonyms: See the entries for SHOW and REVEAL.

---

hire *verb*   To give a job to: Adam's neighbor **hired** him to baby-sit.
My brother drove us to the party because we couldn't afford to **hire** a limousine.

    employ   To pay someone to do work: The school employed more teachers to deal
with the growing number of students.

    engage   To hire: The stores engaged more workers for the holiday rush.

---

hit *verb*   To give a blow to: The truck **hit** the curb but didn't do any damage.
Gavin **hit** the ball over the fence.

    beat   To hit again and again; pound: He beat the drum in time with the music.

    hammer   To strike again and again; pound: I hammered a nail into the wall to hang a picture.

    pound   To hit with heavy blows: She pounded on the door.

    punch   To hit a person or thing with a fist or hand: The boxers punched each other.

    strike   To give a blow to; hit: My bike struck the curb and fell over.

For more choices see the entries for CRASH and KNOCK.

---

hobby *noun*   Something done regularly in one's spare time for pleasure: You might be surprised what an exciting
hobby watching birds can be.
My **hobbies** are collecting foreign stamps and coins.

    activity   A thing to do or done for pleasure: I have activities after school on Tuesdays and Thursdays.
Phil's activities include soccer practice and glee club.

    pastime   Something that makes the time pass in a pleasant way: Riding a bike and playing tennis are my favorite pastimes.
Baseball is sometimes called the national pastime.

    pursuit   A hobby or other interest: Learning to cook is one of my favorite pursuits.

Antonyms: See the entry for WORK¹.

hold *verb*   To take and keep in the hands or arms: *Please **hold** the keys while I carry the boxes. They **held** the birthday cake between them.*

   clasp   To hold or grasp tightly: *Alexa clasped Jerry's hand and pulled him up.*

   clutch   To grasp tightly: *I clutched the rail as the roller coaster started.*

   grip   To take hold of firmly and tightly: *She gripped the baseball bat and stepped up to the plate.*

For more choices see the entries for SEIZE and TAKE[1].
Antonyms: See the entry for MISS.

WORDS from Words

HOLD is often combined with other words to form expressions that have special meanings. These expressions also have synonyms. *For example:*

to hold back means to keep from moving on or continuing: *The fence **held back** the ferocious dog. Dawn tried to **hold back** her laughter.* Useful synonyms are **harness**, **hinder**, and **restrain**.

to hold out means to last or keep fighting: *They **held out** as long as they could but finally had to surrender.* Useful synonyms are **continue**, **persist**, and **resist**.

to hold up means to keep from falling: *The walls **hold up** the roof.* Useful synonyms are **brace**, **prop up**, and **support**. **Hold up** can also mean to rob someone: *The police arrived in time to catch the robbers who **held up** the bank.*

hole *noun*   A hollow place or gap in something solid: *I almost didn't notice that there was a **hole** in my shirt. My dog keeps digging **holes** in the garden.*

   cavity   A hollow place; hole: *Woodpeckers dig cavities in trees for their nests.*

   crater   A hollow area that looks like the inside of a bowl: *There are many large craters on the moon that can be seen from earth.*

   hollow   A hole or empty space: *My bike rattled as I rode over a hollow in the road.*

   pit   A hole in the ground: *They used a bulldozer to dig a pit for the swimming pool.*

honest *adjective*   Fair and upright; not cheating, lying, or stealing: *He had an **honest** look on his face.*

   honorable   Showing a sense of what is right and proper: *It is not honorable to cheat.*

   truthful   Telling the truth: *She gave truthful answers to the teacher's questions.*

   upright   Good; honest: *An upright citizen is sure to obey the law.*

For more choices see the entry for RESPONSIBLE.

hope *verb* — To wish for something very much: — *Angela hoped that her guests would arrive on time.*
We hope that Shannon will get well soon.

    anticipate — To look forward to; expect: — *We anticipated having a good time at the party.*

    expect — To look forward to: — *I expect to see my best friend tomorrow.*

    look forward to — To wait eagerly: — *We looked forward to our vacation.*

    wish — To want something very much: — *I wish summer would never end.*

---

horse *noun* — A large animal used for riding and pulling heavy loads: — *That horse has a beautiful mane.*
Knights rode to battle on horses.

    colt — A young horse or similar animal, often a male: — *A young donkey or zebra is also called a colt.*

    filly — A young female horse: — *We named the filly Blaze because of her color.*

    foal — A young horse shortly after birth: — *The foal struggled to stand up soon after it was born.*

    mare — A female horse, donkey, or zebra: — *The mare looked after her colt.*

    pony — A small kind of horse: — *There are ponies you can ride at the park.*

    stallion — An adult male horse: — *The stallion protected the herd of mares and colts.*

WORD BANK

Sometimes you can make things clearer and more interesting for your reader by naming the particular **HORSE** you mean. Some **horses** are:

Arabian	draft horse	palomino	steed
bronco	hack	pinto	thoroughbred
carriage horse	mustang	quarter horse	warhorse
charger	nag	racehorse	workhorse
circus horse	packhorse	saddle horse	yearling

There is also a great deal of equipment used for riding or working with **horses**. The names of some of this equipment are:

bit	draft horse	reins	stable
bridle	halter	saddle	stall
cinch	harness	saddle blanket	stirrup

hot *adjective*   Having a high temperature: *It is nice to have a breeze on **hot** summer days. The oven is **hot**.*

fiery   As hot as fire; burning: *The volcano's lava left a fiery trail.*

scalding   Hot enough to burn, often said of liquids: *A pot of scalding water spilled on the floor.*

scorching   Hot enough to burn the outside of something: *The fire in the furnace was scorching hot.*

torrid   Extremely hot, often said of weather: *A torrid summer wind swept across the desert.*

For more choices see the entry for WARM.
Antonyms: See the entries for COLD and RAW.

---

house *noun*   A place where people or animals live: *We are moving to a new **house** next week. A hermit crab uses an empty snail shell for its **house**.*

dwelling   A place where a person lives: *We live in a two-family dwelling.*

home   The place where a person lives: *Our home is in an apartment house.*

residence   A place where a person lives: *The entrance to our residence is on the third floor.*

For more choices see the entries for CABIN and HUT.

WORD BANK

Sometimes you can make things clearer and more interesting for your reader by naming the particular **HOUSE** you mean. Some **houses** are:

castle	*estate*	*manor*	*plantation*
chateau	*hacienda*	*mansion*	*villa*

---

humanity *noun*   All human beings; people: *Cleaning up pollution will help all **humanity**.*

humankind   All human beings: *Scientists study the origin of humankind.*

man   A human being or the human race: *Early man lived in caves.*

mankind   The human race; human beings as a group: *The landing on the moon is one of the great achievements of mankind.*

For more choices see the entries for PEOPLE and PERSON.

humble *adjective* — Not proud: — He was a **humble** man who gave credit to others for his achievements.

modest — Not thinking too highly of oneself: — A modest person does not show off or brag.

unassuming — Modest: — The people were charmed by the unassuming attitude of the movie star.

Antonyms: See the entry for PROUD².

---

hungry *adjective* — Wanting or needing food: — The **hungry** goldfish swam to the surface of the water when Kyle came near.
They had dinner early because they were so **hungry**.

famished — Very hungry; starving: — We were famished by dinnertime because we missed lunch.

ravenous — Very hungry: — I am so ravenous, I could eat anything.

starving — Very hungry: — I'm starving; let's eat.

---

hunt *verb* — To look hard for something or someone: — We helped Spencer **hunt** for the book he wanted.
People **hunted** eagles until they were protected by law.

chase — To run after and try to catch: — We chased the bus but couldn't catch it.

pursue — To follow in order to catch or capture: — The dog pursued the cat across the yard.
The police pursued the suspect.

stalk — To follow someone or something quietly and carefully: — The cheetah stalked a zebra.

track — To follow the marks left by a person or animal: — The hunters tracked the bear into the mountains.

trail — To follow the path or scent of: — The photographer trailed the deer with the help of his hound.

For more choices see the entry for LOOK².

---

hurry *verb* — To move faster than usual: — They **hurried** to the movie so they wouldn't miss the beginning.
You will have to **hurry** if you want to catch up.

hasten — To move quickly; hurry: — They hastened to keep up with the experienced hikers.
Let me hasten to say how right I think you are.

hustle — To move or do something very quickly: — The team hustled onto the field, ready to play.

rush — To move, go, or come quickly: — The cars rushed by on the highway.
We rushed to catch the train.

For more choices see the entries for RUN and ZOOM.

hurt *verb* To cause pain or injury:

*I **hurt** my leg roller-skating.*
*That bump really **hurts**.*
*They weren't **hurt**, because their seat belts protected them.*
*Her remark **hurt** my feelings.*

ache To hurt with a dull, constant pain:

My legs ached after trying those new exercises.

smart To cause or feel a sharp, stinging pain:

My hand smarted from the bee sting.

suffer To hurt from pain or sorrow:

I suffered from a sore throat.

For more choices see the entry for INJURE.
Antonyms: See the entry for HELP.

---

hut *noun* A small, roughly built house or shelter:

*They put up a flimsy **hut** to live in while they built a house.*
*He wrote in a little **hut** near a pond.*

shack A small, roughly built hut or cabin:

We built a shack out of some boards left over from building the garage.

shed A small building used for storing things:

All our gardening tools are in the shed.

For more choices see the entries for CABIN and HOUSE.

idea *noun* — A picture formed in the mind; a belief or opinion: — *The **idea** for Velcro came from noticing how burrs catch on clothing.*
*We all had different **ideas** about what to do.*

concept — A general idea; thought: — *Our country honors the **concept** that everyone is equal under the law.*

notion — An idea or belief: — *Do you have any **notion** of where we are?*

thought — The product of thinking; an idea: — *My **thought** is that home is in that direction.*
*What are your **thoughts**?*

For more choices see the entry for BELIEF.

ideal *noun* — The best and most perfect result; model: — *Our laws are based on certain **ideals**.*
*His teacher became his **ideal**.*

dream — A hope or ambition to do or succeed at something: — *Richard has a **dream** of becoming a great actor.*
*If he works hard, his **dream** may come true.*

model — A person or thing that is a good example: — *Parents are the **models** for their children's behavior.*

standard — Anything used to set an example: — *The **standards** for taking honors courses are very high at this school.*

For more choices see the entry for PURPOSE.

imagination *noun* — The ability to create ideas or images: — *It takes a lot of **imagination** to write science fiction.*
*In his **imagination** he was a star athlete.*

creativity — The ability to make something in a new way: — *The chef's **creativity** was best shown by his delicious desserts.*

fancy — The picturing of things in the mind; imagination: — *It was just her **fancy** that she had an invisible friend.*

fantasy — Playful or wishful imagination: — *Nelson had a **fantasy** about flying to the moon on a huge bird.*

originality — The ability to do or think of something new: — *The artist showed great **originality** in her work.*

imitate ↔ impolite

imitate *verb* | To act like another person or thing: | Everyone was amused when the child **imitated** the singer. Many teenagers **imitate** people they admire.

copy | To make or do something that is exactly like something else: | Some fans copied the way the rock star dressed.

mimic | To imitate: | The comedian mimicked famous people to make fun of them.

reproduce | To produce, form, or bring about again: | This computer program reproduces the experience of flying a jet fighter.

---

immediate *adjective* | Done right away, without delay: | The teacher wanted an **immediate** answer. Danielle's **immediate** response to the party invitation was joy.

instant | Without delay; immediate: | Our computer gave an instant reply to our question.

prompt | Quick or on time: | The restaurant always gives us prompt service.

punctual | On time; prompt: | Ian is always punctual for appointments.

Antonyms: See the entry for LATE.

---

imperfect *adjective* | Having mistakes or faults: | Her **imperfect** vision was corrected by eyeglasses. The jacket was **imperfect** because one sleeve was longer than the other.

defective | Having a flaw or weakness; not perfect: | The defective appliance wouldn't even turn on.

faulty | Having something wrong: | The flat tire on my bicycle was caused by a faulty valve.

flawed | Having scratches, cracks, or slight defects: | The flawed mirror made me look short.

Antonyms: See the entry for PERFECT.

---

impolite *adjective* | Showing bad manners: | It is **impolite** to talk with your mouth full of food. I don't want to introduce Ralph to my friends because he is so **impolite**.

discourteous | Impolite; rude: | It is discourteous to interrupt others when they are speaking.

disrespectful | Showing lack of respect: | Some disrespectful people booed the mayor when he started his speech.

inconsiderate | Not thoughtful of others; rude: | The inconsiderate guest left without thanking his hosts.

rude | Having or showing bad manners: | They asked her to leave because of her rude behavior.

104

important
adjective

Having great value or meaning:

It is **important** to take care of your health.
There will be an **important** meeting at school to decide what the new mascot will be.

crucial	Very important; decisive:	The *crucial* championship game is next week.
prominent	Well-known or important:	The city council is made up of *prominent* citizens.
serious	Important:	Failing the math test is a *serious* problem.
significant	Having special value or meaning:	A presidential election is a *significant* event.

For more choices see the entries for KEY, MAIN, and URGENT.
Antonyms: See the entry for UNIMPORTANT.

---

incomplete
adjective

Not complete or finished:

You can't play cards with an **incomplete** deck.
Her homework was **incomplete** when it was due.

deficient	Lacking something needed:	He became ill because his diet was *deficient* in vitamins.
unfinished	Not finished or complete:	Don't turn in an *unfinished* project.

Antonyms: See the entry for COMPLETE.

---

incorrect
adjective

Not right or correct:

I had so many **incorrect** answers on my math test, the paper was covered with red marks.
They took an **incorrect** turn and got lost.

false	Not true or correct:	The guide gave us a *false* idea of where to go.
inaccurate	Not correct; wrong:	We followed the directions, but they were *inaccurate*.
mistaken	Wrong; in error:	We had a *mistaken* idea about where we were and we got lost.

For more choices see the entry for WRONG.
Antonyms: See the entries for CORRECT, RIGHT, and TRUE.

---

incredible
adjective

Hard to believe:

Dylan's **incredible** story made the teacher laugh.
He spends an **incredible** amount of money on clothes.

amazing	Surprising; astonishing:	The child had an *amazing* gift for playing the cello.
astonishing	Very surprising:	Shelly has an *astonishing* ability to recall details.
remarkable	Worthy of being noticed; unusual:	Hurricane winds have *remarkable* force.
unbelievable	Hard to believe:	The magician made an *unbelievable* escape from a locked jail cell.

For more choices see the entry for UNUSUAL.
Antonyms: See the entry for USUAL.

indifference •◆ infuriate

indifference
noun

Lack of interest, concern, or care:

*Her supposed **indifference** to other people turned out to be shyness.*

   apathy

Lack of feeling, interest, or concern:

*Many people didn't bother to vote because of their **apathy** about the election.*

   inattention

Lack of interest or care:

*He missed the homework assignment because of his **inattention**.*

   unconcern

Lack of interest or concern:

*His **unconcern** about the time made him miss his appointment.*

Antonyms: See the entry for INTEREST.

---

informal *adjective*

Not formal; without ceremony:

*She e-mailed the invitations to the **informal** party. Even though the president was there, the meeting was very **informal**.*

   casual

Informal:

*The camp counselor had a **casual** attitude about the rules and was not strict.*
*The guests wore **casual** clothes to the barbecue.*

   easygoing

Not strict; easy to please:

*The official's **easygoing** manner made us comfortable.*

   relaxed

Not strict or severe:

*The vacation resort had a very **relaxed** atmosphere.*

---

information
noun

Knowledge and facts about something:

*The **information** Jan found on the Web was wrong. New **information** made Randy change his mind.*

   evidence

Proof of something:

*The fossil bones scientists found are **evidence** that dinosaurs once lived here.*

   fact

Something known to be true or real:

*It is a **fact** that the earth is round.*

   news

Information about something that happened recently:

*The **news** of the discovery excited everyone.*

For more choices see the entries for DATA and KNOWLEDGE.

---

infuriate *verb*

To make angry or furious:

*Jennifer's teasing **infuriated** Brianna. It **infuriates** me when my computer crashes.*

   anger

To make or become angry:

*The teacher was **angered** by our bad behavior.*

   enrage

To make angry; put into a rage:

*The other team's poor sportsmanship **enraged** the fans.*

   incense

To make very angry:

*The audience was **incensed** by the speaker's obvious falsehoods.*

   madden

To make angry or crazy:

*The constant interruptions when I was trying to study **maddened** me.*

Antonyms: See the entry for EASE.

injure *verb* To cause physical damage: *Jon fell and **injured** his leg.*
*Spreading false stories can **injure** someone's reputation.*

damage To injure or harm: *The flood **damaged** many houses.*

harm To injure or damage something: *Those flies can't **harm** you, but they sure are bothersome.*
*A good trainer never **harms** an animal.*

wound To injure or hurt by piercing the skin: *The soldier was **wounded** during the battle.*

For more choices see the entry for HURT.
Antonyms: See the entry for HELP.

---

insect *noun* Any of a large group of small animals without a backbone: *__Insects__ have three pairs of legs, a body divided into three parts, and usually two pairs of wings.*
*Flies, ants, and beetles are **insects**.*
*Spiders have eight legs and are not **insects**.*

arthropod One of a large group of animals with no backbone: *Lobsters, crabs, insects, and spiders are **arthropods**.*

bug A general term for any insect or crawling animal: *A **bug** crawled up a blade of grass.*
*Some people are afraid of **bugs**.*

WORD BANK

Sometimes you can make things clearer and more interesting for your reader by naming the particular **INSECT** you mean. Some **insects** are:

ant	cockroach	gnat	mantis
bee	cricket	grasshopper	midge
beetle	dragonfly	hornet	mosquito
butterfly	earwig	housefly	moth
caddis fly	firefly	ladybird beetle	termites
cicada	flea	locust	wasp

---

inside *adjective* On or in the inner side: *Although I wanted a window, I had to take an **inside** seat on the plane.*
*Do you know the **inside** story?*

inner Farther in: *The biology lab is in the **inner** room.*

interior Having to do with or on the inner side: *The **interior** walls of the house are white.*

internal Having to do with or on the inside: *The heart and the stomach are **internal** organs of the body.*

Antonyms: See the entry for OUTSIDE.

I   inside •→ inspect

inside *noun*   The inner side or part: *The inside of the cave was pitch black.*
Wait until you see the inside of our house.

   interior   The inner side, surface,   *The interior of the car was tan leather.*
                  or part:

Antonyms: See the entry for OUTSIDE.

Word Alert

INSIDES means the internal organs of the body: *My insides ached when I had the flu.* Useful synonyms for **insides** are *innards* and *organs*.

---

insist *verb*   To request or say in a   *The mayor insisted that his plan was the best.*
                        strong, firm manner: *Sometimes, if you insist too much you won't*
                                                 get what you want.

   assert   To insist on; claim: *The witness asserted that his story was true.*

   claim   To say that something   *The old man claimed he was a hero and showed us*
              is true: *his medals to prove it.*

   demand   To ask for forcefully: *The customer demanded a refund for the broken toy.*

   require   To force, order, or demand: *The rules require that we attend school assemblies.*

   urge   To speak or argue strongly   *The speaker urged us to vote.*
             for something:

For more choices see the entries for FORCE and ORDER.

---

inspect *verb*   To look at closely   *The fire department inspects the school every year.*
                         and carefully: *She inspected herself in a mirror to make sure*
                                            she looked her best.

   check   To test to find out if   *The mechanic checked the brakes on our car.*
              something is correct:

   examine   To look at closely   *A doctor examines my eyes once each year.*
                and carefully:

   survey   To look at or study   *The governor surveyed the damage*
               in detail: *caused by the flood.*

insult *noun*

A remark or action that hurts someone's feelings:

*It is an **insult** to call someone a liar. The crowd yelled **insults** at the basketball player when he missed an easy shot.*

affront

Something said or done that is purposely mean or insulting:

Her mean comments were an affront to my character.

offense

The act of causing anger or unhappiness:

I was only joking and meant no offense.

slur

An insulting remark:

His comments are a slur on our town's reputation.

Antonyms: See the entry for PRAISE.

---

insult *verb*

To hurt the feelings or pride of:

*You **insulted** my friends by not showing up for their party. She **insulted** me by ignoring me.*

affront

To insult directly and openly:

The protesters affronted the mayor by shouting him down.

offend

To cause to be angry or unhappy:

Your rude behavior offended me.

outrage

To cause to feel great anger:

Their silly prank outraged many of their neighbors.

scorn

To treat or reject as low or bad:

Many people scorned her for being a gossip.

slander

To utter false and damaging statements about a person:

The senator charged that the newspaper had slandered her.

Antonyms: See the entry for PRAISE.

---

intelligence *noun*

The ability to think, learn, and understand:

*Scientists have shown that animals have more **intelligence** than we realized. There are tests that measure **intelligence**, but they can't measure future achievement.*

brains

Intelligence:

It takes brains to figure out a math problem like this.

cleverness

Alertness and quickness of mind:

We could never trap the squirrel because of its cleverness.

intellect

The power of mind to think, learn, and understand:

Our history professor has a great intellect.

mind

The part of a person that thinks, knows, learns, remembers, understands, and feels:

You can succeed if you put your mind to it.

intend *verb* — To have a purpose or plan in mind: — *What do you **intend** to do with your free time? James **intended** to be home early, but choir practice ran longer than he expected.*

aim — To intend for; direct toward: — *The advertisements were aimed at people interested in baseball.*

expect — To want something because it is right or necessary: — *I expected you to apologize sooner.*

plan — To have an intention: — *We planned the party so it would be a complete surprise for Jennifer.*

propose — To intend or plan to do something: — *Logan proposes to study to become an astronomer. Randi proposed a walk in the park after lunch.*

interest *noun* — A desire to know about something: — *Natalie has a strong **interest** in horses. No one in the class had any **interest** in visiting the box factory.*

attention — Notice, interest: — *A loud noise attracted our attention.*

concern — Serious interest or worry: — *Jade's concern over the sick kitten kept her awake that night.*

curiosity — A wish to learn new things: — *My curiosity got the better of me, and I opened the mysterious package.*

Antonyms: See the entry for INDIFFERENCE.

interesting *adjective* — Causing or holding interest: — *The museum was more **interesting** than I expected. I heard an **interesting** story about pirate treasure.*

absorbing — Holding the interest of: — *Carol lost all sense of time while reading the absorbing book.*

appealing — Interesting or attractive: — *Eating dinner this late is not appealing to me.*

captivating — Capturing and holding the attention of by beauty or excellence: — *Grandpa told us a captivating ghost story.*

fascinating — Causing and holding interest through a special quality or charm: — *The snake charmer's act was fascinating.*

gripping — Attracting and keeping interest: — *The audience was spellbound by the gripping ending of the movie.*

inspiring — Having a rousing effect; arousing interest: — *His speech was so inspiring that I stood up and cheered.*

Antonyms: See the entry for DULL.

interrupt *verb* — To break in upon or stop a person from talking or acting: — *The fire drill **interrupted** the lesson.* / *Please do not **interrupt** my speech until I am done.*

  break in — To interrupt: — *The student **broke in** with a question just as the story was getting interesting.*

  cut off — To put an end to or interrupt: — *The storm **cut off** our electricity.*

  disturb — To break in on; interrupt: — *The ringing of the phone **disturbed** everyone's sleep.*

  interfere — To disturb or interrupt: — *The noise from the street **interferes** with my studying.*

---

introduce *verb* — To make known or acquainted: — *The teacher **introduced** the new student to the class.* / *Let me **introduce** you to your new teammates.*

  acquaint — To make familiar: — *Are you **acquainted** with my cousin?*

  announce — To make something known in a formal way: — *The teacher **announced** that there will be a spelling test on Friday.*

  present — To introduce a person: — *Sabrina **presented** her new friend to her parents.*

---

invent *verb* — To make or think of something for the first time: — *The light bulb was **invented** by Thomas Edison.*

  design — To make a plan, drawing, or outline of: — *Isabel **designed** all the costumes for the play.*

  devise — To invent; plan: — *We **devised** a secret code for our messages.*

  originate — To bring into being: — *The idea for the play **originated** from a short story.*

---

invite *verb* — To ask someone to go somewhere or do something: — *Make sure you **invite** Rachel to the party.* / *Everyone we **invited** is coming.*

  ask — To invite: — *We **asked** all our friends to the game.*

  request — To ask for: — *The chairperson **requested** that you attend the meeting.*

  summon — To ask to come: — *The principal **summoned** the senior class to her office.*

---

irritate *verb* — To make angry or impatient: — *Your teasing **irritates** me.* / *Christopher was **irritated** by the constant interruptions.*

  annoy — To bother or disturb: — *Loud music **annoys** me.*

  bother — To give trouble to; annoy: — *A small fly **bothered** me until I brushed it away.*

  pester — To trouble or bother again and again: — *Don't **pester** me with dumb questions.*

  provoke — To make angry or impatient: — *He **provoked** her with his teasing.*

jagged *adjective* — Having sharp points that stick out: — *Many seabirds build their nests on **jagged** cliffs.*

bumpy — Covered with bumps; rough: — *The bus rattled as it traveled down the bumpy road.*

irregular — Not smooth; bumpy: — *We sanded the table to smooth out its irregular surface.*

uneven — Not straight, smooth, or regular: — *You can see how uneven the coast is by looking at a map.*

For more choices see the entry for ROUGH.
Antonyms: See the entries for FLAT and SMOOTH.

---

jail *noun* — A building where people who are awaiting trial or have been found guilty of breaking the law are kept: — *The police kept the outlaws in **jail**.*

brig — A prison on a ship: — *Sailors are sentenced to the brig when they have been accused or convicted of a crime.*

penitentiary — A prison for people found guilty of serious crimes: — *Prisoners in a penitentiary are guarded twenty-four hours a day.*

prison — A place where people accused or convicted of crimes are forced to stay: — *Inmates of a prison wear uniforms and follow very strict rules.*

---

jealous *adjective* — Having envy of a person or his or her accomplishments: — *Olivia was surprised to learn that Victoria was **jealous** of her dancing ability.*
*The older child was **jealous** of the new baby.*

envious — Feeling or showing envy: — *She was envious when her friend got a beautiful new coat.*

resentful — Feeling or showing anger or bitterness: — *Adrian was resentful about the race because he thought the winner cheated.*

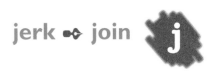

jerk *verb* — To move with a sudden, sharp motion: — The magician **jerked** the curtain away and the flowers were gone.
Katrina **jerked** the fishing pole and pulled out a fish.

jolt — To move with a sharp jerk: — Our car jolted along the rough road.

lurch — To move unsteadily: — The boat lurched from side to side in the strong wind.

tear — To move very quickly: — When we opened the door, the cat tore outside.

For more choices see the entries for PULL and YANK.

---

job *noun* — Something that has to be done: — Your most important **job** is to look after your little sister.
William had two **jobs** during the summer.

chore — A small job or task: — One of Andy's chores is feeding the cat.

duty — Something a person is supposed to do: — One of the manager's duties is to open the shop in the morning.

errand — Something a person is supposed to do: — We have several errands to run while we are downtown.

task — A piece of work to be done: — Your task is to put away all the books.

For more choices see the entry for WORK.

---

jog *verb* — To run or move at a slow, steady pace: — I **jog** with my parents every morning before school.

lope — To run with long, easy strides: — A wolf loped along the trail looking for prey.

trot — To run slowly; jog: — Jacqueline trotted to practice because she was a little late.

For more choices see the entry for RUN.

---

join *verb* — To put or come together: — We all **joined** hands and sang the school song.
Two roads **join** the highway about a mile from here.

combine — To join together; unite: — We combined all the ingredients in a large bowl.

connect — To join loosely: — The two poles were connected with a piece of rope.

enroll — To make or become a member; join: — Rebecca enrolled in a swimming class.

link — To join or be joined: — The class linked arms and formed a circle.

unite — To bring things together so that they become like one: — Two small school districts were united into one large district.

For more choices see the entry for MIX.
Antonyms: See the entry for DIVIDE.

joke *noun* — Something said or done to make people laugh; something not taken seriously:

He told a joke to put everyone at ease.
The exam was so easy it was a joke.

gag — A joke:

We laughed at the comedian's gags.

jest — A playful joke; prank:

His jests were meant to be funny, but they hurt her feelings.

prank — A playful or mischievous act meant to trick or tease somebody:

On April Fool's Day we all played pranks on each other.

---

jolly *adjective* — Full of fun:

His broad smile and funny costume made the clown look very jolly.

joyful — Feeling or causing great happiness:

A family reunion is a joyful occasion.

merry — Happy and cheerful:

Everyone had a merry time on the sleigh ride.

For more choices see the entry for HAPPY.
Antonyms: See the entries for SAD, SULLEN, and UNHAPPY.

---

journey *noun* — Traveling from one place to another; a long trip:

The long journey took us across a desert and over a range of mountains.
We were exhausted by our journey.

expedition — A journey made for a particular reason:

An expedition is being sent to the jungles of Mexico to search for a lost city.

tour — A trip with several stops that usually returns to where it started:

Our tour of the city took us to the park and the harbor, and then back to the hotel.

trip — A brief journey:

My family took a quick trip to the market.

voyage — A long journey:

Magellan made the first voyage around the world.

---

judge *noun* — A person who decides questions or chooses the winner in a contest or dispute:

After listening to all the evidence, the judge made a decision.
The judges selected a winner from among the contestants.

justice — A judge of the Supreme Court of the United States:

There are nine justices on the Supreme Court.

magistrate — A judge:

The magistrate ruled that the accused was innocent.

official — A person who holds a certain office or position:

The referees at a sporting event are often called officials.

jumble *noun* · A confused mixture or condition: · *After the earthquake, there was a **jumble** of books on the floor of the library. My socks were in a **jumble** after I washed them.*

chaos · Complete confusion; great disorder: · *The tornado left the town in complete chaos.*

confusion · The condition of being mixed up; disorder: · *When the lights went out, everyone shouted in confusion. The confusion ended when the lights came back on.*

disorder · A lack of order; confusion: · *My room was in complete disorder after my friends visited.*

mess · An untidy group of things: · *Your desk is such a mess I don't see how you can find anything.*

muddle · A confused condition; mess: · *My school papers were in a terrible muddle after I dropped my notebook.*

For more choices see the entry for MESS.

---

jumble *verb* · To mix or throw into confusion: · *All my pens and pencils were **jumbled** in a drawer. I **jumbled** all my papers together and took them home to organize them.*

confuse · To throw into disorder; mix up: · *At first, the new neighborhood confused me.*

mess up · To make dirty or disorderly: · *We messed up the kitchen trying to make spaghetti sauce.*

muddle · To make a mess of: · *We muddled the job of trying to straighten up the library books.*

scramble · To mix together; mix up: · *I scrambled my notes and couldn't figure them out.*

For more choices see the entry for MIX.
Antonyms: See the entry for ARRANGE.

---

jump *verb* · To spring into the air: · *Danielle **jumped** off the high diving board. The cat was so surprised, it **jumped** straight up into the air.*

bound · To spring back or up: · *A gazelle bounded over the bushes to escape a lion.*

hop · To move by jumping: · *A rabbit hopped across the grass. We hopped over the fence.*

leap · To jump: · *We leaped to our feet when the bell rang. A squirrel leapt from branch to branch.*

vault · To jump over something: · *The runner vaulted the hurdles to win the race. We learned how to vault in gym.*

For more choices see the entry for DIVE.

keep *verb*

To continue to have, hold, or do; to not get rid of something:

Hannah **kept** all her old book reports.
My mother **keeps** pictures of me in an album.
I **keep** trying to call her at home, but there is no answer.

hold   To keep in or not let out: That plastic bottle **holds** one gallon.

reserve   To keep for a special purpose:

My parents **reserved** a table at a restaurant for my birthday party.
The recipe said to **reserve** the chopped onion for later use.

retain   To keep after it has been used:

I didn't **retain** my sales receipt so I couldn't return the shoes to the store.

save   To set aside money or anything else for future use:

Suzanne **saved** all the money she earned baby-sitting.
We **saved** part of our lunch for later.
Squirrels **save** nuts to eat in winter.

store   To put away for future use: My mother **stores** cans of food in our basement.

Antonyms: See the entry for RETURN².

---

key *adjective*

Very important; chief:

The principal holds a **key** position in a school.
The **key** question is not why it was done, but who did it.
Hannah's performance was a **key** factor in the orchestra's success.

cardinal   Of greatest importance; chief: One of my **cardinal** rules is to always tell the truth.

chief   Most important; main: Apples are one of the **chief** crops grown in Washington state.

fundamental   Serving as a basis; essential: Kicking a ball is a **fundamental** skill in soccer.

major   Bigger and more important: The **major** expense for our vacation is getting there.

For more choices see the entries for IMPORTANT and MAIN.
Antonyms: See the entry for UNIMPORTANT.

key *noun* | Something that solves or explains: | The papers Janet found turned out to be the **key** to the mystery.
The **key** to solving these puzzles is in the back of the book.

answer | The solution to a problem: | Can you find the answer to this math problem?

clue | Something that helps to solve a mystery or problem: | The detective looked for clues at the scene of the crime.

guide | A person or thing that explains: | I need a guide to help me fix my computer.

WORDS from Words

KEY can be combined with other words to form expressions that have special meanings. These expressions also have synonyms. *For example:*

keyed up means very excited: *The children were so **keyed up**, they couldn't stand still. If you get too **keyed up** before bedtime, you won't sleep well.* Useful synonyms are **agitated** and **stimulated**.

to key in means to enter information into a computer: *I had to **key in** my report all over again after the computer crashed.* Useful synonyms are **enter**, **input**, and **type in**.

kind *adjective* | Gentle, generous, and friendly. | It was **kind** of you to help.
Pam was always **kind** to stray cats.
He was a **kind** person.

caring | Having concern about others: | She is a caring person who volunteers to work at the hospital.

considerate | Thoughtful of other people and their feelings: | It was considerate of you to let me know you would be late.

humane | Having sympathy for others: | The humane nurses took care of the victims of the flood.

sympathetic | Feeling the sorrow or trouble of others: | A sympathetic friend called every day while I was sick.

For more choices see the entries for FRIENDLY and NICE.

kindness *noun* | The quality of being kind or helpful to others: | *Everyone admired Kaylee for her acts of* **kindness**. *Pets should be treated with* **kindness**.

charity | Kindness and forgiveness toward others: | *I try to show* charity *to people who are unkind to me.*

compassion | Sympathy for someone else's misfortune: | *They felt* compassion *for the poor and collected food for them.*

good will | Kindness and friendliness: | *Our neighbors showed their* good will *by inviting us to a picnic.*

sympathy | The ability to feel and understand the troubles of others: | *Camilla had* sympathy *for the injured dog and took it to a vet.*

---

king *noun* | A man who rules a country; a person or thing that is the most important or best: | *Only a few countries have* **kings** *today. The lion is said to be the* **king** *of the beasts, but the elephant might be a better choice.*

Majesty | A title used in speaking to or about a king, queen, or other royal ruler: | *Thank you, Your* Majesty. *Their* Majesties *have invited us for tea.*

monarch | A king or queen of a country: | *The* monarch's *birthday was celebrated with a parade.*

ruler | A person who rules: | *A king is the* ruler *of a country.*

For more choices see the entry for QUEEN.

---

knock *verb* | To strike with a sharp, hard blow: | *They* **knocked** *on the door when they arrived. We were wrestling and* **knocked** *the lamp off my desk.*

bang | To make a sudden, loud noise: | *The chairwoman* banged *her gavel to call the meeting to order.*

rap | To knock or tap sharply: | *Our guests* rapped *on the door when they arrived.*

tap | To hit or strike lightly: | *We* tapped *on the window to get the clerk's attention.*

thump | To make a dull, heavy sound by knocking: | *My books fell off my desk and* thumped *loudly on the floor.*

For more choices see the entries for CRASH and HIT.

knot *noun*   A tangle or lump of string, rope, or hair: *The rope was tied with a tight* **knot**. *She had to comb the* **knots** *out of her hair after she washed it.*

    snarl   A tangled or knotted mass: *The electric cord had twisted into a terrible* snarl.

    tangle   A twisted, confused mass: *The wind blew my hair into a* tangle.

For more choices see the entry for JUMBLE.

WORD BANK

Sometimes you can make things clearer and more interesting for your reader by naming the particular **KNOT** you mean. Some **knots** are:

bow	*hangman*	*noose*	*splice*
braid	*hitch*	*plait*	*square*
granny	*loop*	*slip*	*tie*

---

know *verb*   To understand clearly: *Do you* **know** *how to play chess?* *I* **know** *the neighborhood like the back of my hand.*

    comprehend   To understand: *It took me a while to* comprehend *how to multiply fractions, but now I understand.*

    grasp   To see the meaning of: *I* grasped *the meaning of the poem as soon as I read it out loud.*

    perceive   To understand, comprehend: *Casey soon* perceived *that she was speaking so softly, no one in the audience could hear her speech.*

For more choices see the entry for UNDERSTAND.

---

knowledge *noun*   An understanding gained through experience or study: *Christian's* **knowledge** *of puppies came from working at a pet store.* *He doesn't have enough* **knowledge** *about cars to fix an engine.*

    awareness   Knowledge: *There was an increasing* awareness *that our deadline was approaching.*

    learning   Knowledge gained through study: *Men and women of great* learning *have made our lives better.*

    wisdom   Good judgment; knowing what is right, good, and true: *We grow in* wisdom *as we gain experience.*

For more choices see the entry for EDUCATION and INFORMATION.

land *noun*

Any part of the earth's surface that is not covered with water:

The **land** stretches from sea to sea.
This is good **land** for growing corn.

earth — Dry land; the ground: — The quake caused the earth to shake.

grounds — The land around a building: — We planted flowers to decorate the school grounds.

property — A piece of land: — My aunt bought some property near the lake.

real estate — Land together with buildings, trees, and other things on it: — He owns real estate in the city.

---

large *adjective*

Big in size or amount:

The **large** airplane carried more than 400 passengers.
The outdoor concert drew a **large** crowd.
Our library has a **large** selection of magazines.

ample — Large in size or capacity: — There was ample room for our whole family in the dining room.

considerable — Great in amount or extent: — That computer costs a considerable amount.
We had considerable trouble walking on the icy sidewalk.

extensive — Large; great; broad: — The mansion had extensive gardens.
The tornado caused extensive damage.

massive — Very large and solid: — The massive football player filled the doorway.
The safe at the bank has a massive door.

sizable — Quite large: — A sizable amount of my allowance is spent on snacks.

For more choices see the entries for BIG, GIANT, and WIDE.
Antonyms: See the entries for LITTLE, SMALL, and TINY.

last [1] *adjective* — Coming at the end:
The mystery was solved in the **last** chapter.
Tammy was always **last** in line.

concluding — Last:
The concluding song at the concert
was one of my favorites.

final — Coming at the end; last:
The final problem on the math test is for extra credit.
The team celebrated after the final game.

ultimate — Last; final:
The ultimate question on the test was too tough for me.
The ultimate result of careless behavior
may be an accident.

---

last [2] *adjective* — Coming just before this; most recent:
The **last** time I saw Emma was two days ago.
How old were you on your **last** birthday?

latest — Happening not long in the past:
Brooke always dressed in the latest style.
Have you seen the latest version of that
computer program?

most recent — Happening closest to now:
I read the most recent book in the series,
and I can't wait for the next one.

newest — Having recently come into a certain state or relationship:
Leslie is the newest member of the chorus.

Word Alert

When used as a verb, **LAST** means to go on or to continue: *The boring movie seemed to last forever.* Synonyms for this meaning of **last** can be found at the entries for **CONTINUE** and **WAIT.** When **last** is used as a noun it means the final: *He was the last in line.* Useful synonyms for this meaning of **last** are **closing**, **concluding**, and **final**.

---

late *adjective* — Coming after the usual time:
Mackenzie wanted to stay up for the **late** show,
but I was too tired.
We were **late** for school because of the rain.

delayed — Not on time; late:
All the flights were delayed because of the snowstorm.

overdue — Not on time; late:
The plane from London is overdue.

tardy — Arriving or happening after the appointed time:
Several students were tardy for class because
of the traffic.

Antonyms: See the entry for IMMEDIATE.

laugh *verb* — To make the sounds and facial expressions that show amusement:

*We all **laughed** at the funny cartoon.*
*Our confident team **laughed** at the thought of losing.*

chuckle — To laugh softly, especially to oneself:

*Carla **chuckled** when she read my note.*

giggle — To laugh in a silly, high-pitched, or nervous way:

*Josie **giggled** at the joke.*

guffaw — To laugh loudly:

*Dan **guffawed** so hard he had to hold his sides.*

roar — To laugh loudly:

*The crowd **roared** at the tricks the clowns did.*

snicker — To laugh in a sly way:

*The sneaky child **snickered** when someone else got into trouble.*

Antonyms: See the entry for CRY.

WORD BANK

There are many other ways to describe a **LAUGH** beyond the synonyms listed above. Some possible choices are:

be in stitches	*chortle*	*roll in the aisle*	*slap one's thighs*
belly laugh	*crow*	*scream*	*split one's sides*
break up	*howl*	*shriek*	*titter*
bubble	*laugh one's head off*	*snigger*	*twitter*
cackle	*laugh till one cries*	*snort*	*whoop*

law *noun* — A rule made by a government for the people of a town, state, or country:

*The same **laws** apply to every citizen, no matter how rich or poor.*
*The police enforce traffic **laws** on the highway.*

bill — A suggested law:

*A **bill** must be passed by Congress and signed by the president before it becomes a federal law.*

code — A set of laws or rules that people live by:

*The local traffic **code** requires that a person riding a bicycle wear a safety helmet.*

ordinance — A rule of law made by an authority; decree:

*Many cities have **ordinances** controlling the level of pollution automobiles are allowed to produce.*

statute — A law:

*You can read the **statutes** in the library to find out what the law says.*

For more choices see the entry for RULE.

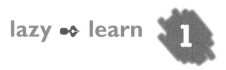
lazy *adjective*   Not willing to work: *When the mouse appeared, the lazy cat stretched and went back to sleep.*
She's too lazy to clean up her room.

   idle   Not wanting to be active; lazy: *The idle children were no help with the chores.*

   inactive   Idle; sluggish: *Most reptiles are inactive during cold weather.*

   listless   Inactive or not caring: *The exhausted players were in a listless mood after losing the game.*

   sluggish   Not energetic or alert: *Lack of sleep made me sluggish.*

Antonyms: See the entry for BUSY.

---

lead *verb*   To show the way or be head of: *The usher led us to our seats in the front row.*
You can lead if you know the way.
A conductor leads a symphony orchestra.

   command   To have power over; rule: *The general commanded his troops to stand at attention.*

   conduct   To direct or show the way: *Our history teacher conducted our class in the art museum.*
Our music teacher conducts the chorus.

   direct   To manage or control; guide: *The air controllers direct the planes from the airport tower.*

   escort   To go along to protect or show honor: *The queen was escorted by several dignitaries on her visit.*

   manage   To direct or control: *The president of a company manages the people who work for him.*

   supervise   To watch over and direct: *Our coach supervises all our team practices.*

For more choices see the entries for GUIDE and GOVERN.

---

learn *verb*   To get to know through study or practice; to gain knowledge or skill: *We will learn about computers in class tomorrow.*
She learned to swim before I did.

   acquire   To get; learn: *I want to acquire the ability to speak Italian.*

   find out   To learn: *Find out where we are supposed to meet.*
Nancy found out what the assignment is.

   master   To become an expert in: *It can take years to master physics.*
Jackson mastered algebra easily.

   pick up   To learn: *We hoped we would pick up a little French when we visited Paris.*

For more choices see the entry for STUDY.

least *adjective* — The smallest amount; littlest: — *When we compared our homework, I had the **least** mistakes. Of all our plants, the cactus requires the **least** care.*

fewest — The smallest number of things: — *Our team won the math contest because we made the fewest mistakes.*

slightest — The least amount or importance; smallest: — *There is only the slightest chance of snow today.*

smallest — The least amount; littlest: — *Brendan is the smallest and fastest boy in class.*

tiniest — The smallest: — *The baby shoes were the tiniest Marsha had ever seen.*

WORDS from Words

LEAST is often combined with other words to form expressions that have special meanings. These expressions also have synonyms. *For example:*

at least means not less or fewer than: *At least thirty people attended the meeting. Brush your teeth at least twice a day.* A useful synonym is **no less than**. **At least** also means no matter what happens: *We may not succeed, but at least we tried.* Useful synonyms are **anyway**, **at any rate**, and **in any case**.

---

leave *verb* — To go from a place; to go away: — *They must **leave** for the airport at noon. You can **leave** the table if you are finished eating. David **left** before the end of the play.*

depart — To go away; leave: — *The school bus departs for the museum right after lunch.*

exit — To go out; leave: — *The class exited by the back door during the fire drill.*

go — To move away: — *Don't go yet. He went away.*

set out — To begin a trip; leave: — *Tony set out from school for Harry's house. The ocean liner set out for Japan.*

WORDS from Words

LEAVE is often combined with other words to form expressions that have special meanings. These expressions also have synonyms. *For example:*

to leave behind means to forget to bring: *I left my book behind, and I need to get it. Don't leave anything behind when you go home.* Useful synonyms are **abandon** and **forget**.

to leave off means to stop: *Where did we leave off in our discussion?* Useful synonyms are **cease**, **quit**, and **suspend**.

to leave out means to not to do, say, or put in: *Don't leave out any of your friends on the list for the party. She left out the best part of the story.* Useful synonyms are **omit** and **skip**. **Leave out** can also mean to ignore or suppress: *He felt left out at the party because he couldn't dance.* Useful synonyms are **ignore**, **neglect**, and **overlook**.

legend *noun* A story from the past that people believe but may not be entirely true: *The **legend** that alligators are living in the sewers of New York is not true.*
*The **legend** of King Arthur may be based on fact.*

fable A story meant to teach a lesson: *Fables are often about animals that behave like humans.*
The fable about the boy who cried wolf teaches a lesson about the danger of false alarms.

folklore Traditional tales, beliefs, and customs: *Folklore is passed down from one generation to another.*

folktale A traditional story that has been handed down among the common people: *My grandfather has told me many folktales that he heard from his grandfather.*

myth A story that tells about people's beliefs: *Myths usually feature gods and heroes as characters.*
Myths help explain how nature works or how certain customs came to be.
Larry loved reading the Greek myth about Zeus hurling lightning bolts from the sky.

leisure *noun* The time to do what one likes; free time: *Gail has so many activities that she doesn't have much time for **leisure**.*

free time Time available to do what one likes, not used: *Larry used some of his free time to read and then went swimming.*

spare time Time free to do what one wants; extra time: *In his spare time Drake likes to go fishing.*
If you have some spare time, we can play chess.

lengthen *verb* To make something longer; to become longer: *She was growing so fast that her mother had to **lengthen** her pants.*
*The days **lengthened** as summer grew near.*

extend To make longer; stretch out: *We enjoyed our visit so much that we wanted to extend it as long as possible.*
The host extended his hand in greeting.

prolong To make longer, especially in time: *We prolonged our vacation as long as we could.*

stretch To extend; make longer: *I stretched the neck of my shirt so that it would fit better.*
Molly stretched her muscles before she exercised.

let ⬝⟷ lie

let *verb*	To give permission to; to allow:	*The teacher **let** them go to the library.* *Let the dog have a biscuit.*
allow	To grant permission to or for, often in relation to rules:	*Fishing is not allowed at the beach.*
authorize	To give authority to; allow:	*The teacher authorized us to study in the library.*
permit	To allow a person to do something:	*My parents won't permit me to stay out late.* *The teacher permitted Gavin to go to the library.*

For more choices see the entry for AGREE.
Antonyms: See the entries for FORBID and PREVENT.

Word Alert

LETS and **LET'S** have different meanings but are sometimes confused. **Lets** is a form of the verb **to let**, meaning to allow or permit, as in: *This key lets you open the door.*

Let's is a shortened form of **let us**. Instead of saying *Let us go to the game together,* or *Let us go for a walk,* we say *Let's go to the game together,* or *Let's go for a walk.*

WORDS from Words

LET is often combined with other words to form expressions that have special meanings. These expressions also have synonyms. *For example:*

to let down means to fail to live to someone's hopes: *You will **let down** the whole team if you don't show up. I know you won't **let me down**.* Useful synonyms are **betray**, **disappoint**, and **fail**.

to let off means to set free with little or no punishment: *The principal **let us off** but warned us not to do it again.* Useful synonyms are **excuse** and **pardon**.

to let on means to show that one knows something: *Megan didn't **let on** that she knew about the surprise.* Useful synonyms are **admit**, **confess**, and **reveal**.

to let out means to allow someone to leave a place: *The class was **let out** for recess.* Useful synonyms are **free**, **dismiss**, and **release**. **Let out** can also mean to utter: *At the scariest part of the movie, Grace **let out** a scream.* Useful synonyms are **say**, **shout**, and **speak**.

lie *noun*	Something a person says that he or she knows is not true:	*I was fooled by his **lies**.* *She said she never tells **lies**, but that story sounds like a **lie** to me.*
deception	A trick or lie that fools someone:	*The shopping trip was a deception to keep Sharon away while we got ready for her surprise party.*
falsehood	An untrue statement; a lie:	*The rumor is a complete falsehood.*
fib	A lie about something unimportant:	*He told a fib about meeting a famous soccer player.*
untruth	A false statement:	*His statement that he has been to Mars is an untruth.*

lie[1] *verb* — To say something that is not true: — He got in trouble when he **lied** about his age. Justin didn't **lie** about winning a medal at camp.

  deceive — To make someone believe something that is not true; mislead: — An opossum can sometimes deceive a predator by playing dead.

  fib — To tell a lie about something unimportant: — She fibbed when she said she had already brushed her teeth.

  mislead — To lead into a mistaken thought or wrong action: — The advertisement for this product misled us.

lie[2] *verb* — To put oneself in a flat position on a surface; to rest on something: — It's fun to **lie** on the grass and watch the clouds. When he had the flu, he felt so bad he just **lay** on his bed. The basketball was **lying** in a corner.

  lie down — To move to a flat position: — I think I will lie down and take a nap. Joe lay down his books and opened his lunch.

  recline — To lean back; lie down: — Georgia reclined on the sofa to watch television.

  stretch out — To spread one's body or limbs; to lie down: — Why don't you stretch out on the bed for a while and rest?

Word Alert

The verbs **LAY** and **LIE** are easy to confuse. **Lay** means to put or place something. It is always followed by a noun or pronoun used as a direct object: *I lay the boxes over there. I laid my coat on the chair.* **Lie** means to recline and does not take a direct object: *I want to lie in bed and read my book. Yesterday I lay on the grass and watched the clouds.* Here are the various forms of **lay** and **lie**:

Present Tense	Past Tense	Present Participle	Past Participle
lay (to put)	laid	laying	lays
lie (to recline)	lay	lying	lies

like *verb* — To be fond of: — Did you **like** the movie? Robert **likes** playing with his dog.

  care for — To like or enjoy: — I don't care for sour lemonade.

  delight in — To take pleasure from: — My grandmother delights in telling me stories.

  enjoy — To get joy or pleasure from: — Our whole family enjoyed our vacation.

  relish — To take pleasure in; enjoy: — Patrick relished going to his favorite restaurant.

For more choices see the entry for LOVE.

Word Alert

LIKE also means almost the same as: *My dress is like yours.* Synonyms for this meaning of **like** can be found at the entry for **SIMILAR**.

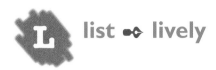

list *noun* | A written series of names, numbers, or other items: | *He kept a **list** of his friends' telephone numbers in his wallet.*
*My mother forgot to put milk on the grocery **list**.*

    catalog | A list: | *The library catalog lists all the titles and authors of all their books.*
Our library catalog is available on a computer.

    index | An alphabetical list: | *The last pages of this book contain an index to its contents.*

---

little *adjective* | Small in size or amount; short in time or distance: | *Jacob is **little**, but he can hit a baseball out of the park.*
*We used a microscope to see the **little** animals in a drop of water.*
*There is only a **little** time left, so we'd better hurry.*
*We only walked a **little** way.*

    limited | Kept within bounds; restricted: | *We only have only a limited time before the bus leaves.*

    slight | Not much or important; little: | *There is only a slight chance of rain.*

    wee | Very small: | *The kitten was just a wee thing when it was born.*

For more choices see the entries for SHORT, SMALL, and TINY.
Antonyms: See the entries for BIG, GIANT, and LARGE.

---

live *verb* | To make one's home: | *I **live** in the city, but my cousin **lives** on a farm.*
*Huge herds of bison once **lived** on the Great Plains.*

    dwell | To make one's home; live in a place: | *My family dwells in an apartment.*
A squirrel dwells in that tree.

    inhabit | To live in or on: | *Many fish inhabit the sea.*

    reside | To make one's home for a long period of time: | *My family has resided here for three generations.*

    stay | To occupy for a short time: | *We stayed in a hotel for a week.*

Antonyms: See the entry for DIE.

---

lively *adjective* | Full of life or spirit: | *They had a **lively** argument about who won the game.*
*The **lively** kitten played for hours with a ball of yarn.*

    active | Doing something much of the time; lively: | *Laurie was very active in the glee club.*
Alex took an active interest in soccer.

    energetic | Full of energy: | *Nancy was an energetic partner on my project.*
We felt energetic after eating.

    vigorous | Active and lively; strong: | *My grandparents keep healthy by taking a vigorous walk every day.*
The candidate gave Bob a vigorous handshake.

lock *verb* | To fasten something with a lock: | Did you **lock** the back door?
The pirate's treasure was **locked** in a huge chest.

   bolt | To fasten with a bolt: | We **bolted** the gate at night.

   latch | To fasten or close with a latch: | We **latched** the door so the cat couldn't get out.

   padlock | To fasten with a padlock: | I put my books in my locker and **padlocked** it.

For more choices see the entries for CLOSE and SHUT.
Antonyms: See the entry for OPEN.

---

lonely *adjective* | Unhappy from being alone; away from others; alone: | Hailey felt **lonely** when she was away from her friends.
The **lonely** old barn stood by itself on a hill.

   homesick | Sad because of being away from one's home: | When I went to camp the first time, I was **homesick** for my family.

   lonesome | Unhappy with being alone: | I was **lonesome** while you were away.

   solitary | Alone; without companions: | The forest ranger led a **solitary** life at the lookout tower deep in the woods.

For more choices see the entry for ALONE.

---

long *adjective* | Having great length; having or lasting for a certain length: | It took a **long** time to roll up the **long** hose.
How **long** can you hold your breath?

   drawn out | Long: | The story was so **drawn out**, we thought it would never end.

   lengthy | Long or too long: | The **lengthy** speech made the crowd bored and restless.

   prolonged | Long, especially in time: | There was a **prolonged** silence while we waited for the show to begin.

Antonyms: See the entry for SHORT.

---

look[1] *verb* | To use one's eyes: | **Look** both ways before you cross the street.
Jasmine carefully **looked** at her homework to make sure there were no mistakes.

   gaze | To look at something for a long time: | We all **gazed** at the stars.

   peer | To look closely: | Jeremy **peered** at the map but could not find the street.

   scrutinize | To look at very carefully: | Charles **scrutinized** the newspaper in search of a summer job.

   stare | To look at for a long time: | Sue was so surprised, she just **stared** at me.

For more choices see the entries for PEEK, SEE, and WATCH[1].

look

look² *verb*   To make a search: We **looked** everywhere for the lost book.
    Can you **look** at my computer and tell me what's wrong?

    explore   To go over carefully: We **explored** the house from the basement to the attic.

    search   To look through; examine carefully: Carlos **searched** everywhere for his lost jacket.

    seek   To look for; try to find; go in search of: I will **seek** an answer to your question on the Web.
    Early explorers were **seeking** the Fountain of Youth.
    We **sought** our friends on the playground.

For more choices see the entries for HUNT and STUDY.

---

look³ *verb*   To come into sight; be seen: The house **looked** old and dilapidated.
    The two brothers **looked** alike.

    appear   To come into sight; be seen: The buildings of the city **appeared** in the distance.

    resemble   To look like or be similar to: The puppies all **resembled** their mother.

    seem   To appear to be: Although they **seemed** just alike, the two sisters had very different personalities.

Word Alert

LOOKS is a noun that means physical appearance, especially when pleasing: *He inherited his good **looks** from his mother.* Synonyms for **looks** are **appearance** or **demeanor**.

WORDS from Words

LOOK is often combined with other words to form expressions that have special meanings. These expressions also have synonyms. *For example:*

to look after means to take care of: *The baby-sitter **looked after** the three children. Miranda **looks after** her brother after school.* Useful synonyms are **oversee** and **supervise**.

to look down on or **upon** means to hate or scorn: *The nobles **looked down on** the peasants.* Useful synonyms for look down on can be found at the entry for **HATE**.

to look forward to means to wait for eagerly: *Everyone was **looking forward** to the party. Jake **looked forward** to skateboarding after school.* Useful synonyms are **anticipate** and **expect**.

to look into means to ask questions about: *We will **look into** the problem of the missing bicycles.* Useful synonyms are **examine**, **investigate**, and **search for.**

to look out or **to look out for** means to take care: *Look out for the broken step on the stairway.* Useful synonyms are **be careful**, **take care**, and **be watchful**.

to look up means to search and find information: *I always **look up** unfamiliar words in a dictionary. They **looked up** Aztec culture in the library for their report.* Useful synonyms are **research** and **search**.

to look up to means to respect: *Joanne **looks up to** her mother. Many people **look up to** doctors.* Useful synonyms are **admire** and **respect**.

loose *adjective* | Not tight; not fastened or attached firmly: | He wore **loose** pants for karate practice. A **loose** page fell out of my notebook.

 baggy | Hanging loosely: | His baggy pants made him look sloppy.

 slack | Not tight or firm; loose: | The slack rope swung in the breeze.

Antonyms: See the entry for TIGHT.

Word Alert

LOOSE can mean free: *Our cat got loose again. The little boy ran loose on the playground.* Synonyms for this meaning of **loose** are *free* and *released*. **Loose** can also mean not careful: *The witness gave only a loose account of the accident.* Useful synonyms for this meaning of **loose** can be found at the entries for *CARELESS* and *RECKLESS*.

---

lose[1] *verb* | To no longer have; to fail to keep: | Please don't **lose** your key again. Be careful not to **lose** your temper. Lynn keeps **losing** her pen. Ed **lost** his glasses but found them in a drawer.

 mislay | To put something in a place that is later forgotten: | I mislaid my new sweater and couldn't find it for days.

 misplace | To put something somewhere and forget where it is: | I seem to misplace my glasses all the time. Joseph misplaced his homework and had to do it over.

For more choices see the entry for FORGET.
Antonyms: See the entries for FIND and GET.

---

lose[2] *verb* | To fail to win: | The team **lost** by only one point. The candidate with the least supporters will **lose** the election.

 be defeated | To lose a contest: | Our team was defeated in the finals last year. The South was defeated in the Civil War.

 forfeit | To lose or give up because of some accident or mistake: | We had to forfeit the game because several of our players were out sick.

 yield | To give up; surrender: | The knight yielded after he was knocked off his horse.

Antonyms: See the entry for WIN.

loss *noun* — The act or condition of losing or having lost something:

The **loss** of the close game disappointed the fans.
The **loss** of the library book worried me.
Our team now has four wins and three **losses**.

damage — Harm that makes something less valuable or useful:

The storm caused great **damage**.

defeat — The condition of being defeated in a contest:

The game ended in a **defeat**.

reverse — A change in luck from good to bad:

He had several **reverses** when he was starting out, but he is successful now.

setback — A sudden change from better to worse:

Our vacation plans suffered a **setback** when the weather turned bad.

Antonyms: See the entry for VICTORY.

WORDS from Words

LOSS is sometimes combined with other words to form expressions that have special meanings. These expressions also have synonyms. *For example:*

at a loss means puzzled or confused: *Their sudden departure left me **at a loss**.* Useful synonyms are **baffled**, **bewildered**, and **unsure**.

at a loss for words means so surprised or puzzled one cannot speak: *When they announced I had won, I was **at a loss for words**.* Useful synonyms are **dumbfounded**, **flabbergasted**, and **shocked**.

---

lost *adjective* — That which cannot be found; missing:

Juliet never found her **lost** pen.
I thought my jacket was **lost** until it turned up at school.

mislaid — Having put something in a place and forgotten where it is; lost:

My wallet was **mislaid**, and I couldn't go out until I found it.

misplaced — Having put something somewhere and forgotten where it is; lost:

My **misplaced** jacket finally turned up in my closet.

missing — Lost; not to be found:

Our dog was **missing** last night.
Our neighbors found our **missing** dog in their yard.

loud *adjective* — Having a strong sound:

The music was so **loud**, I couldn't hear what my friend was saying.
We heard a **loud** crash from the kitchen.

deafening — Extremely loud:

The dam broke with a **deafening** roar.

noisy — Full of sounds, often unpleasant:

The **noisy** crowd kept yelling for their team.
The street party was so **noisy** it kept us awake.

Antonyms: See the entry for QUIET.

love *noun* | A strong, tender feeling: | Tom's **love** for reading started in first grade. *The* **love** *of a friend is special.*

   affection | A feeling of tenderness, fondness, or love: | *I feel a deep* affection *for my sister. Richard has* affection *for his dog.*

   devotion | A strong affection; faithfulness: | *Shelby felt great* devotion *to her parents.*

   fondness | A liking or loving feeling: | *Chet showed his* fondness *for his classmates by inviting them all to a party.*

---

love *verb* | To have a strong, warm, or tender feeling: | *Hannah* **loved** *her home and couldn't wait to get back from vacation. I* **love** *music.*

   adore | To love and admire very much: | *I* adore *my little brother even though he annoys me sometimes.*

   cherish | To love and treat tenderly: | *She* cherishes *her cat.*

   like | To be fond of; enjoy: | *I* like *movies, but I love books. Do you* like *sports?*

For more choices see the entry for LIKE.
Antonyms: See the entry for HATE.

---

luck *noun* | What seems to happen to a person by chance: | *We had the good* **luck** *to meet Beth on the street. Some people say bad* **luck** *is better than no luck at all.*

   chance | The possibility of something happening: | *I took the* chance *that you might be home and came over. There is a small* chance *of rain tonight.*

   fortune | Something either good or bad that will happen to a person; luck: | *It was my good* fortune *to be here when you arrived.* Fortune *was against us and we lost.*

---

lucky *adjective* | Having or bringing good luck: | *She was* **lucky** *to win the prize. I always carry my* **lucky** *four-leaf clover.*

   fortunate | Having or resulting from good luck: | *It was very* fortunate *that we met by accident. The* fortunate *man won the lottery twice.*

Antonyms: See the entry for UNLUCKY.

---

luxurious *adjective* | Giving much comfort and pleasure: | *On vacation we spent the night in a* **luxurious** *hotel. My room seemed* **luxurious** *after living in a tent.*

   elegant | Rich and fine in quality: | *In the play the king and queen wore* elegant *costumes.*

   ornate | Having much decoration: | *The throne room was decorated with* ornate *furniture.*

   sumptuous | Costly; rich: | *A long table was filled with a* sumptuous *banquet.*

For more choices see the entries for EXCESSIVE and EXPENSIVE.
Antonyms: See the entry for CHEAP².

magnificent *adjective* — Very beautiful and grand: *The queen lived in a **magnificent** palace.*
*The view from the top of the mountain was **magnificent**.*

    glorious — Very beautiful; splendid: *They held a glorious parade to honor the heroes.*

    grand — Large and impressive; most important: *The royal family lives in a grand house.*
The grand prize is a trip to the tropics.

    splendid — Very beautiful; magnificent: *A splendid display of fireworks filled the sky.*

For more choices see the entries for BEAUTIFUL, HANDSOME, and PRETTY.

---

main *adjective* — Greatest in size or importance: *The **main** branch of the library is much larger than our local branch.*
*Charles explained the **main** idea of the story.*

    central — Very important; main: *Our central concern is making sure everyone has an equal chance to speak.*
The central office of the telephone company is downtown.

    leading — The first position or most important: *The leading causes of obesity are overeating and lack of exercise.*

    primary — First or greatest in importance: *Our primary concern is reaching our destination safely.*

    principal — Greatest or first importance: *Detroit is the principal city in Michigan.*
Diamonds are a principal product of South Africa.

For more choices see the entry for KEY and IMPORTANT.
Antonyms: See the entry for UNIMPORTANT.

Word Alert

The nouns **PRINCIPAL** and **PRINCIPLE** are often confused. A **principal** is a person who heads a school or who plays an important role in some activity: *After the performance the principals in the play took separate bows.* A **principle** is an idea; a basic truth, law, or belief: *Our laws are based on the principles contained in the Constitution.*

make[1] *verb*

	To put something together or cause to happen:	*The class **made** cookies for the party.* *My sweater is **made** of wool.* *Don't **make** trouble.*
create	To cause something to exist or happen:	*Melanie **created** some amazing drawings in art class.*
fashion	To give form to; shape; make:	*Antonio **fashioned** an airplane out of paper and wood.*
produce	To make or create something:	*Cows **produce** milk.* *These computers are **produced** in California.*

For more choices see the entry for BUILD.
Antonyms: See the entry for DESTROY.

---

make[2] *verb*

	To add up to; amount to:	*Elaine **made** the money to buy her bike by baby-sitting.* *Three feet **make** a yard.*
amount to	To add up to; to equal:	*The bill **amounts to** twelve dollars.* *Their story **amounted to** nothing more than gossip.*
equal	To be the same in amount, size, or value:	*I could never **equal** the school record in high jump.*
total	To add up or find the sum of; to amount to:	*I **totaled** a long column of numbers to get my answer.* *By the end of the game the score **totaled** thirty-one to thirty.*

WORDS from Words

MAKE can be combined with other words to form expressions that have special meanings. These expressions also have synonyms. *For example:*

to make believe means to pretend: *The boys like **to make believe** they are musicians in a rock band.* Useful synonyms are **contrive**, **imagine**, and **pretend**.

to make it means to succeed: *He is good enough **to make it** in the big leagues.* Useful synonyms are **flourish**, **prevail**, and **succeed**.

to make off with means to take without permission: *The game stopped when my dog **made off** with the ball.* Useful synonyms are **pilfer**, **snatch**, and **steal**.

to make up can mean to become friends again: *We **made up** after our fight and went to the movies together.* A useful synonym is **apologize**. **To make up** can also mean to invent something in your mind: *Angel **makes up** stories to amuse his younger sister.* Useful synonyms are **create** and **imagine**. **To make up** also means to put cosmetics on the face, sometimes to prepare for a role on the stage. Those cosmetics are known as **makeup**.

man *noun* An adult male person: When a boy grows up, he becomes a **man**. Our biology teacher is a **man**, and our coach is a woman.

gentleman A man who is polite, kind, and honorable: My brother always shakes hands like a *gentleman*.

guy A boy or man; fellow: A *guy* I know told me this story.

fellow A man or boy: Be a good *fellow* and bring me that book.

male A male person or animal: A *male* deer is called a buck.

For more choices see the entries for HUMANITY, PERSON, and WOMAN.

Word Alert

GUY is considered very informal and should only be used as a synonym for man in casual conversation. **GUYS** is an informal term meaning persons of either sex or several people: *Do you guys want to go to the movies tonight?*

many *adjective* A large number: There are **many** books in a library. Juan's family has lived here for **many** years.

countless Too many to be counted: There are countless grains of sand on a beach.

numerous A great many: I have asked you numerous times.

plenty Enough or more than enough; a large number: We have plenty of sodas for all your friends.

several More than a few but less than many: We saw several squirrels in the park, but not as many as last year.

Antonyms: See the entry for FEW.

mature *adjective* Having reached full growth: A **mature** colt is a horse, and a **mature** puppy is a dog.

adult Having grown to full size; mature: An adult giraffe is over ten feet tall. Adult clothing is sold on the second floor.

full-grown Having grown to full size: A full-grown elephant is huge.

grown-up Fully grown; adult: My cousin is a grown-up person now.

maybe *adverb* Possibly; perhaps: I disagree, but **maybe** you are right. **Maybe** I can visit next week.

perhaps Maybe; possibly: If you have time, perhaps we can go shopping together on Tuesday. Perhaps I was wrong about that issue.

possibly Perhaps; maybe: I can see you tomorrow, or possibly on Friday.

136

meal *noun* — Food served and eaten at one time: — *Many people try to eat three meals each day. We went for a walk after our meal.*

banquet — A formal dinner given on special occasions: — *Our school holds an awards banquet to honor students at the end of every school year.*

feast — A large, rich meal on a special occasion: — *Our family has a feast each year to celebrate the holidays.*

WORD BANK

There are many names for **MEALS** and words related to **meals**: Some that you might use are:

after-school snack	chow	fare	midnight snack
breakfast	dinner	lunch	spread
brunch	entree	mess	supper

---

mean *adjective* — Not kind or nice: — *A mean woman told us to get away from her yard. Teasing animals is mean.*

malicious — Caused by the desire to harm or hurt someone: — *Their malicious lies are completely untrue.*

nasty — Resulting from hate: — *That was a nasty trick he played on us.*

rude — Showing bad manners; not polite: — *The child's rude behavior was very offensive. That was a rude remark.*

For more choices see the entries for CRUEL and VICIOUS.
Antonyms: See the entry for FRIENDLY.

Word Alert

MEAN also means something halfway between two extremes: *The mean between 1 and 10 is 5. The mean temperature in our town is 57°.* Useful synonyms for this meaning of **mean** are *average* and *middle*.

---

measurement *noun* — Something found or shown by measuring: — *A measurement tells the size, height, or amount of something. I used a ruler to find the measurements of my shelves. Astronomers make precise measurements of the distance to other planets.*

dimensions — The measurement of length, width, or height: — *The dimensions of our classroom are 32 feet long, 24 feet wide, and 7 feet high.*

proportion — The size or dimensions of something: — *We measured the proportions of the room.*

size — The length, width, and height of something: — *Your room is about the same size as mine.*

WORD BANK

There are many kinds of **MEASUREMENTS** and words related to **measurement**. Some that you might find useful are:

acre	degree	knot	pint
bit	fathom	league	pound
bushel	foot	light-year	quart
byte	furlong	liter	rod
carat	gallon	man-hour	second
centimeter	gram	meter	ton
century	hertz	metric ton	volt
cup	horsepower	millimeter	watt
day	hour	millennium	week
decade	inch	minute	yard
decibel	kilometer	month	year

meet[1] *verb*		To come upon or find by chance:	Let's meet after school. We met two years ago.
	come upon	To meet:	At the grocery store, I came upon a friend whom I haven't seen in months. Did you come upon any seashells while you were walking on the beach?
	encounter	To meet, usually unexpectedly:	I encountered an old friend at the ball game.
	run across or run into	To meet or find by chance:	Will ran across several bargains while shopping. Luisa ran into an old friend in town.
meet[2] *verb*		To get together:	You should meet my friend Marisa. The student council meets on Tuesday.
	come together	To meet:	Our team comes together before each game to plan our strategy.
	contact	To get in touch with:	We contacted Dan by e-mail.
	join	To get together with:	We joined our friends at their table.
	unite	To bring or join together:	The couple was united in marriage.

Word Alert

When two lines **meet** or cross, they are said to *intersect*. A place where lines or streets **meet** is called an *intersection*.

melt *verb* — To change from solid to liquid by heating; to slowly dissolve: — The ice **melted** in the bright sun. Sugar **melts** in water.

  dissolve — To mix thoroughly with liquid: — The ice **dissolved** in the warm drink. The syrup **dissolved** in the milk.

  thaw — To become free of frost or ice: — You must **thaw** the turkey before you cook it. During the day the snow in the streets **thawed**.

---

mess *noun* — A disorderly or dirty condition: — Don't leave your room in a **mess**. He made a **mess** of his affairs by not paying his bills.

  clutter — A messy collection of things; litter: — I couldn't do my homework because of all the **clutter** on my desk.

  disorder — A lack of order; confusion: — The room was in complete **disorder** after the birthday party.

  litter — Scraps of paper or other rubbish: — The vacant lot was covered with broken bottles and other **litter**.

For more choices see the entry for JUMBLE.

---

message *noun* — Words or information sent from one person or group to another: — Lucas left a **message** on Lorraine's answering machine. There were no new **messages** on the e-mail server.

  communication — A shared message or news: — The latest **communication** from the airline said the plane would be late.

  note — A short message or letter: — The **note** told us where to look for the treasure. I just finished writing the thank-you **notes** for my birthday presents.

  statement — Something stated in words: — The police took **statements** from the witness.

---

messy *adjective* — In a sloppy or dirty condition; untidy: — How can you stand such a **messy** room? The streets were very **messy** after the storm.

  cluttered — Covered with a messy collection of things; littered: — My desk is so **cluttered** I can't find anything.

  disheveled — Very messy; mussed: — My gym clothes were **disheveled** after the game. He looked **disheveled** when he got off the crowded bus.

  sloppy — Not neat; messy; careless: — We cleaned up the **sloppy** kitchen after we made breakfast. There were many mistakes because of **sloppy** work.

For more choices see the entries for DIRTY and UNTIDY.
Antonyms: See the entries for CLEAN and NEAT.

middle *noun* — A point halfway between two things: — We sat in the **middle** of the audience. / There is a line down the **middle** of the road.

  center — The middle part of a circle or sphere: — The center is the same distance from any point on the circumference of a circle or the surface of a sphere.

  core — The central, most important, or deepest part of anything: — The core of the president's statement was that we must control needless waste. / Luis is honest to the core.

  heart — The center or middle of anything: — Ferocious piranhas live in the heart of the Amazon jungle.

  inside — The inner side or part: — The inside of the house was painted white.

---

mind *noun* — The part of a person that thinks, learns, and remembers: — His **mind** was filled with facts about computers. / Keep your **mind** on your work.

  brain — The main part of the nervous system of animals that controls the actions of the body. — The brain is the center for thought, memory, learning, and emotions.

  intellect — The power of the mind to think, learn, and understand: — Madame Curie, the discoverer of radium, was a woman of great intellect.

  intelligence — The ability to think, learn, and understand: — Many schools give tests that measure intelligence.

---

minor *adjective* — Small importance or size: — The teacher marked only a few **minor** errors on my term paper. / Who goes first is really a **minor** problem.

  slight — Not much or not important: — There is only a slight chance of rain tomorrow.

  trivial — Of little or no importance: — Don't get bogged down in trivial details.

For more choices see the entry for UNIMPORTANT.
Antonyms: See the entries for KEY and MAIN.

---

miss *verb* — To fail to catch; to let fall or slip by: — I **missed** several catches during practice. / We **missed** our ride and had to walk.

  bumble — To act in a clumsy or awkward way: — He bumbled around and dropped the cup he was holding.

  drop — To fall or let fall: — He dropped a glass because his hands were wet.

  fumble — To handle clumsily or drop: — The player fumbled the ball, and the other team grabbed it.

  muff — To handle awkwardly: — He muffed his catch, and the ball rolled between his feet. / The team really muffed that play.

Antonyms: See the entries for CATCH and SEIZE.

Word Alert

TO MISS can mean to feel the absence of someone or something: *I missed my parents when I was away.* Useful synonyms for this meaning of **miss** can be found at the entry for **WANT**.

---

mistake *noun*	Something not done correctly:	There was only one spelling mistake on Dakota's homework. I was in a hurry and used your towel by mistake.
blunder	A careless or stupid mistake:	Forgetting my sister's birthday was a real blunder.
error	Something that is wrong; a mistake:	The teacher found five spelling errors in my book report.
oversight	A careless mistake not made on purpose:	Forgetting to buy milk at the market was an oversight.
slip	A mistake or error:	It took only one slip for the criminal to reveal himself to the wily detective. My remark was a slip of the tongue.

For more choices see the entries for DISADVANTAGE and FAULT.

---

mix *verb*	To put two or more different things together:	We mixed flour, water, milk, and eggs to make a cake. If you mix red and blue, you get purple.
blend	To mix together completely:	The recipe says to blend all the ingredients for the cookies in a bowl and then add water.
merge	To join and become one; come together:	The two roads merged and became a single highway. The fishing is good where the two creeks merge.
stir	To mix something by moving it around with a spoon or stick:	Bethany stirred milk into her hot tea.

For more choices see the entries for JOIN and JUMBLE.
Antonyms: See the entry for DIVIDE.

WORDS from Words

MIX can be combined with **UP** to form to **mix up**, meaning to confuse: *I got so mixed up I skipped three questions on the test.* Useful synonyms are **mistake** and **misunderstand**. **Mix up** can also mean to involve: *They got mixed up in some real estate scheme, but it fell through.* Useful synonyms are **entangle** and **involve**.

modern *adjective* — Having to do with the present or recent times: — *Their **modern** furniture was uncomfortable.*
***Modern** medicine has saved thousands of lives.*

contemporary — Modern; up-to-date: — *The homes featured in the magazine were decorated with contemporary furniture.*

current — Belonging to the present time: — *She always dressed in the current fashion.*
Remind me to send you my current e-mail address.

up-to-date — Showing the latest developments or style: — *The up-to-date version of this computer program no longer has that bug.*

For more choices see the entry for NEW.

---

money *noun* — Coins and paper used to buy things: — *Do you have enough **money** to pay for the book?*
*She has worked hard for her **money**.*

cash — Money in the form of coins and bills: — *My mother got some cash at an ATM to pay for the movies.*
Some people carry little cash and pay for things with checks or credit cards.

currency — Money used in a country: — *Angela collects currency from foreign countries.*

funds — Money that is ready to use: — *We have saved enough funds to pay for your college.*

riches — Much money, land, or other valuable things: — *The museum has a display of the riches that were found hidden in an ancient king's tomb.*

valuables — Things worth much money: — *The miser stored his valuables in a vault and never let anyone see them.*

wealth — A great amount of money or valuable things; riches: — *Her family has great wealth.*

WORD BANK

Sometimes you can make things clearer and more interesting for your reader by naming the particular kind of **MONEY** you mean. Some kinds of **money** are:

cent	euro	pence	rand
centavo	franc	penny	riyal
centime	guilder	peseta	ruble
dime	kopek	peso	rupee
dinar	lira	pfennig	shekel
dirham	mark	piaster	shilling
dollar	nickel	pound	yen
drachma	öre	quarter	zloty

moral *adjective* | Good and honest in character and behavior; having to do with what is right and wrong: | She was a *moral* person who never told a lie. Whether to report someone for cheating is a *moral* question.

scrupulous | Very careful to do what is right or proper; moral: | Our teacher is very *scrupulous* in grading her students

upright | Good; honest: | An *upright* citizen obeys the law.

virtuous | Morally good: | He was a *virtuous* gentleman who was always fair to others.

For more choices see the entry for GOOD.

---

more *adjective* | A greater number, amount, or degree: | I can always find room for *more* ice cream. A meter is *more* than a yard.

additional | More; extra: | You can find *additional* information for your report at the library. Do you need *additional* help?

another | One more; an additional: | Would you like *another* glass of milk?

extra | More than usual, expected, or needed; additional: | We needed *extra* practice before the big concert. Shannon brought *extra* pencils for the test.

---

most *adjective* | Greatest in number, amount, or degree: | The winner is the one who receives the *most* votes. Kelly did more work, but Molly took *most* of the credit.

greatest | Largest in size, number, or amount: | China has the *greatest* population of any country. The person with the *greatest* number of votes wins.

majority | The largest number; more than half: | She received a *majority* of the votes and won the election.

maximum | The greatest possible number or amount: | Five dollars is the *maximum* amount we can spend.

---

mostly *adverb* | For the most part: | The dress was *mostly* green, except for the white collar. We have one more task, but our work is *mostly* done.

chiefly | Mainly; mostly: | Computer chips are *chiefly* made out of silicon.

largely | Mostly; to a great extent: | The earth is *largely* covered with water.

mainly | For the most part; chiefly: | Amanda is *mainly* interested in art.

move *verb*	To change the place or direction of something:	He had to **move** his books off the couch so we could sit down. I **moved** one checker, and he jumped me three times.
advance	To move forward:	The heavy traffic *advanced* slowly. The army *advanced* on the enemy.
convey	To take from one place to another:	The bus *conveys* passengers from home to work. A dictionary *conveys* information about words.
propel	To move forward or onward:	Some airplanes are *propelled* by jet engines.
shift	To move or change:	We *shifted* our desks to the new classroom. Public opinion *shifted* back and forth between the candidates.

For more choices see the entries for BRING and CARRY.

---

music *noun*	A pleasing combination of sounds:	We listen to **music** on the radio after school. Do you know the name of that piece of **music** being played on the piano?
melody	A rhythmic arrangement of musical notes:	Ian whistled his favorite *melody*.
song	A piece of music that has words set to it:	Do you know the words to that *song*?
tune	A melody:	He hummed the *tune* because he didn't know the words.

WORD BANK

Sometimes you can make things clearer and more interesting for your reader by naming the particular kind of **MUSIC** you mean. Some types of **music** and musical terms include:

anthem	country music	march	scherzo
bluegrass	fanfare	minuet	sonata
blues	folk music	opera	soul
cantata	fugue	overture	suite
chorale	hymn	pop	symphony
concert	jazz	rock	waltz

WORD BANK

Just as there are many kinds of **music**, there are many ways to make **music**. **Musical instruments** include:

accordion	electric guitar	marimba	timpani
banjo	fife	oboe	triangle
bassoon	flute	organ	trombone
castanets	French horn	piano	trumpet
cello	gong	piccolo	tuba
clarinet	guitar	recorder	viola
cymbals	harmonica	saxophone	violin
drum	harp	synthesizer	xylophone

Musical groups include:

band	ensemble	military band	steel band
brass band	folk group	orchestra	string quartet
chamber orchestra	jazz band	quartet	symphony orchestra
duet	marching band	rock band	trio

---

mysterious
adjective — Hard to explain or understand; full of mystery: — We heard **mysterious** noises echoing in the dark cave. The **mysterious** note came from Jessica.

hidden — Out of sight; secret: — The old map showed the location of hidden treasure.

obscure — Hard to understand; not clearly expressed: — I had trouble understanding the obscure poem. For some obscure reason he doesn't like cats.

puzzling — Hard to understand; confusing: — The puzzling riddle turned out to have a simple answer.

For more choices see the entries for UNBELIEVABLE and UNCERTAIN.
Antonyms: See the entry for OBVIOUS.

---

mystery *noun* — Something that is not known, explained, or understood: — How creatures live at the bottom of the ocean is a **mystery** that is slowly being solved.

puzzle — Something that confuses: — We solved the puzzle of where our cat was hiding when we found her in the closet.

question — Something asked to find out something: — The visitor asked many questions about our town.

secret — Something known only to oneself or a few: — The location of the pirate's treasure was a secret.

For more choices see the entries for PROBLEM and QUESTION.

narrow *adjective* — Not wide or broad:

*The passage was so **narrow**, they had to turn sideways to get through.*
*Stephanie easily stepped across the **narrow** stream.*

   snug — Fitting very closely or tightly:

My old sweater is too snug for me now.
She felt comfortable in her snug sleeping bag.

   tight — Fitting closely:

My jeans felt tight after I ate too much.
The opening to our attic is a very tight fit.

For more choices see the entry for THIN.
Antonyms: See the entry for WIDE.

---

natural *adjective* — Produced by nature or closely following nature; not artificial:

*She had no problems expressing her **natural** feelings.*
*The painting of flowers looked very **natural**.*

   inborn — Born in a person; natural:

Julie seems to have an inborn talent for singing.

   instinctive — Born in a person or animal; not learned:

Building a nest is an instinctive behavior for most birds.

   lifelike — Like something alive or real:

The statue is so lifelike you expect it to speak.

   realistic — Showing things as they are in everyday life:

Her painting was so realistic, I felt I could step right into it.

---

nature *noun* — All things not made by people:

*The mountains and the oceans are part of **nature**.*
*Chris loved looking at **nature** when he was hiking.*

   environment — The air, water, soil, and all the things that surround a person, animal, or plant:

Our zoo tries to recreate a natural environment for each of its animals.
Problems in the environment can affect your health.

   outdoors — The world outside houses or other buildings; the natural world:

National parks protect special areas of the great outdoors.

   wilderness — A natural place where no people live:

Pioneers cleared the wilderness to plant their crops.
Today many people think that the wilderness is disappearing too quickly.

naughty *adjective* — Behaving badly: — *The teacher made the **naughty** boys stay after school.*
*The **naughty** puppy chewed my shoes.*

disobedient — Refusing or failing to obey: — *My disobedient dog never comes when he is called.*

mischievous — Playful but naughty; full of mischief: — *The mischievous child put sugar in the salt shaker.*

unruly — Hard to control or manage: — *I need to comb my unruly hair after I shower.*

For more choices see the entry for BAD³.
Antonyms: See the entry for GOOD.

---

near *adjective* — Not far or distant: — *The **nearest** store is over there.*
*Will I see you in the **near** future?*

adjacent — Next to: — *The garage is adjacent to our house.*

close — With little space between: — *We live close to the park.*
Mario sat close to his friends.

immediate — Close in time or space: — *The fire station is in the immediate vicinity.*

nearby — A short distance away: — *My uncle lives in a nearby town.*

Antonyms: See the entry for FAR.

---

neat *adjective* — Clean and kept in order: — *All the books were lined up in **neat** rows.*
*Kurt has **neat** handwriting.*

orderly — Arranged in a certain way: — *The class marched to the library in an orderly line.*

organized — Put together in an orderly way: — *My coin collection is organized by country.*

tidy — Neat and clean; well-organized: — *She likes to keep her room tidy.*

well-groomed — Carefully dressed and groomed: — *Kevin always looks well-groomed.*

For more choices see the entry for CLEAN.
Antonyms: See the entries for DIRTY, MESSY, and UNTIDY.

---

necessary *adjective* — Must be had or done: — *He had all the **necessary** parts to fix his bicycle.*
*A pencil is **necessary** to take this test.*

essential — Very important or necessary: — *Flour and milk are essential ingredients for making pancakes.*

indispensable — Absolutely necessary: — *Studying is indispensable to doing well in school.*

required — Necessary: — *This book is required reading in my class.*

necessity *noun* | Something that is needed; requirement: | *The school nurse spoke to us about the **necessity** of good nutrition.*
*Food, clothing, and shelter are some of the **necessities** of life.*

need | Something that is necessary, useful, or desired: | *In the snowstorm their **need** was for a warm fire.*
*What are the **needs** for our trip?*

requirement | Something that is necessary: | *Practice is a **requirement** for learning to play a musical instrument.*
*The coach listed the **requirements** for joining the team.*

---

need *verb* | To lack or require; to have to: | *Ian **needs** just two more points to win the game.*
*Marissa and Jack **need** to buy new shoes.*
*I **need** to finish my homework before dinner.*

lack | To need something: | *The game **lacked** excitement because one team was so much better than the other.*

require | To have need of something: | *Everyone **requires** food and sleep.*

---

nervous *adjective* | Not able to relax, uneasy: | *Jeffrey was **nervous** about giving his speech.*
*The **nervous** cat ran away at the first noise.*

apprehensive | Worried; fearful: | *We were **apprehensive** about taking the test.*

fidgety | Restless; nervous: | *Sitting too long makes me **fidgety**.*

restless | Not able to rest or keep still: | *The audience became **restless** during the long speech.*

tense | Showing strain: | *I was **tense** before our play began.*

For more choices see the entry for UPSET.
Antonyms: See the entry for CALM.

---

new *adjective* | Recently grown or made; seen for the first time: | *The **new** shows on television aren't very original.*
***New** leaves sprout on trees in spring.*

novel | New and unusual: | *Katie had a **novel** idea for framing her drawings.*

original | New; not a copy or imitation: | *We saw **original** paintings by famous artists at the museum.*

recent | Done, made, or happening not long ago: | *The television program was interrupted to report the most **recent** news.*
*Our **recent** vacation was the best ever.*

For more choices see the entries for FRESH and YOUNG.
Antonyms: See the entries for COMMON and OLD.

next *adjective* — Following immediately in time or order:
Our computer is in the next room.
We have a date to go shopping next week.

   coming — Approaching; next:
Our movie theater shows the coming attractions before every show.
I hope to visit my grandmother this coming summer.

   following — Coming after in order or time:
We packed on Tuesday night and left the following morning.

---

nice *adjective* — Pleasing or satisfactory; thoughtful:
We had a nice time at Grandmother's.
Our nice neighbor baked an apple pie for my family.

   agreeable — Pleasant; pleasing:
Fortunately, the medicine had an agreeable taste.

   pleasant — Friendly and agreeable:
She has a pleasant way of making us feel welcome.
Our meal was served by a pleasant waiter.

   sweet — Having or marked by agreeable or pleasing qualities:
Jenny has a sweet personality.

For more choices see the entries for FRIENDLY and KIND.

---

noise *noun* — A loud and harsh sound:
The noise from outside made it hard to concentrate.
The planes flying overhead make a horrible noise.

   clamor — A loud continuous noise:
The clamor of car horns and sirens kept me awake all night.

   din — A loud noise that goes on for some time:
We could hear the din of the excited crowd even before we got into the sports arena.

   sound — What can be heard:
Sounds are vibrations moving through the air.
A warbler's song is a very beautiful sound.

For more choices see the entry for RACKET.
Antonyms: See the entries for QUIET and SILENCE.

WORD BANK

Sometimes you can make things clearer for your reader by naming the particular **NOISE** you mean.
Some **noises** are:

bang	cluck	hoot	wham
bong	crunch	klipklop	whomp
boom	ding	splat	whoosh
burble	glug	sploosh	zap
chug	honk	twitter	zing

 normal ◆◆ number

normal *adjective* — Most common; usual:
The **normal** temperature for a human is 98.6 degrees Fahrenheit.
My eye doctor said my eyes are **normal** so I don't need glasses.

    commonplace — Ordinary; not interesting:
Snow is commonplace in Alaska but not in Hawaii.
We found his stories commonplace.

    everyday — Fit for normal days:
We dressed up for the party instead of wearing our everyday clothes.

    standard — Widely used or usual:
It is standard practice to take attendance at school each morning.

For more choices see the entries for COMMON, REGULAR, and USUAL.
Antonyms: See the entries for ODD and UNUSUAL.

---

notice *verb* — To become aware of:
Alexa didn't **notice** the cold until she took off her sweater.
Did you **notice** the full moon last night?

    note — To take careful notice of:
Please note the new rules posted by the door.

    observe — To see or notice:
Sean observed a small blue bird sitting on the feeder.

    perceive — To become aware of through seeing, hearing, tasting, smelling, or feeling:
I perceived a faint sound from behind the door.

For more choices see the entries for DISCOVER, FIND, and SEE.

---

numb *adjective* — Lacking feeling or the power to move:
My mouth was **numb** for several hours after I left the dentist.
Victor could barely move his **numb** fingers in the cold.

    asleep — Without feeling; numb:
My foot fell asleep because I sat on it too long.

    dull — Not bright, clear, or distinct:
I had a dull pain in my elbow after I bumped it.

---

number[1] *noun* — A symbol that tells how many or which one:
Did you write down the telephone **number**?
We learned how to divide **numbers** in class.

    digit — One of the numerals:
Sometimes 0 is not counted as a digit, but 1, 2, 3, 4, 5, 6, 7, 8, and 9 always are.

    figure — A symbol that stands for a number or an amount given in numbers:
The most recent population figures show that our town is growing.

    numeral — A figure or group of figures that stand for a number:
The numerals 7 and VII both stand for "seven."

number[2] *noun* The total amount of things in a group:

> The *number* of active players on a basketball team is five.
>
> If you guess the correct *number* of marbles in the jar, you will win a prize.

amount The sum of two or more numbers or quantities:

> What is the *amount* of time you spend on your homework each week?

quantity A number or amount:

> The recipe calls for a *quantity* of milk.
>
> If we double the recipe, what *quantities* will we need of all the ingredients?

sum The number that results from adding two or more numbers together:

> The *sum* of 5 and 6 is 11.

WORD BANK

There are many words used to describe particular kinds of **NUMBERS**. Sometimes you can make things clearer for your reader by naming the particular kind of **number** you mean. Some kinds of **numbers** are:

Arabic numeral	even number	numerator	rational number
binary system	exponent	odd number	real number
cardinal number	fraction	ordinal number	remainder
cube root	imaginary number	percentage	Roman numeral
decimal system	infinity	power	square root
denominator	integer	prime number	whole number

obey *verb* — To carry out orders, wishes, or instructions: — *If everyone **obeyed** the speed limit, there would be fewer accidents.*
*Chuck's dog has been trained to **obey** his commands.*

   carry out — To obey or follow: — *We **carried out** the coach's plays during the game.*

   comply — To act in agreement with a request or rule: — *Jerry **complied** with the teacher's request to revise his report.*

   follow — To obey: — *The students **followed** the instructions on the test.*

   observe — To follow, obey, or celebrate: — *The bus driver **observed** all the safety rules.*
*Our family **observes** holidays with my grandparents.*

---

object *verb* — To be against; to raise objections: — *Many people **object** to loud noise late at night.*
*The lawyer **objected** to the judge's decision.*

   complain about — To make an accusation or charge: — *We **complained** to our neighbors **about** their dog's howling at night.*

   dispute — To argue against; disagree with: — *We **disputed** the statement that their team is better than ours.*

   protest — To object to: — *The students **protested** against the closing of the library.*

For more choices see the entries for BLAME and DISAPPROVE.

---

obvious *adjective* — Easily seen or understood: — *The answer to the question seemed **obvious** to me.*
*Her frown made it **obvious** that she didn't want to go to the party.*

   clear — Easily seen or understood; plain: — *The directions were perfectly **clear**.*

   distinct — Easy to see, hear, or understand: — *The teacher saw a **distinct** improvement in our performance on the second test.*

   evident — Easily seen or understood; clear: — *It was **evident** that they weren't enjoying the movie because they left before it ended.*

   plain — Clearly seen, heard, or understood: — *We made it **plain** that we did not agree with him.*
*The car turned the corner and came into **plain** view.*

Antonyms: See the entries for MYSTERIOUS and UNCERTAIN.

odd *adjective* — Different from the usual or normal:

There was an **odd** noise coming from the broken radio.
It seemed **odd** that no one was in the cafeteria at lunch time.
She wore a very **odd** hat with a floppy brim to the party.

curious — Odd or unusual:

There was a *curious* smell in the air.
Tamara found a *curious* old box in her grandmother's attic.

outlandish — Not familiar; strange or odd:

The singer wore an *outlandish* costume during the show.

weird — Strange or odd in a frightening or mysterious way:

The *weird* lights in the sky turned out to be helicopters.
A *weird* look came over his face.

For more choices see the entries for STRANGE, UNFAMILIAR, and UNUSUAL.
Antonyms: See the entries for COMMON, NORMAL, and USUAL.

---

offer *verb* — To present to be accepted or turned down; to show a desire to do or give something:

I was **offered** a chance to sing in the show.
My friends **offered** to help me.

provide — To give what is needed or wanted:

The school *provided* the equipment for our team.

supply — To provide with something needed or wanted:

The art teacher *supplied* paper, paints, and brushes for our watercolor lessons.

volunteer — To give or offer:

Noah *volunteered* an answer to the teacher's question.

---

often *adverb* — Many times:

I **often** talk to my friends about school.
We went to the pool **often** during the summer.

commonly — Often; regularly:

It is *commonly* understood that the earth is round.

frequently — Often:

Sparrows are *frequently* seen at our bird feeder.
We listen to music *frequently*.

regularly — Normally; usually:

We *regularly* go to the movies on Fridays.

For more choices see the entry for USUALLY.
Antonyms: See the entries for RARELY and SCARCELY.

old *adjective* | Having lived or existed for a long time: | An **old** man told us about the history of our town. The **old** fort dates back to the Civil War.

   aged | Old; having lived a long time: | We visit our aged grandparents on Sunday.

   dated | Too old: | The information we found on the Web was so dated, it was completely useless.

   elderly | Rather old: | Our elderly neighbor walks five miles every day.

For more choices see the entry for ANCIENT.
Antonyms: See the entry for YOUNG.

---

once *adverb* | In a time now past: | Caroline **once** had a collection of dolls, but she gave them to her little sister. It is hard to believe that my aloof cat was **once** a cuddly kitten.

   at one time | In the past; once: | At one time it was believed that the stars were only a short distance away from the earth.

   formerly | Some time ago: | Our principal formerly taught at another school.

   previously | Before, earlier: | We were previously introduced at last week's meeting.

---

only *adverb* | No more than: | I have **only** two dollars. Gabriella has three sisters but **only** one brother.

   barely | Only just; scarcely: | There was barely enough food to go around.

   just | No more than; only: | It looks painful, but it's just a scratch.

   merely | Nothing more than; only: | I am merely a member of the team, not the coach. Although he looked sick, he was merely tired.

Word Alert

ONLY is also an adjective that means alone of its kind: *This is the only copy of this book in the library. Randy is an only child.* Synonyms for this meaning of **only** are *lone* and *solitary*.

---

open *adjective* | Allowing movement in or out; not shut: | The dog escaped through the **open** door. Chloë poured three glasses of milk from the **open** container.

   ajar | Partly open: | The classroom door was ajar, and we could hear noise coming from the hall.

   uncovered | Without a cover; open: | The water in the uncovered pan began to boil.

   unlocked | With the lock open: | We left the door unlocked so my brother could get in.

Antonyms: See the entries for CLOSE, LOCK, and SHUT.

operate *verb* — To be at work or to control the working of something: — My computer doesn't **operate** very well.
Don wants to learn how to **operate** the copier.

    function — To work or serve: — The old truck *functions* best when it has time to warm up first.

    run — To operate; work: — Our old lawnmower *ran* on gas, but the new one *runs* on electricity.

    work — To operate: — Can you *work* the fax machine?
Did the medicine *work*?

---

opposite *adjective* — On the other side; across from another person or thing: — The two teams lined up on **opposite** sides of the field.
Sour is the **opposite** of sweet.

    contradictory — Opposing; inconsistent: — There are two *contradictory* versions of what happened.

    contrary — Entirely different; opposite: — Her taste in music is *contrary* to mine.

    facing — Across from another person or thing: — Morgan and Joseph sat in *facing* seats.

    opposing — Opposite; contrasting: — The *opposing* sides in the debate sat across from each other.

---

order *verb* — To tell what to do: — The coach **ordered** us to jog around the track.
The fire marshall **ordered** everyone out of the building.

    command — To give an order: — The general *commanded* his soldiers to march in the parade.

    direct — To manage or control: — Our teacher *directed* us to take out a pencil and paper.

    instruct — To give directions or orders: — The doctor *instructed* me to stay off my sore foot for a few days.

For more choices see the entries for FORCE and INSIST.

---

original *adjective* — Made or done for the first time: — People from Asia were the **original** settlers of North America.
Kelsey had an **original** idea for the school play.

    first — Before all others: — Neil Armstrong was the *first* human to walk on the moon.

    imaginative — Showing imagination and original thought: — Chris came up with an *imaginative* solution to the problem.

    initial — Coming at the beginning; first: — The *initial* letter of the English alphabet is "a."
The *initial* idea for the project came from Karen.

    novel — New and unusual: — Sandra had a *novel* suggestion for the party.

For more choices see the entry for NEW.

outside *adjective* | The side or surface that is out: | *The **outside** lights go on automatically when it gets dark.*
*Her **outside** layer of clothing was a plastic raincoat.*

exterior | The outer part: | *The exterior walls of our school building are made of brick.*

external | On or having to do with the outside: | *The peel of a banana is its external covering.*

outdoor | Used or done in the outside: | *Soccer is an outdoor game.*

outer | On the outside: | *The outer walls of our house are wood.*

Antonyms: See the entry for INSIDE.

---

outside *noun* | The side or surface that is out: | *We went **outside** when the rain stopped.*
*The paint on the **outside** of the house is peeling.*

exterior | The outer part: | *The exterior of our library is made of stone.*

Antonyms: See the entry for INSIDE.

---

own *verb* | To have as a belonging: | *The city **owned** the land it wanted to turn into a park.*
*Jack **owns** many books.*

have | To own; possess: | *I have two backpacks.*
Everyone in our class has their own calculator.
Do you have a dog?

possess | To have or own: | *Everyone in our family possesses a cell phone so we can all keep in touch.*
Makayla possesses great artistic talent.

pack *noun* — A sturdy bag used to carry things on the back or over the shoulder:

Evan's pack was too heavy to lift when it was loaded with all his books.
The mountain climbers carried sturdy packs filled with their gear.

bag — Something made of paper, plastic, or other soft material, used to hold things:

Andrew carried two bags of groceries into the kitchen.

bundle — A number of things tied or wrapped together:

Sierra put a bundle of newspapers into the recycling bin.

package — A thing or group of things packed, wrapped, or tied together; a box, case, or container:

A big package arrived in the mail.
We made pancakes by following the directions on the package.

For more choices see the entry for BOX.

WORDS from Words

PACK is sometimes combined with other words to form expressions that indicate where the **pack** is carried. Examples are **backpack** and **shoulder pack**. **Pack** is also combined with other words to tell you what the **pack** carries. An example is **ice pack**.

pack *verb* · To fill up with things: · *Veronica **packed** so many things she couldn't lift her suitcase.*
Pack only what you need for your stay overnight.

cram · To force or crowd into a tight space; to fill with more than is normally held: · *My locker is crammed with books and papers.*

crowd · To fill too full: · *The bus was so crowded that the door wouldn't close.*

load · To put a load in or on something: · *Our car was loaded with suitcases for the trip.*

squeeze · To force by pushing or shoving: · *We squeezed four of us into the back seat of the car.*
Lauren couldn't figure out how her cat squeezed under the fence.

pain *noun* · A feeling of being hurt: · *I went to the dentist to see about the **pain** in my mouth.*
*Running gave me a **pain** in my side.*

ache · A dull constant pain: · *Dave got an ache in his stomach from eating too much.*

soreness · A mild pain: · *I had a little soreness in my legs after we did the new exercises.*

twinge · A sudden, sharp pain: · *I felt a twinge in my sore shoulder when I picked up my backpack.*

pamper *verb* · To treat too well: · *The new owners **pampered** their poodle puppy.*
*My mother **pampers** me on my birthday.*

baby · To treat like a baby: · *My parents babied me when I was sick.*

humor · To give in to what a person wants: · *My parents sometimes humor my little brother to keep him quiet.*

indulge · To give in to the wishes of someone: · *Grandparents often indulge their grandchildren with special treats.*

particular *adjective* · Taken by itself; apart from others: · *This **particular** chair is uncomfortable.*
*Did you have a **particular** reason for your visit?*

certain · Known but not named; some; particular: · *The low scores on the test show that certain students did not read the assignment.*

specific · Exact; particular: · *We have specific instructions to go to the auditorium.*
What is the specific reason for your argument?

unique · Not having an equal; being the only one of its kind: · *Meeting the president was a unique experience.*

For more choices see the entries for DIFFERENT and UNUSUAL.
Antonyms: See the entries for COMMON, NORMAL, and USUAL.

party *noun* — People getting together to have a good time; a group of people doing something together:

*Alexandria's **parties** are always fun.*
*They formed a search **party** to find the missing dog.*

celebration — Festive activities in honor of someone or something special:

A celebration is being planned to honor the founders of our school.

festivity — Rejoicing and fun:

The party was full of festivity.

gathering — A meeting, assembly, or crowd:

We had a family gathering to celebrate my grandfather's birthday.

social — A party or friendly gathering:

Do you want to go to the social at the gym tonight?

---

pass *noun* — A written permission; ticket:

*Students are not allowed in the halls during class without a **pass**.*
*Walter has a free **pass** to the movies.*

license — A card or paper showing that a person has legal permission to do or have something:

My sister just passed the test for her driver's license.

permit — A written order giving permission to do something:

We bought a fishing permit at the lake.

---

pass *verb* — To complete a course of study; be successful on an examination:

*Elise **passed** first year Spanish.*
*Our whole class **passed** the math test.*

complete — To finish; pass:

I completed a lifesaving course over the summer.

fulfill — To meet or satisfy:

Catherine fulfilled her language requirement by taking French.

satisfy — To fulfill or meet a demand:

You can satisfy the math requirement by passing a written test.

Antonyms: See the entry for FAIL.

Word Alert

The verb **PASS** also means to go past or to move: *We pass the park on the way to my uncle's house.* Synonyms for this meaning of **pass** can be found at the entry for **GO**. **Pass** also means to move or hand something from one person to another: *Please pass the butter.* Synonyms for this meaning of **pass** can be found at the entry for **HAND**.

 **past**

WORDS from Words

PASS is often combined with other words to form expressions that have special meanings. These expressions also have synonyms. *For example:*

to pass away or **to pass on** means to die: *The famous scientist passed away at the age of ninety-one.* Useful synonyms can be found at the entry for **DIE**.

to pass on also means to give to one's heirs: *My grandfather passed on this watch to my father, who will pass it on to me.* Useful synonyms are **bequeath**, **hand down**, and **will**.

to pass out means to distribute or give out: *The teacher passed out the test.* Useful synonyms for this meaning of **pass out** are **distribute**, **hand out**, and **issue**. **To pass out** can also mean to lose consciousness: *Several marchers in the parade passed out because of the heat.* Useful synonyms for this meaning of **pass out** are **black out** and **faint**.

to pass over means to leave out: *The teacher accidentally passed over James and Jill when she was calling roll.* Useful synonyms are **leave out** and **omit**. **Pass over** also means to move over lightly or swiftly: *We saw several airplanes pass over.* Synonyms for **pass over** can be found at the entry for **SLIDE**.

to pass through means to filter: *The air conditioner cleans the air as it passes through it.* Useful synonyms are **filter**, **strain**, and **trickle through**. **To pass through safely** means to live through something: *The passengers passed through the shipwreck safely.* Useful synonyms are **endure** and **survive**.

to pass up means to do without: *Don't pass up this chance to take a trip.* Useful synonyms are **give up**, **miss**, and **refuse**.

past *adjective*	Gone by; over; just ended:	We learned about *past* events in our history class. The *past* two weeks have been very hectic.
early	In or near the beginning:	In *early* history a way was found to make tools out of metal.
former	Belonging to or happening in the past:	In *former* times people used candles rather than electric lights.
preceding	Gone or coming before:	The photo of our class is on the *preceding* page. The *preceding* program has been a commercial presentation.

Word Alert

The noun **PAST** means a time gone by or history: *Dinosaurs lived in the past. We study our country's past.* Synonyms for this meaning of **past** are **antiquity**, **history**, and **long ago**. A useful antonym is **future**.

patient
adjective

Able to put up with pain, trouble, or delay without getting angry or upset:

*The **patient** crowd waited quietly for the concert to start.*
*You have to be **patient** when you are waiting in line.*

tolerant

Willing to let other people do as they please:

This tolerant neighborhood lets people sell things on the sidewalk.

understanding

Able to feel and show sympathy:

My teacher gave me an understanding look when I missed a word in the spelling bee.

For more choices see the entry for CALM.
Antonyms: See the entry for UPSET.

---

pause *noun*

A short stop or rest:

*There was a **pause** as my computer searched the Web.*
*After a **pause** for rain, the game began again.*

delay

A putting off to a later time:

There will be a delay until the other team gets here.
The delay lasted only fifteen minutes.

interruption

Something that stops a person who is speaking or doing something:

There were so many interruptions I couldn't get my homework done.
The concert continued without interruption.

For more choices see the entry for BREAK.

---

pause *verb*

To stop for a short time:

*The computer **paused** while it loaded a new program.*
*Maybe we should **pause** and let the others catch up.*

interrupt

To break in upon something in progress:

The network interrupted my favorite show for a special report.

postpone

To put off until later:

The baseball game was postponed because of rain.

For more choices see the entries for DELAY and HESITATE.

---

peace *noun*

Freedom from fighting or conflict:

*After the war ended, a period of **peace** began.*
*The people prospered during the **peace**.*

accord

Agreement; harmony:

The two countries reached an accord on the location of their border.

agreement

The condition of agreeing; harmony:

Our family is in agreement about where to go for vacation.

armistice

A temporary stop in fighting agreed upon by those who are fighting a war:

An armistice was declared while peace talks took place.

harmony

Friendly agreement or cooperation:

We live in harmony with our neighbors.

truce

A short stop in fighting:

The opposing armies called for a truce while their leaders met to discuss peace terms.

Antonyms: See the entry for FIGHT.

PEACE also means calm: *We love the peace and quiet of the park.* Synonyms for this meaning of **peace** can be found at the entries for **CALM** and **QUIET**.

peek *verb*	To look quickly or secretly:	*We all try to **peek** at our presents before the holidays. The teacher gave my father a **peek** at my score on the test.*
glance	To look quickly:	*Kenny glanced at the book and put it aside.*
glimpse	To look quickly; glance:	*Olivia glimpsed Vicki going into the store.*
peep	To look secretly or quickly through a narrow opening or from a hiding place:	*The children peeped through the curtains to see if anyone was nearby.*

For more choices see the entries for LOOK¹, SEE, and WATCH¹.

PEEK is sometimes confused with **peak**. **Peek** means to take a quick look: *I peeked through the window to see if anyone was outside.* **Peak** means the top of something, especially a high mountain: *We could see for miles from the peak of the mountain.* Useful synonyms for **peak** can be found at the entry for **TOP**.

people *noun*	Men, women, and children:	*A crowd of **people** waited for the store to open. Downtown was filled with **people** having a good time.*
folk	People:	*Country folk often go to the city to shop.*
humans	People; human beings:	*Humans have large brains.*

For more choices see the entry for HUMANITY.

perfect *adjective*	Without mistake or fault:	*Diana studied hard and got a **perfect** score on her spelling test. It was a **perfect** day to go to the park.*
exact	Without anything wrong; accurate:	*My watch is supposed to keep exact time. The recipe calls for an exact amount of salt.*
flawless	Perfect:	*At the concert the musician gave a flawless performance.*
ideal	Being exactly what one would hope for; the perfect type:	*A warm, sunny beach is an ideal place for a vacation.*

For more choices see the entries for RIGHT and TRUE.
Antonyms: See the entry for IMPERFECT.

period *noun* — A portion of time:
A year is a **period** of twelve months.
The team scored three times in the second **period**.
Janet lived in Europe for a **period** of time.

age — A particular period of history:
Much of North America was covered with glaciers during the Ice **Age**.

era — A period of time or history:
An **era** is often associated with a great event.
In the history of the United States, the Civil War **era** was followed by the **era** known as Reconstruction.

span — A space of time:
The Internet was developed over a **span** of about twenty years.

stretch — A continuous length of time:
We worked for a long **stretch** and then rested.

---

person *noun* — A man, woman, or child; a human being:
Any **person** who wants to go to the movie should stand by the door.
Gene wants to be the first **person** to solve the math problem.

human — A person:
Every man, woman, and child is a **human**.

human being — A human; person:
Under our laws every **human being** has certain rights that cannot be taken away.

individual — A single person or thing:
That tall **individual** certainly stands out in a crowd.

For more choices see the entries for HUMANITY and PEOPLE or MAN and WOMAN.

WORDS from Words

IN PERSON is an adverb that means someone is physically present: *The movie star will appear in person at the opening of her new movie.* A useful synonym is ***personally***.

---

personal *adjective* — Not public; private:
I keep my **personal** journal hidden in a safe place.
I prefer not to talk about **personal** things with a stranger.

individual — Of or for one person or thing:
Each student received **individual** instruction from the teacher.

intimate — Very personal; private:
My diary contains my **intimate** thoughts.

private — Belonging to a particular person or group:
That book is my **private** property.
We were having a **private** conversation.

Antonyms: See the entry for PUBLIC.

personality
noun

All of a person's characteristics, habits, and other qualities:

*Your **personality** makes you different from everyone else.*
*Shannon has a very friendly **personality**.*

    character

All the qualities that make a person or thing different from others:

She has a very honest character.
The rocks from the desert have a different character from rocks found in the mountains.

    disposition

A person's usual way of acting, thinking, or feeling:

Charlotte always has a pleasing disposition, even when she is tired.

    identity

Who a person is; what a thing is:

Can you tell me the identity of the stranger?

    nature

The basic character or quality of a person or thing:

Our principal has a kindly nature.
It is the nature of water to be wet.

---

persuade *verb*

To cause someone to do or believe something by pleading or arguing:

*Joanne **persuaded** us to vote for her for class president.*
*Advertisements try to **persuade** you to buy a product.*

    coax

To persuade or influence by mild urging:

I tried to coax my parents into letting me go out on a school night.
Sarah coaxed her puppy out from under the bed.

    convince

To cause a person to believe or do something:

My friends convinced me that I should go to the movie.

    influence

To have an effect on:

My parents have influenced my behavior in many ways.

    sway

To change the thinking of; influence:

The class was swayed by Hunter's presentation.

For more choices see the entries for ENCOURAGE and URGE.
Antonyms: See the entry for DISCOURAGE.

---

pet *verb*

To stroke or pat in a loving way:

*Have you ever **petted** a llama?*
*It is best not to **pet** a strange dog.*

    caress

To touch or stroke gently:

My cat purrs when you caress it.

    rub

To move with pressure back and forth on something:

I rubbed my sore elbow.
My father rubs my head when he is pleased with something I've done.

    stroke

To rub gently:

Marilyn stroked her hair with a brush.

---

pick *verb*

To take from a number offered; to pull away with your fingers:

***Pick** a number between one and ten.*
*Sally had to **pick** a color for her new dress.*
*We **picked** flowers in the garden.*

    decide

To make up one's mind:

Natasha decided she liked blue better than red.

    gather

To collect; choose:

We gathered seashells on a sandy beach.

For more choices see the entry for CHOOSE.

WORDS from Words

PICK is often combined with other words to form expressions that have special meanings. These expressions also have synonyms. *For example:*

to pick on means to treat someone smaller or weaker in a mean way: *The class bully tried* **to pick on** *the littlest girl, but we stood up to him.* Useful synonyms are **harass**, **pester**, and **tease**.

to pick out means to choose: *You can* **pick out** *any book you want at the library.* Useful synonyms are **choose** and **select**.

---

picture *noun*	A painting, drawing, or photograph of a person or thing; an image on television or in a movie:	*We all dressed up for our class* picture. *The* picture *on Dalton's television is very clear.*
image	A picture or likeness of a person or thing:	*An* image *of George Washington is on one side of a quarter.*
movie	A series of pictures that is projected on a screen; a motion picture:	*My grandmother showed us a* movie *of my mother when she was a child.*
photograph	A picture made with a camera:	*We took dozens of* photographs *on the day we got our digital camera.*
portrait	A picture of someone:	*Before cameras were invented, many people had their* portrait *painted. Sandy drew a* portrait *of her dog.*

piece *noun*	A part that has been separated from something; a fragment:	*We each had a* piece *of cake. There were* pieces *of the broken window on the floor.*
part	Something less than the whole:	*The last* part *of our trip was the best. Larry ate only* part *of his lunch. Do you want* part *of my dessert?*
portion	A part or share of something:	*We spent a* portion *of our weekend cleaning up around the house.*
section	A part taken from a whole; portion:	*They planted vegetables in one* section *of the garden, flowers in another. The* section *of the book I liked best was the airplane race.*
segment	One of the parts of a whole:	*Jasmine broke her tangerine into* segments *and shared them with her friends. A worm's body is divided into* segments.

For more choices see the entry for ATOM.

pity ↔ plain

pity *noun* — Sympathy for the troubles of another:

*We felt **pity** for the victims of the fire.*
*Nicole took **pity** on the new student and invited him to sit next to her at lunch.*

compassion — Sympathy for someone else's troubles, with a desire to help:

The people of the town had compassion for the flood victims and took them in.

mercy — Kindness or forgiveness greater than is expected or deserved:

The king had no mercy for the rebels.
Our neighbor showed us mercy when our ball broke his window.

sympathy — The ability to feel and understand the sorrows or troubles of others:

Aaron felt sympathy for the injured dog.

---

place *noun* — A part of space occupied by a person or thing:

*Yvonne couldn't decide which **place** she wanted to visit first.*
*The **place** where the mosquito bit me is itchy.*

area — A particular space, region, or section:

All the theaters are located in this area of the city.

location — The place where something is located; site:

Can you tell me the location of the party?
The location of our house gives us a beautiful view of the lake.

site — The position or location of something:

This field was the site of a famous Civil War battle.
That corner will be the site of the new library.

---

plain *adjective* — Clearly seen, heard, or understood:

*The police overlooked the clue, even though it was in **plain** sight.*
*Our teacher made the rules very **plain**.*

clear — Easily seen, heard, or understood:

Is the plan clear to you?
Her report of the accident was very clear.

obvious — Easily seen or understood:

The answer to the riddle was obvious to Janice but not to me.
My desk was the obvious place to look for my pen, but I found it in the kitchen.

simple — Easy to understand or do:

Our spelling test was easy because the words were simple.
Learning to ice skate is not as simple as it looks.

uncomplicated — Not complicated; easy to understand or do:

The plans were so uncomplicated it only took ten minutes to put the bookshelf together.

plan *noun* | Something a person intends to do; a way of doing something that has been thought out ahead of time: | Mia had no **plans** for the weekend.
The **plan** for the surprise party was kept secret.

intention | Something in mind as a purpose or plan: | His *intention* was to finish his homework before dinner.

scheme | A plan or plot for doing something: | Scientists have developed a *scheme* for protecting wolves in the wild.
The detectives unraveled the criminal's *scheme* for stealing money.

strategy | A plan for achieving a goal: | The coach had a *strategy* for winning the game.

For more choices see the entry for PURPOSE.

---

plant[1] *noun* | A living thing that stays in one place and is not an animal: | Trees, bushes, vines, grasses, and vegetables are **plants**.
Most **plants** need sunlight and water to survive.

bush | A low shrub, smaller than a tree: | The *bush* was covered with berries.
A rabbit hid in the *bushes*.

flower | A plant grown for its showy petals: | Roses, daisies, and dandelions are *flowers*.
We painted pictures of colorful *flowers* to give to our mothers.

shrub | A woody plant that is smaller than a tree: | Several birds nested this year in the *shrubs* in our garden.

tree | A plant with a stem or trunk made of solid, woody tissue: | We like to sit in the shade of the old *tree* near school.
The branches of the *trees* blew in the wind.

---

plant[2] *noun* | A building or group of buildings containing equipment used to make something: | My father works at a **plant** that makes computer chips.
The old furniture **plant** has been turned into a shopping mall.

factory | A building or group of buildings where things are manufactured: | The huge *factory* outside of town makes refrigerators.

shop | A place where a particular kind of work is done: | There is an auto repair *shop* behind the gas station.

workshop | A room or building where work is done by hand or with machines: | There was sawdust all over the floor of the carpenter's *workshop*.
Matt's father has a *workshop* in his garage.

play ◆◆ pleasure

play *noun* — A story written to be acted out onstage: — Anyone can try out for a part in the school **play**.
We wrote a **play** about George Washington at Valley Forge for our history class.

drama — A story written for actors to perform on a stage: — We saw a drama put on by a local theater group.

entertainment — Something that keeps people interested or amused: — The entertainment for tonight is a troupe of dancers.

show — Any program of entertainment: — Did you watch your favorite show on television last night?
I missed the show at the movies because I was too busy.

---

play *verb* — To be in a game or to do something for fun: — You can **play** on my team.
We **played** soccer on Saturday.
Jeremy likes **playing** his guitar.

compete — To try to win something from another or others: — The teams competed for a silver trophy.
All students must compete in the spelling bee.

entertain — To keep someone interested or amused: — The singer entertained her fans.

portray — To play the part of: — The actor portrayed Abraham Lincoln as a young man.

---

please *verb* — To give pleasure to: — Our report **pleased** the teacher.
Do you think a clown will **please** your friends at the party?

delight — To give great pleasure or joy to: — The magician delighted the children.

gratify — To give pleasure to; please: — We were gratified to hear that our team had won.

satisfy — To make contented; please: — We were satisfied by our success.
Are you satisfied now?

---

pleasure *noun* — The feeling of enjoyment or happiness: — Sidney finds swimming a **pleasure**.
It was a great **pleasure** to meet our new neighbors.

enjoyment — Pleasure; joy: — Christian gets great enjoyment out of his coin collection.

fun — Enjoyment or amusement: — We always have fun riding our bicycles.

satisfaction — Something that makes us feel pleased: — Winning the contest gave the team great satisfaction.

For more choices see the entry for DELIGHT.
Antonyms: See the entries for SADNESS and SUFFERING.

plentiful
adjective
More than enough; abundant:
*Whales used to be **plentiful**, but their numbers have declined because of hunting.*

  abundant
More than enough; plentiful:
We have an abundant supply of ice cream for the party. Robins seem unusually abundant this year.

  profuse
Very abundant; plentiful:
That bush is covered with profuse blossoms in spring.

For more choices see the entry for PRODUCTIVE.
Antonyms: See the entries for BARREN and EMPTY.

---

point *noun*
A fine, sharp end:
*I need to sharpen the **point** of my pencil. Knives and arrows often have dangerous **points**.*

  apex
The highest point of anything:
The top of a triangle is its apex.

  tip
The end part or point:
You can feel the bumps on a surface with the tips of your fingers. The tip of my penknife is sharp.

For more choices see the entry for TOP.

WORDS from Words

POINT is often combined with other words to form expressions that have special meanings. These expressions also have synonyms. *For example:*

beside the point means not related to the subject; not worth mentioning: *Since we are talking about soccer, his question about baseball is **beside the point**.* Useful synonyms are **minor** and **unimportant**.

to point out means to show or call attention to: *Our guide **pointed out** the homes of famous people. Ralph's question **points out** the problem with our plan.* Useful synonyms are **indicate**, **mark**, and **show**.

To the point means related to the subject: *His comments were **to the point**.* Useful synonyms are **appropriate**, **proper**, and **suitable**.

---

polite *adjective*
Showing consideration of others:
*It is **polite** to say "thank you" and "please." The **polite** boy gave his seat to an older woman on the bus.*

  civil
Polite, but not friendly:
Even though Joe was very upset, he managed to give a civil answer.

  courteous
Polite:
The courteous students listened quietly.

  respectful
Having or showing respect:
George is always respectful when he talks to adults.

Antonyms: See the entry for RUDE.

pollution *noun* — Harmful materials that make the air, water, or soil dirty or impure: — *Pollution is caused by certain chemicals, gases, and waste materials.*
Pollution killed a large number of fish near our shore.

    contamination — Impure because of contact or mixing with pollution: — *The source of the contamination was a broken sewer pipe.*

    impurity — An impure or dirty thing: — *Impurities in the water made it dangerous to drink.*

---

poor *adjective* — Having little money: — *During the Middle Ages the poor peasants could barely afford to feed themselves.*

    broke — Having no money: — *We felt broke after paying for our new bicycles.*

    destitute — Without food, shelter, or money: — *If you can't get a job, you may end up destitute.*

    needy — Not having enough to live on; very poor: — *The church helps needy families.*

    penniless — Having no money at all; poor: — *After paying my bills, I felt penniless.*

Antonyms: See the entry for RICH.

---

popular *adjective* — Liked by many people: — *The most popular candidate won the election.*
Soccer is becoming more popular all the time.

    adored — Loved very much: — *The public adored the movie star.*

    beloved — Loved very much: — *The old man was beloved by the whole neighborhood.*

    well-liked — Liked by many people: — *The mayor was so well-liked he was elected for another term.*

---

possible *adjective* — Capable of happening or being done: — *It is not possible to be in two places at the same time.*
There are several possible ways to solve this problem.

    conceivable — Capable of being thought of: — *We searched every conceivable place for my lost jacket.*

    potential — Possible but not yet actual: — *Those piles of old newspapers are a potential fire hazard.*

    probable — Likely to happen or be true: — *It is probable that we will win the game because our opponent's best player is out sick.*

    workable — Possible to do: — *Your ideas for making this a joint project seem workable.*

possibility *noun* | Something that may happen or is possible: | *There is a **possibility** of showers tomorrow.* *Lauren studied hard because of the **possibility** of a pop quiz.*

chance | The possibility of something happening: | *There is a chance of rain tonight.*

likelihood | The condition of being expected: | *There is little likelihood that it will snow here in May.* *In all likelihood the plane will leave on time.*

prospect | Something looked forward to; expected: | *The prospect of playing for the championship was very exciting.*

---

powerful *adjective* | Having great power: | *Big airplanes need **powerful** engines to fly.* *William made a **powerful** suggestion, and everyone agreed.* *The presidency is a **powerful** position.* *Freedom is a **powerful** idea.*

forceful | Having much strength and power: | *Vanessa made a forceful speech.* *Her arguments were very forceful.*

influential | Having the power to produce an effect on others: | *Some influential teachers convinced the principal to change the new rules.*

strong | Having much power, force, and energy: | *Are you strong enough to carry that heavy suitcase?* *A strong wind almost knocked us over.*

For more choices see the entries for STRONG and TOUGH.
Antonyms: See the entries for DELICATE and WEAK.

---

praise *noun* | Words that show high regard and approval: | *Good work deserves **praise**.* *We considered the governor's letter of commendation high **praise**.*

acclaim | Enthusiastic praise: | *The returning astronaut received much acclaim.*

applause | Approval or praise: | *The audience's spirited applause made the pianist return to the stage for two curtain calls.*

approval | Favorable opinion: | *The plan for a new school received the approval of the voters.*

compliments | Something said out of praise or admiration: | *He received several compliments for his science project.*

recognition | Favorable attention or notice: | *Each class will receive recognition for their good work at the awards assembly.*

Antonyms: See the entry for INSULT.

praise *verb* — To express high regard and approval: — *The judges for the contest **praised** Barbara's singing.*

acclaim — To welcome with praise: — *The swimmers were widely acclaimed when they won medals in the Olympics.*

admire — To look at or speak of with appreciation and pleasure: — *We all admired Tobi's new coat.* *People admire our teacher.*

approve — To have or express a favorable opinion: — *My parents approve of my jogging in the morning before school.*

commend — To speak with approval; praise: — *The principal commended us on our high test scores.*

compliment — To express praise or admiration: — *My teacher complimented me on my short story.*

Antonyms: See the entry for INSULT.

---

predict *verb* — To tell beforehand: — *The weather report predicted sunshine all week.* *No one could predict how the election would come out.*

forecast — To tell what will happen; predict: — *The weather service forecasts hurricanes.* *Pollsters try to forecast elections.*

foresee — To know ahead of time: — *No one can really foresee the future.*

foretell — To tell ahead of time; predict: — *Who could foretell that such a strange thing would happen?*

prophesy — To say something will happen in the future: — *People have been prophesying the end of the world for centuries.*

---

prejudice *noun* — An opinion formed before all the facts are known: — *A judge must ignore any **prejudices** in order to make a fair decision.* *Racial **prejudice** has caused much suffering.*

bias — A strong feeling for or against a person or thing that keeps someone from being fair: — *A member of a jury must put aside any bias before reaching a judgment.*

intolerance — An unwillingness to respect different opinions, practices, or people: — *His intolerance toward others made him lose all his friends.*

one-sidedness — Supporting only one side; unfair: — *The contestants complained about the one-sidedness of one of the judges.*

partiality — Showing more favor than is fair: — *The judge showed so much partiality, the contest officials had to find an impartial replacement for him.*

prepare *verb* To make or get ready: *Lloyd **prepared** for his report by making illustrations to show to the class.*
*Did you **prepare** for the test?*

   arrange To prepare for; plan: *The meeting is arranged for Tuesday.*

   fix To get ready or arrange: *Liz fixed herself a snack.*
Can we fix a date for the party?

   get ready To prepare: *I get ready for school around eight o'clock.*

pretend *verb* To give a false show: *Suzie **pretended** to be asleep.*
*I sometimes **pretend** I'm a sports announcer.*

   fake To take on the appearance of; pretend: *They faked the photo by using a computer.*

   feign To put on a false show; pretend: *In the movie the hero feigned illness to escape his captors.*

   pose To take on a false manner: *The thief posed as an electrician to get into the house.*

pretty *adjective* Pleasing or attractive, often said of something small or dainty: *Monica picked **pretty** spring flowers for her room.*
*Joan has **pretty** eyes.*
*What a **pretty** doll!*

   adorable Cute; very sweet; lovable: *The little puppies are adorable.*

   cute Delightful or pretty: *Everyone loved the cute little kitten.*

   sweet Pleasing; agreeable: *That baby is such a sweet child.*

For more choices see the entries for BEAUTIFUL, HANDSOME, and MAGNIFICENT.
Antonyms: See the entry for UGLY.

prevent *verb* To keep something from happening: *The fence **prevented** the animals from escaping.*
*You can **prevent** accidents by being careful.*

   block To get in the way of; obstruct: *The road was blocked so we couldn't pass.*
A tall building blocks our view of the park.

   check To bring to a sudden stop: *I checked my dog's lunge by holding tightly to his leash.*

   head off To get ahead and try to cause something to stop or turn back: *The cowboys headed off the stampeding cattle.*

   hinder To hold back the progress of: *Darkness hindered the search for the lost dog.*

   obstruct To stand or be in the way of: *A large crowd obstructed the entrance to the museum, so we waited outside until it was clear.*

For more choices see the entries for FORBID and STOP.

pride ◂▸ problem

pride *noun* | A feeling of worth or importance: | Benjamin took great **pride** in his ability to play the violin. We showed our **pride** in our school by making sure the halls were neat.

satisfaction | The condition of being satisfied: | I got great *satisfaction* when my speech was a success.

self-esteem | Pride in oneself; self-respect: | Good *self-esteem* comes from doing something right.

vanity | Too much pride in one's looks, abilities, or accomplishments: | Her *vanity* made her so boastful, no one wanted to talk to her.

---

prize *noun* | Something won in a contest or game: | The **prize** for winning the tournament was a gold medal. *Prizes* will be awarded to the three best spellers.

award | Something that is given after careful thought: | Our school won an *award* for academic achievement.

honor | Something given or done to show great respect: | A trophy was one of the *honors* given to our debate team.

reward | Something given in return for something done: | The *reward* for hard work on your lessons is good grades.

---

problem *noun* | A difficult question that must be solved or dealt with: | David couldn't figure out what the **problem** was with his computer. There were twelve **problems** on the arithmetic test.

difficulty | Something that is hard to do: | I had *difficulty* fitting everything into my suitcase.

dilemma | A hard choice to make between two or more things: | My *dilemma* is deciding which colleges to consider.

riddle | A question or problem that is hard to figure out or understand: | We used to tell each other *riddles* when we were children.

For more choices see the entries for MYSTERY and QUESTION.

productive
adjective

Making or yielding large amounts of something:

*This farmland is very **productive**.*
*I had a **productive** time in the library and finished my report.*

> **fertile**
>
> Able to produce crops and plants easily and plentifully:
>
> *The fertile soil of the Great Plains produces tons of wheat and corn each year.*

> **lush**
>
> Thick, rich, and abundant:
>
> *The land this city is built on was once covered with lush forest.*

> **luxuriant**
>
> Having thick or abundant growth:
>
> *The explorers had to cut a path through the luxuriant undergrowth in the jungle.*

> **rich**
>
> Able to produce much; fertile:
>
> *The soil is so rich our roses don't need fertilizer to grow.*

For more choices see the entry for PLENTIFUL.
Antonyms: See the entries for BARREN and EMPTY.

---

promise *noun*

A statement by a person that something will or will not be done:

*The teacher kept her **promise** that we could have a celebration if our team won.*
*I was upset when my sister broke her **promise** to take me to the movies.*

> **oath**
>
> A statement or promise in which a person swears that what he or she says is true:
>
> *The witness took an oath to tell the truth in court.*

> **pledge**
>
> A serious promise:
>
> *My friends pledged that everything I told them would be kept secret.*

> **vow**
>
> A solemn promise or pledge:
>
> *The members of the club took a vow of secrecy.*

> **word**
>
> A promise or vow:
>
> *I gave my word that I would help my cousin on Saturday.*

---

proof *noun*

Facts showing that something is true:

*The fingerprints gave the police the **proof** they needed to arrest the burglar.*
*You need **proof** that you are old enough to enter this contest.*

> **documentation**
>
> Written or printed evidence; written proof:
>
> *My family had all the documentation we needed to get passports.*

> **evidence**
>
> Proof of something:
>
> *The broken window was evidence of how the thief got in.*

> **verification**
>
> Proof of the truth of something:
>
> *We needed verification of our new address before the movers could schedule delivery of our furniture.*

protect *verb*	To keep from harm:	*The Constitution **protects** our right to free speech.* *A seat belt **protected** Zachary on the roller coaster.*
look after	To take care of:	*Our neighbors asked me to look after their cat while they are away.*
shelter	To cover and protect:	*The old barn sheltered us from the cold wind and rain.*

For more choices see the entries for CONSERVE **and** DEFEND.

proud[1] *adjective*	Feeling satisfaction with something you have done; having pride:	*It was a **proud** day for our school when we won the state championship.* *Megan was **proud** of the scrapbook she had made.*
dignified	Showing proper dignity or pride:	*The class took their seats at graduation in a dignified manner.*
self-respecting	Having a proper respect for oneself:	*No self-respecting person would allow our waters to become polluted.*

proud[2] *adjective*	Having a high opinion of yourself or your achievements; showing excessive self-esteem:	*The **proud** noble refused to talk to the other guests at the party.* *They were too **proud** to ask for help even though they needed it.*
arrogant	Having or showing too much pride:	*The arrogant visitors were surprised and upset when they lost the game to our team.*
conceited	Having too high an opinion of oneself:	*Shelly is too conceited to talk to me.*
haughty	Having or showing too much pride in oneself:	*He acts haughty because he has an expensive bike.*
vain	Overly concerned with or proud of oneself:	*He is so vain that he spends hours in front of the mirror.*

Antonyms: **See the entry for** HUMBLE.

public *adjective*	Having to do with or for all the people:	*Each year the city holds a fair in a **public** park.* *The mayor made a **public** announcement.*
common	Belonging equally to all; shared by all alike:	*It is common knowledge that the earth is round.*

Antonyms: **See the entry for** PERSONAL.

WORDS from Words

IN PUBLIC is an adverb that means to be visible to people or where people are present: *The dancers will give a free performance in **public**. The rich financier rarely appears in **public**.* Useful synonyms are **openly** and **publicly**. An antonym is **in private**.

pull *verb* | To move something toward oneself: | Mackenzie **pulled** the door open.
We used our car to **pull** a trailer.

   drag | To pull or move along slowly: | We *dragged* the heavy trunk across the room.

   draw | To move by pulling: | Oxen were once used to *draw* plows, but now tractors are used.

   haul | To pull or move with force: | Wally *hauled* a boat trailer with his car.

   tow | To pull or drag behind: | The speedboat *towed* two water-skiers over the water.

For more choices see the entries for JERK and YANK.

---

punish *verb* | To make a person suffer for doing something wrong: | The parents had to **punish** the naughty child.
The law **punishes** criminals.

   discipline | To train to be obedient, sometimes by punishing: | We *disciplined* our dog to make him stop barking all night.

   penalize | To give a punishment to: | Our team was *penalized* for committing fouls.

   scold | To speak sharply to: | The teacher *scolded* the student for misbehaving.

---

pure *adjective* | Not mixed with anything else: | The necklace was made of **pure** gold.
The diver had to breathe **pure** oxygen.

   genuine | Being what it claims to be; real: | The necklace is made with *genuine* pearls.
My belt is *genuine* cowhide.

   undiluted | Not thinned or weakened by adding liquid; pure: | The drink was made with *undiluted* orange juice.

---

purpose *noun* | The reason for which something is done: | What is the **purpose** of your question?
She made that mistake on **purpose**.

   aim | A goal or purpose: | Eddie's *aim* is to become a doctor.

   end | What is aimed at in doing something; a purpose, goal, or outcome: | The *end* she had in mind was to win the contest.
All her hard work was toward that *end*.

   goal | Something a person wants and tries to get or become: | Rose's *goal* was to read ten books by the end of summer.
My *goal* is to become an artist.

   objective | Something one wants to achieve; purpose: | The *objective* of her campaign was to become class president.

   point | The main idea or purpose: | What is the *point* of the story?
I missed the *point* of the joke.

For more choices see the entries for EFFECT and PLAN.

push ◆◇ puzzle

push *verb*   To press on something to move it: *Wyatt **pushed** all the buttons, but nothing seemed to work.*
*You **push** and I'll pull, and maybe we can open the door.*

    nudge   To push or touch gently to get attention: *I **nudged** my friend when he didn't answer the teacher.*

    press   To push on something: *You have to **press** the button to start the machine.*

    shove   To push along: *We **shoved** my desk nearer to the window.*

    thrust   To push or shove suddenly or with force: *He **thrust** his book into his backpack.*

---

put *verb*   To cause a thing or person to be in a certain place: *Donna **put** all her pencils in a row.*
*I always **put** sugar in my tea.*

    deposit   To put or set down: *The ocean **deposits** sand on beaches.*
*Wendy **deposited** her packages on the chair.*

    lay   To put or place: *May I **lay** my books on this table?*
*I **laid** my coat over there.*
*Maria was **laying** down her purse.*

    place   To put in a particular spot: *We **placed** our desks in alphabetical order according to our last names.*
*Please **place** the glasses on the kitchen table.*

For more choices see the entry for ARRANGE.

---

puzzle *verb*   To be hard to understand or solve: *Warren **puzzled** over the last question until the answer suddenly came.*
*We were **puzzled** by how the dog got out.*

    baffle   To be too confusing for someone to understand: *The math problem **baffled** us.*

    confuse   To mix up; bewilder: *The street signs **confuse** many drivers passing through here.*

    mystify   To confuse or puzzle: *The audience was **mystified** by the magician's tricks.*

quality *noun*   Something that makes a person or thing what it is: *Sweetness is a **quality** of sugar.*
*Nancy has all the **qualities** of a leader.*

   characteristic   A quality that belongs to and helps identify a person or thing: *Honesty is one of my friend's best **characteristics**.*

   feature   A part or quality of something, often one that stands out: *I like some of the **features** of your plan, but not others.*
*Dryness is a **feature** of the desert.*

   merit   The goodness, worth, or value of someone or something: *Your grade will be determined by the **merit** of your work.*

   worth   The quality that makes a person or thing good or useful: *The man measured his **worth** in terms of the friends he had.*
*Eric proved his **worth** to the team when he hit a home run.*

---

quarrel *noun*   An angry disagreement: *We settled our **quarrel** by flipping a coin.*
*My friends haven't spoken since they had a **quarrel**.*

   dispute   An argument or quarrel: *There was a **dispute** over where to put the new firehouse.*
*A judge had to settle the **dispute** between the two businessmen.*

   feud   A bitter quarrel that lasts a long time: *The **feud** between the two old men had lasted so long they couldn't remember how it started.*

   fight   A quarrel: *The two girls had a **fight** over which movie to see.*

   squabble   A trivial, noisy quarrel: *You will regret it if you let a little **squabble** turn into something worse.*

For more choices see the entry for ARGUMENT.

queen *noun* — A woman who rules a kingdom; the wife or widow of a king: — Everyone bowed as the **queen** walked by. A woman who becomes **queen** usually rules until she dies.

   empress — A woman who is the ruler of an empire or the wife or widow of an emperor: — Over the several centuries of its history, the Roman Empire had many *empresses*.

   sovereign — A king or queen; ruler: — The *sovereign* declared her wishes in a royal proclamation.

For more choices see the entry for KING.

---

question *noun* — Something asked to obtain information: — Brent asked a **question** about the assignment. There were twenty **questions** on the test.

   doubt — A feeling of not believing or trusting: — Casey had *doubts* about finishing, but she kept working anyway. The weatherman expressed *doubts* about whether the storm would hit our town.

   issue — A subject being discussed or questioned: — The *issue* of slavery divided the United States in the 1800s. The members spent so much time discussing when to hold their next meeting, they never got to the important *issues*.

   query — A question: — Pete had a *query* about how long the trip would take.

   subject — Something thought or talked about: — The *subject* of our discussion was where to put the new library.

---

quick *adjective* — Happening in a short time: — Victoria made a **quick** trip to the store. The cat was so **quick**, it was gone in a flash. That was a **quick** game.

   brisk — Quick and lively: — The hikers set a *brisk* pace at first but slowed down as the day got hotter.

   hurried — Faster than usual: — He took a *hurried* look at his ticket and ran to catch his plane.

   rush — Done quickly; urgent: — The mechanic did a *rush* job on our car so we could have it for our trip.

   speedy — Quick or fast: — The *speedy* painters finished our whole house in three days. The mayor made a *speedy* decision.

For more choices see the entry for FAST.
Antonyms: See the entry for SLOW.

quiet *adjective* — Making little or no noise: *The library is a good place to study because it is quiet. The quiet crowd waited for the concert to begin.*

peaceful — Calm; undisturbed: *The park is so peaceful when I jog in the early morning.*

silent — Completely quiet; without noise: *We stood in the silent field after the snow stopped falling.*

soundless — Without a sound: *The antelope didn't notice the soundless footsteps of the lion until it was too late.*

still — Without sound or movement; silent: *Stevie listened for crickets on a still evening.*

For more choices see the entry for CALM.

---

quiet *noun* — Having little or no noise: *I love the peace and quiet of the mountains. The quiet of the street at midnight was a little eerie.*

calm — A time of quiet or stillness: *As the violent storm moved away, the calm returned to the forest.*

peace — A lack of noise or disorder; quiet or calmness: *Once the dogs stopped barking, peace returned to our neighborhood.*

peacefulness — Quiet and calmness: *We love the peacefulness of the woods after it snows.*

serenity — Calmness and peacefulness: *The serenity of the lake made me feel very peaceful.*

tranquillity — A condition of calmness and quiet; peacefulness: *Howard finds the tranquillity of the desert very restful.*

For more choices see the entry SILENCE.
Antonyms: See the entries for NOISE and RACKET.

---

quit *verb* — To stop doing something: *Alexandra quit reading to go outside. The computer quit, and we couldn't get it restarted.*

abandon — To give up completely: *We abandoned one project and started another when we couldn't find enough information.*

give up — To stop trying: *After several tries, I gave up trying to call her.*

For more choices see the entries for END and STOP.
Antonyms: See the entry for BEGIN.

---

quote *verb* — To repeat words exactly: *The newspaper usually quotes the complete text of the president's speech. Dylan quoted several sources in his report.*

cite — To repeat the words of another person exactly; quote: *Jeffrey cited the encyclopedia to support his theory.*

mention — To speak about or refer to: *She mentioned my ideas to our friends.*

refer to — To speak about or mention: *Mel referred to what he had read in his report.*

racket *noun*   A loud or confusing noise: *I dropped a bag of empty soda cans and made a horrible* **racket**.
The **racket** *from the ball game could be heard blocks away.*

commotion   A noisy confusion; disorder: *There was a* commotion *in the audience when the rock star appeared onstage.*

noise   A loud and harsh sound: *The* noise *of a passing jet made it hard for me to hear what Dick was saying.*

uproar   A noisy and exciting disturbance: *The crowd was in an* uproar *when our team broke the tie and won the game.*

For more choices see the entry for NOISE.
Antonyms: See the entry for QUIET.

---

rage *noun*   Violent anger: *The coach flew into a* **rage** *when the umpire made a bad call.*
Her voice quivered with **rage**.

fury   Violent anger: *The man seethed with* fury *when his car window was broken.*

tantrum   An outburst of temper or anger: *The spoiled child threw a* tantrum *when he didn't get what he wanted.*

wrath   Very great anger: *In our play, the hero had to face the* wrath *of the evil king.*

For more choices see the entry for ANGER.

Word Alert

RAGE also means a temporary fashion or style: *That song was all the* rage *last summer, but now you never hear it.* Synonyms for this meaning of **rage** can be found at the entry for *FASHION*.

ragged *adjective* — Worn or torn into rags: — *His old running shoes were so **ragged** he finally threw them away.*
*My stuffed rabbit may be **ragged**, but I still love it.*

frayed — Showing loose threads: — *The cuffs on my old jacket were so **frayed**, my mother got me a new one.*

tattered — Torn; ragged: — *My favorite pants have become too **tattered** to wear.*

torn — Pulled apart; having holes or cuts: — *My jacket has a **torn** sleeve.*

worn-out — Used or worn so much that it should not be used anymore: — *I had to replace my **worn-out** gym shoes.*

---

rain *noun* — Water that falls in drops from clouds: — *The team couldn't practice because the **rain** had soaked the field.*
*Crops need **rain** to grow.*

downpour — A very heavy rain: — *The **downpour** quickly flooded the streets.*

shower — A brief fall of rain: — *The weather forecast says there will be scattered **showers** today.*

sprinkle — A gentle rain: — *We had a few **sprinkles** but no real rain.*

---

raise *verb* — To move or cause to be moved to a higher position, place, or amount: — *Andrea **raised** her hand to ask a question.*
*My parents **raised** my allowance.*

hoist — To lift; raise; pull up: — *We **hoisted** the flag up the pole.*

lift — To raise or be raised: — *Can you help me **lift** this box?*
*The cheerful music **lifted** my spirits.*

pick up — To take and lift up: — *I **picked up** my clothes and put them away.*

---

rare *adjective* — Seldom happening, seen, or found: — *Ancient Roman coins are **rare**, but ancient Greek coins are **rarer**.*
*A warm, sunny day is **rare** here in winter.*

infrequent — Not happening often; not frequent: — *Her **infrequent** visits disappointed her relatives.*

scarce — Difficult to find: — *Water is **scarce** in the desert.*

uncommon — Unusual; rare: — *That butterfly is **uncommon** in this part of the country.*

For more choices see the entries for FEW and UNUSUAL.
Antonyms: See the entries for COMMON, NORMAL, and USUAL.

rarely *adverb* — Not often; seldom: — We **rarely** see big trucks in our neighborhood.
Gary **rarely** gets off work before six o'clock.

infrequently — Not happening often: — It rains **infrequently** in the desert.
Unfortunately, we get to the museum very **infrequently**.

seldom — Not often; rarely: — We **seldom** see each other since she changed to another school.
I **seldom** go to the movies without my friends.

For more choices see the entry for SCARCELY.
Antonyms: See the entries for OFTEN and USUALLY.

---

rattle *verb* — To make a series of short, sharp sounds: — Coins **rattled** in Natalie's purse.
The door **rattled** in the wind.

bang — To make a sudden, loud noise: — The child **banged** on her little drum.

clatter — To make or cause a loud, rattling noise: — We heard the dishes **clatter** in the kitchen.

jingle — To make or cause a tinkling or ringing sound: — The bell on the cat's collar **jingles** to warn birds away.

---

raw *adjective* — Damp and cold: — A **raw** wind seemed to cut through my winter coat.

biting — Sharp and stinging: — We bundled up against the **biting** north wind.

bitter — Sharp and raw: — The winter storm brought **bitter** cold.

bleak — Cold and gloomy: — The last leaves fell to the ground on a **bleak** February day.

For more choices see the entry for COLD.
Antonyms: See the entries for HOT and WARM.

Word Alert

RAW sometimes means uncooked: *We ate raw carrots.* A useful synonym is **fresh**. **Raw** can also mean inexperienced: *The raw recruits had to learn how to march.* Useful synonyms are **green**, **unskilled**, and **untrained**.

reach *verb* — To get or come to: — *The train **reached** the station early.*
*I hope we can **reach** an agreement soon.*

   arrive at — To come to or reach: — *Nora **arrived at** the gate just as the train was leaving.*
*Has the jury **arrived at** a decision yet?*

   attain — To arrive at; reach: — *She **attained** her goal when she became editor of the school newspaper.*

   get to — To reach; arrive: — *We will talk when we **get to** school.*

Word Alert

REACH also means to get in touch with someone: *I tried to **reach** you on the phone yesterday, but there was no answer.* Synonyms for this meaning of **reach** can be found at the entry for **COMMUNICATE**.

---

ready *adjective* — Prepared for use or action: — *The car was loaded and **ready** to go.*
*Jose was **ready** to study for the test.*
*Everything is **ready** for the party.*

   prepared — Ready or fit for a particular purpose: — *Colette was **prepared** to take the exam.*

   set — Ready or prepared to do something: — *Robin was all **set** to go to camp.*

---

real *adjective* — Not imagined or imitation: — *What is the **real** story behind the legend of Daniel Boone?*
*The flowers were **real**, not plastic.*

   actual — Real; existing: — *There are many copies, but this is the **actual** painting.*

   existing — Real: — *The book was about **existing** people, not imaginary ones.*

   genuine — Being what it seems; real: — *Her purse is **genuine** leather.*
*The witness's story seemed **genuine**.*

   true — Agreeing with the facts; not false, wrong, or made up: — *The **true** facts are stranger than fiction.*
*The movie was based on a **true** story.*

---

reason *noun* — A cause or motive: — *Michael had no **reason** to doubt Zachary.*
*Is there a **reason** why you were late?*

   cause — A person or thing that makes something happen: — *What was the **cause** of his outburst?*
*Heavy rain was the **cause** of the flood.*

   explanation — A reason or meaning: — *The **explanation** for why things fall is gravity.*
*What is the **explanation** for your behavior?*
*Ted has an **explanation** for everything.*

   motive — The reason that a person does something: — *Jerry's **motive** for practicing was his desire to get on the team.*

rebel *verb*	To fight against authority:	Some slaves **rebelled** against their owners and escaped to the North before the Civil War. Teenagers sometimes **rebel** against being told what to do.
resist	To fight against or overcome:	The people of the country **resisted** the dictator's harsh rule. I **resisted** eating the ice cream until I finished my dinner.
revolt	To rebel against a government or other authority:	The American colonists **revolted** against the British.
rise up	To rebel:	The people **rose up** against the injustices of the government.

reckless *adjective*	Not careful:	Justin made a **reckless** move with his queen and lost the chess game. **Reckless** driving causes many accidents.
heedless	Not paying attention to; careless:	In his **heedless** rush to get up, Jack almost knocked over his desk.
impetuous	Acting without planning or thought:	His **impetuous** behavior caused him to make mistakes.
rash	Too hasty; not careful:	He made a **rash** decision and has been sorry ever since. It is **rash** not to wear a seat belt in a car.

For more choices see the entry for CARELESS.
Antonyms: See the entry for CAREFUL.

refuse *verb*	To say no to:	Holly **refuses** to do any more work unless her friends help. The teacher **refused** to favor some students over the rest of the class.
decline	To refuse politely:	I had to **decline** the invitation to the party because I would be away on that day.
dismiss	To send away or allow to leave:	Our teacher **dismissed** class early.
reject	To refuse to accept, allow, or approve:	The inspector **rejected** any apple that had a bruise. The voters **rejected** the school board's plan.
turn down	To refuse:	The student council **turned down** our plan for the dance. I was **turned down** by one college but accepted by another.

regular *adjective* | According to custom or rule: | We took our **regular** way home from school. Our **regular** teacher is absent.

ordinary | Commonly used, regular: | On an ordinary day we get out of school at three o'clock.

routine | According to the regular way of doing something: | Feeding our cat is one of my routine chores.

typical | Showing the qualities of a group or type: | My typical lunch is a peanut butter sandwich.

For more choices see the entries for COMMON, NORMAL, and USUAL.
Antonyms: See the entries for ODD, UNFAMILIAR, and UNUSUAL.

---

religion *noun* | A particular system of belief and worship: | Christianity, Judaism, Islam, Hinduism, and Buddhism are some of the world's major **religions**. Freedom of **religion** is guaranteed by the Constitution.

creed | A statement of belief by a person or group: | "Honesty is the best policy" is my creed.

faith | Belief or trust without proof: | I have faith in your ability and know you will succeed.

For more choices see the entry for BELIEF.

---

religious *adjective* | Showing devotion to a religion: | Many of my classmates have different **religious** beliefs from mine. Is your family **religious**?

devout | Very religious: | Devout believers gathered at their place of worship every week.

pious | Very religious; devout: | The pious monks worked hard to help the poor.

spiritual | Having to do with the spirit: | Priests, ministers, and rabbis are spiritual leaders.

---

remark *noun* | Something said in a few words: | My grandfather always makes a few **remarks** at holiday meals. The teacher wrote a few **remarks** on my report.

comment | A remark or note: | We listened carefully to the coach's comments after the game.

observation | Something said; comment; remark: | Sheila made an observation about how much she loved the beach.

statement | Something expressed or explained in words: | The president made an important statement about the environment.

remember ◈ report

remember *verb* | To bring back to mind: | *Can you **remember** where we parked the car?*
*Who **remembers** how to play gin rummy?*
*The old man **remembered** every word to the song.*

recall | To bring back to mind; remember: | *I know we have met, but I can't recall your name.*

recollect | To remember; recall: | *Can you recollect our visit to the zoo?*

think of | To call to mind; remember: | *Is there anyone you can think of who can help with this problem?*

---

remove *verb* | To take or move away or off: | *They **removed** their coats when they came inside.*
*The turpentine will **remove** all the old paint.*

eliminate | To get rid of; remove: | *We are all working to eliminate pollution.*

extract | To take, get, or pull out: | *It took a lot of effort to extract the rusted bolt.*
The dentist extracted my wisdom teeth.

take away | To remove: | *The movers took away all our furniture.*

withdraw | To take away; remove: | *I had to withdraw from the race because I hurt my foot.*
My mother withdrew money from the bank to pay for new clothes for school.

For more choices see the entry for ERASE and UNDO.

---

rent *verb* | To pay for the right to use something: | *Patricia and Mark **rented** bicycles and rode around the park.*
*Sometimes we **rent** a house right on the beach.*

charter | To rent or hire by charter: | *I would love to charter a yacht and sail around the world.*

hire | To get the temporary use of something in return for payments; rent: | *The high school seniors hired limousines to take them to the prom.*

lease | To rent: | *We leased a car for our trip.*

---

report *noun* | An account, statement, or announcement: | *Beth turned in her book **report**.*
*The principal prepared a **report** for the school board.*
*Many **reports** are prepared for the public each year.*

account | A spoken or written statement; report: | *Did you read the account of the big game in the newspaper?*

record | A written account of something: | *The court keeps a record of the testimony of every witness.*

summary | A brief account that contains the main points of something: | *The radio station gives a summary of the news every hour.*
I wrote a summary of the game for the school newspaper.

For more choices see the entry for STORY.

report *verb* — To make or give an account of:

The newspaper *reported* on the election.
Each night the sports announcer *reports* all the scores.
You are supposed to *report* all auto accidents to the police.

announce — To state or make known publicly or formally:

Our principal *announced* that she would be leaving.

relate — To tell or report events or details.

Paul *related* the story of how we got lost in the woods.

summarize — To give a brief report that contains the main points of something:

She *summarized* the book's plot in the first few paragraphs of her report.

For more choices see the entries for DESCRIBE and TELL.

Word Alert

As a verb, **REPORT** also means to present oneself to: *Several students were asked to report to the principal's office.* Synonyms for this meaning of **report** can be found at the entry for **VISIT**.

---

respect *noun* — High regard or consideration:

The mayor earned our *respect* by doing a good job.
Respect for the rights of others is an important principle.

esteem — High respect or admiration:

Most Americans hold the Constitution in high *esteem*.

praise — Words that show high regard or approval:

Good work deserves *praise*.

regard — Respect or affection:

I hold our friendship in high *regard*.

---

responsible *adjective* — Able to be trusted:

The class elected Martha treasurer because she was so *responsible*.

dependable — Reliable or trustworthy:

We need a *dependable* person to be a school crossing guard.

reliable — Able to be depended upon and trusted:

A *reliable* person should handle the money.
There are some very *reliable* players on our team.

trustworthy — Able to be trusted; reliable:

Only tell your secrets to *trustworthy* people.

For more choices see the entry for HONEST.

restless *adjective* — Unable to rest; not still:
*We were all **restless**, waiting to give our speeches.*
*The **restless** wind blew leaves across the pavement.*

  agitated — Disturbed or excited:
The agitated dogs barked wildly.
The wind stirred the agitated water.

  nervous — Not able to relax; tense:
Loud noises make my cat nervous.

  uneasy — Worried; nervous; restless:
I was uneasy about the test because I hadn't studied hard enough.
After tossing and turning, I finally dropped off into an uneasy sleep.

---

restrict *verb* — To keep within limits:
*We were **restricted** from going into the construction site.*
*The contest rules **restrict** each entry to twenty-five words or less.*

  confine — To hold or keep in; limit:
Our dog is confined to the backyard by a fence.
The doctor confined me to my bed while I was sick.

  cramp — To limit; confine:
Space on the small boat was cramped.

  limit — To keep within bounds; restrict:
We have to limit the time we watch television so we can get our homework done.

Antonyms: See the entry for ASSIST.

---

result *noun* — Something that happens because of something else:
*The accident was the **result** of carelessness.*
*Did you hear the **results** of the game?*

  conclusion — Something decided after thinking:
Eventually we came to the conclusion that she was right.

  consequence — The result of an action:
He turned in his report a week late and as a consequence his grade was lowered.

  end — Goal; purpose; outcome:
He was working toward a good end — getting into college.

  outcome — Something that happens because of something else; a consequence:
The outcome of the school election was a surprise.

---

return[1] *verb* — To come or go back:
*I **returned** home from the library.*
*They will **return** from vacation tomorrow.*

  come back — To return:
Our cat came back home.
Please come back when you can.

  go back — To return:
We must go back to pick up my books.
They went back to the grocery store for more food.

  revisit — To visit again; return:
Larry wants to revisit the museum sometime.

return² *verb* | To take, bring, send, give, or put back: | *I returned several books to my grandmother.*
Please return my calculator when you are finished with it.

give back | To return: | *Mike thanked Lauren and gave back her CD.*

hand back | To return: | *The teacher handed back our papers.*

replace | To put back: | *Harriet replaced the book on the shelf.*

restore | To give or put back: | *My lost wallet was restored by the person who found it.*

Antonyms: See the entry for KEEP.

---

reveal *verb* | To make known: | *Hope was worried that Brittany might reveal her secret to their friends.*
The secret entrance to the cave could only be revealed when the sun was in the right place.

disclose | To make known: | *He didn't disclose where he had heard the rumor.*

divulge | To reveal; tell: | *Please don't divulge the plot of the novel until I've had a chance to read it.*

expose | To make something known; reveal: | *The reporter exposed the dangerous pollution in our river.*

Antonyms: See the entry for HIDE.

---

rich *adjective* | Having much money, land, or other valuables: | *Our state is rich in natural resources.*
The rich man lived alone in a huge mansion.
The queen is a rich woman.

affluent | Wealthy, prosperous: | *Affluent customers shop at that expensive store.*

opulent | Showing wealth or affluence: | *Their opulent mansion contained many works of art.*

prosperous | Having success, wealth, and good fortune: | *The prosperous merchants made sure that less fortunate families were taken care of.*

wealthy | Having many material goods or riches: | *Mr. Smith's invention made him a wealthy man.*

Antonyms: See the entry for POOR.

right *adjective* — Free from mistakes; true: — *It turned out that there was only one **right** answer to the problem.*
*Telling the truth is the **right** thing to do.*

    correct — Not having any mistakes: — *Sydney gave the correct answer.*
Alex fumbled through his pocket looking for correct change.

    definite — Certain, clear: — *Her answer was a definite no.*

    faultless — Without anything wrong; unspoiled: — *After checking for every possible error, Walt was sure that his computer program was faultless.*

    precise — Clearly and accurately said or shown: — *The science teacher asked the class to measure the precise amount the jar would hold.*
The precise time the bus arrived was 4:38.

    specific — Exact; particular: — *We need to set a specific time for our meeting.*

For more choices see the entries for PERFECT and TRUE.
Antonyms: See the entries for INCORRECT and WRONG.

---

roomy *adjective* — Having plenty of room; large: — *Their house is very **roomy**.*
*Your new jacket is **roomy** enough for you to grow.*

    extensive — Large; great; broad; roomy: — *The storm caused damage over an extensive area.*
I made extensive revisions to the second draft of my term paper.

    spacious — Having lots of space; roomy: — *They lived in a spacious apartment.*
Our school has a spacious auditorium.

For more choices see the entries for LARGE and WIDE.
Antonyms: See the entry for NARROW.

---

rough *adjective* — Having an uneven surface; not smooth: — *Alexander scraped his knee on **rough** tree bark.*
*The **rough** road was dangerous for bike riders.*

    coarse — Thick and rough: — *The beach was covered with coarse sand.*
My heavy sweater is made out of coarse wool.

    ragged — Rough and uneven: — *We saw a ragged line of mountains in the distance.*

    rugged — Rough and uneven: — *This dirt road goes through some rugged country.*

For more choices see the entry for JAGGED.
Antonyms: See the entries for FLAT and SMOOTH.

round	*adjective*	Shaped like a ball or globe:	*The round orange rolled across the kitchen floor.* *The earth and all the other planets are round.*
	circular	Having the shape of a circle; round:	*The circus was held in a huge circular tent.* *Sue was wearing a small circular pin on her sweater.*
	spherical	Shaped like a ball; round:	*The fat man in the cartoon had a spherical shape.*

WORDS from Words

ROUND is often combined with other words to form expressions that have special meanings. These expressions also have synonyms. *For example:*

roundabout means not straight or direct: *We took a roundabout way home.* Useful synonyms are **long**, **meandering**, and **winding**.

round number means a number given in terms of the nearest whole number, or in tens, hundreds, thousands, and the like: *40, 200, and 1,000 are round numbers; 38, 186, and 959 are not round numbers.* Useful synonyms are **even** and **rounded off**.

to round off means to make into a round number: *58.7 is rounded off to 60.*

to round out means to make complete: *We rounded out our day with dinner and a movie.* Useful synonyms are **complete** and **finish**.

to round up means to drive or herd together: *The cowboys rounded up the cattle. Round up all your friends and we'll go to the park.* Useful synonyms are **bring together**, **call together**, and **gather**. A **roundup** is a gathering together of people or things, especially livestock: *They hold a roundup of wild horses every year. The newscaster gave a roundup of the latest news.* A possible synonym is **gathering**.

rude	*adjective*	Showing bad manners:	*Speaking with your mouth full is rude.* *The teacher punished them for making rude remarks.*
	discourteous	Without good manners:	*You have no reason to be discourteous to our neighbor.*
	impolite	Not showing good manners:	*They were impolite to everyone at the party.*
	sassy	Rude:	*The sassy little girl talked back to her mother.*

Antonyms: See the entry for POLITE.

ruin *verb* — To harm or damage: — Rain could ruin our day at the beach.
Morgan's chances to make the team were ruined when she broke her ankle.

demolish — To tear down or destroy: — The workers demolished the old factory with dynamite.

destroy — To ruin completely; wreck: — The hurricane destroyed several buildings, but no one was injured.

wreck — To destroy or ruin: — Losing our best player wrecked our hopes for winning the game.
Bad weather could wreck our plans for the picnic.

---

rule *noun* — A direction that guides behavior or action: — The referee makes sure everyone plays by the rules of the game.
I always make it a rule to be on time.

decree — An official order or decision: — The emperor sent out a decree that raised everyone's taxes.

principle — A rule of behavior that a person chooses to live by: — One of my principles is to always tell the truth.

regulation — A law, rule, or order: — Running in the halls is forbidden by school regulations.

For more choices see the entry for LAW.

WORDS from Words

RULE is often combined with other words to form expressions that have special meanings. These expressions also have synonyms. *For example:*

as a rule means usually: *As a rule, I don't eat candy this close to dinner.* Useful synonyms can be found at the entry for **USUALLY**.

to rule out means to decide against; exclude from consideration: *After they **ruled out** getting a dog, they had to decide what kind of cat they wanted.* Useful synonyms are **decide against**, **exclude**, and **limit**.

---

rumor *noun* — A story or statement told by one person to another as truth, but without any proof: — There was a rumor that all computers were going to shut down at noon yesterday, but they are still running.
The rumor about free concert tickets turned out not to be true.

gossip — Idle talk or rumors about other people: — Spreading gossip is mean.
The gossip about the singer turned out to be untrue.

hearsay — Information about someone else: — She said the stories were all true, but they turned out to be just hearsay.

run *verb*	To go or cause to go quickly:	*Barry was late and had to **run** to catch the school bus. A cheetah can **run** faster than any other animal.*
dash	To move fast; rush:	*When the dog appeared, our cat dashed into the house.*
race	To move or go very fast:	*We raced across the football field.*
sprint	To run fast for a short distance:	*I sprinted down the stairs and out the door.*

For more choices see the entries for HURRY and ZOOM.

WORDS from Words

RUN is often combined with other words to form expressions that have special meanings. These expressions also have synonyms. *For example:*

in the long run means near the end or in the last part of a course of events: *In the long run, missing one day of school probably won't affect your final grades. Things tend to even out in the long run.* Useful synonyms are **finally**, **in the end**, and **on the whole**.

in the short run means in the near future: *The amount of pollution we create in the short run can have long-term effects on the environment.* Useful synonyms are **before long**, **shortly**, and **soon**.

on the run means running: *She caught the ball on the run. We had so many errands we have been on the run all day.* Useful synonyms are **hurrying**, **running**, and **scrambling**. **On the run** also means trying to escape: *The robbers were on the run from the police.* Useful synonyms are **fleeing**, **running away from**, and **trying to avoid**.

to run across and **to run into** mean to meet someone by chance. *We ran across some old friends at the mall today. I ran into Aunt Teresa, and she asked about you.* Useful synonyms are **come across**, **encounter**, and **meet**. **Run into** can also mean to collide with something: *The car ran into a fire hydrant.* Useful synonyms are **bump**, **crash**, and **hit**.

to run away and **to run off** mean to leave very quickly because you want to get away. *Our dog always runs away whenever it's time for her bath. The boys ran off while I covered my eyes and counted to one hundred.* Useful synonyms are **escape** and **flee**.

to run out means to come to an end: *The clock ran out before the other team could score. We have run out of milk.* Useful synonyms are **deplete**, **exhaust**, and **use up**.

to run out of and **to run through** mean to use up the supply of something. *We have run out of sugar. I can't believe we ran through the whole bag.* Useful synonyms are **consume**, **drain**, and **exhaust**.

to run over means to ride or drive over: *Our car ran over some glass and got a flat tire.* Useful synonyms are **drive over**, **pass over**, and **ride over**. **To run over** also means to overflow: *The sink ran over when I left the water running too long.* Useful synonyms are **flood**, **spill over**, and **swamp**.

sad *adjective*

Feeling or showing unhappiness or sorrow:

Eli was **sad** when his best friend moved away.
It was a **sad** day when my father lost his job.

dejected
Sad or depressed:
Everyone felt **dejected** when our team lost.

depressed
Feeling sad:
Tim was **depressed** when he could not get the lead in the school play.

downcast
Low in spirits; sad:
She was **downcast** when she did not make the team.

melancholy
Low in spirits; sad:
Natasha felt **melancholy** because her trip was ending.

For more choices see the entries for SULLEN and UNHAPPY.
Antonyms: See the entry for HAPPY.

---

sadness *noun*

Sorrow and unhappiness:

A feeling of **sadness** came over me when I had to move to a new school.
Music can make my **sadness** go away.

distress
Great pain or sorrow; misery:
My grandfather's illness was a cause of **distress** for my whole family.

grief
A very great feeling of being sad:
I will always remember my **grief** at the death of my dog.

melancholy
Low spirits; a mood of sadness:
All his songs are too full of **melancholy** for me.

sorrow
A strong feeling of loss:
We all felt **sorrow** when our dog disappeared.

unhappiness
Sadness; sorrow:
My best friend's move caused my **unhappiness**.

For more choices see the entry for SUFFERING.
Antonyms: See the entries for DELIGHT and PLEASURE.

---

safe *adjective*

Free from harm or danger:

Tori hid her diary in a **safe** place.
We feel **safe** in our house at night.

guarded
Kept safe from harm or danger:
They moved the gold to the bank in a **guarded** truck.

protected
Safe from harm:
We found a **protected** place out of the rain.

secure
Safe from harm or loss:
A basement is a **secure** place to be during a tornado.

Antonyms: See the entries for DANGEROUS and DARING.

same
adjective

Like another in every way:

Telling the twins apart was even harder because they wore the **same** clothes.
We came back the **same** way.

   identical

The very same:

At first we were embarrassed when we wore identical dresses to the party, then we decided it was funny.
The identical thing happened to me last month.

   matching

A person or thing very much like another:

The matching sock for this one is lost.
My friends and I bought matching beach towels for summer.

For more choices see the entry for EQUAL.
Antonyms: See the entry for UNEQUAL.

---

sarcastic
adjective

Using sharp words that make fun of someone or something:

Frank's **sarcastic** comments hurt Paige's feelings.

   insulting

Using remarks or actions that hurt someone's feelings:

I can't believe he made such an insulting comment.

   mocking

Making fun of in a mean way:

His mocking imitation of me was so funny, I couldn't help but laugh.

   sneering

Showing hatred or scorn:

His sneering look was replaced by surprise when my magic trick worked.

---

save *verb*

To free from harm; make safe:

We heard that several horses were **saved** from a burning barn.
Kenny was rewarded for **saving** the puppy from getting hit by a car.

   deliver

To save from danger; rescue:

The slaves were finally delivered from bondage.
The Coast Guard delivered the crew by helicopter when their boat ran aground.

   rescue

To save or free:

The lifeguard rescued the child from the water.
I rescued our kitten from up in a tree.

   salvage

To save from being lost or destroyed:

We were able to salvage all our important papers from the flooded basement.

For more choices see the entry for PROTECT.

Word Alert

SAVE also means to set aside for future use: *I save rubber bands, but I never seem to use them. You should save your money for college.* Synonyms for this meaning of **save** can be found at the entry for **KEEP**.

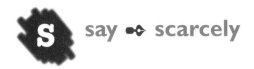

say *verb*	To speak and express in words:	*What did he say?* *They **said** they enjoyed meeting you.* *What are they **saying** now?*
declare	To make known publicly or formally:	*The fire chief declared that our school had done well during the fire drill.*
express	To say or show:	*The Declaration of Independence expresses the idea that all people are created equal.* *I sometimes have trouble expressing exactly what I mean.*
mention	To speak about:	*I forgot to mention my homework when we talked.* *I mentioned the party to my friends.*
remark	To say briefly; mention:	*The principal remarked that our class had done well on the test.*
utter	To give voice to; express out loud:	*Hal uttered a sigh of relief when our teacher said we could have more time on our reports.*

For more choices see the entries for EXPLAIN, TALK, and TELL.

saying *noun*	A familiar statement expressing some truth or common sense:	*She always followed the old **saying**, "a penny saved is a penny earned."*
adage	An old and familiar saying that is believed to be true:	*"The early bird catches the worm" is an adage.*
expression	A common word or group of words:	*"Look before you leap" is a common expression.* *"Smart aleck" is a slang expression.*
motto	A short sentence that says what someone believes in or what something stands for:	*"Don't Tread on Me" was a motto for the patriots in the American Revolution.*
proverb	A short saying that expresses something many people believe to be true:	*"Save your money for a rainy day" is a proverb.*

scarcely *adverb*	Only just or almost not; barely or hardly:	*The bus had **scarcely** gone before another one appeared.* *There was **scarcely** anyone in the restaurant.*
barely	Only just; scarcely:	*There is barely enough dessert for all of us.* *We barely made it to the show in time.*
hardly	Just about; barely:	*We could hardly see who it was in the dim light.*

For more choices see the entry for RARELY.
Antonyms: See the entries for OFTEN and USUALLY.

scare *verb*   To frighten or become afraid: A sudden noise **scared** the whole class.
The roller coaster didn't **scare** me.

alarm   To make afraid; frighten: A spider **alarmed** me, but it quickly scurried away.

frighten   To make or become suddenly afraid or alarmed: All the loud sirens **frightened** us.
Gene **frightens** easily when he is alone in the house.

startle   To frighten or surprise suddenly: The explosion **startled** me.
We **startled** a bird in the bushes, and it flew away.

terrify   To fill with terror; frighten greatly: The child was **terrified** by the bad dream.

---

school *noun*   A place for teaching and learning: Our **school** is located a few blocks from my house.
We attend **school** five days a week.

educational institution   An organization set up to educate or carry on educational research: Our teacher attended an **educational institution** to improve his teaching skills.

WORD BANK

SCHOOL has no exact synonyms, but you can make things clearer for your reader by naming the particular **school** you mean. Some types of **schools** are:

academy	elementary school	junior high school	primary school
boarding school	grammar school	kindergarten	seminary
college	high school	middle school	university

Word Alert

SCHOOL can also mean a large group of fish: *A school of tuna was sighted by the fishermen.* Synonyms for this meaning of **school** can be found at the entry for **GROUP**.

---

scratch *verb*   To scrape or cut with something sharp and pointed: A thorn on the rosebush **scratched** my thumb.
Neal was **scratching** his head while he was thinking.
Our dog loves to be **scratched**.

scrape   To injure or scratch by rubbing against something sharp or rough: I **scraped** my knee on the pavement when my bike crashed into the curb.

scuff   To scratch the surface of something by scraping or wear: The child **scuffed** his new shoes the first time he wore them.

scream *verb* — To make a loud, piercing cry or sound:

The audience **screamed** at the scary parts of the movie.
The siren **screamed** as the fire truck went by.
We **screamed** with laughter at Alexa's joke.

    screech — To make a shrill, harsh cry or sound:

An old lady **screeched** at us about not playing in the street.
The car's brakes **screeched**.

    shriek — To utter a loud, sharp cry or sound:

He was so scared he **shrieked** when the door slammed.
The wind **shrieked** outside the window.

    squeal — To make a loud, shrill cry or sound:

Pigs **squeal** when they are hurt or frightened.
The tires **squealed** as the car turned the corner.

For more choices see the entries for CRY and YELL.

---

see *verb* — To look with the eyes; view:

Do you want to **see** a movie?
We **saw** the parade last Saturday.

    behold — To look at; see:

As the fog cleared, we **beheld** the shapes of the cliffs.
Behold the vastness of the ocean.

    discern — To see clearly; to recognize the difference between things:

We **discerned** a pattern in the woven rug.
There are so many opinions I am having trouble **discerning** who is right.

    spot — To see; recognize:

I **spotted** you in the crowd.

For more choices see the entries for LOOK¹ and NOTICE.

Word Alert

SEE also means to understand: *I see what you mean.* Synonyms for this meaning of **see** can be found at the entries for **KNOW** and **UNDERSTAND**.

WORDS from Words

SEE is often combined with other words to form expressions that have special meanings. These expressions also have synonyms. *For example:*

to see off means to go with someone to a place of departure: *We **saw** our guests **off** at the airport.* Useful synonyms are *say farewell*, *say good-byes*, and *take leave of*.

to see through means to continue to the end of a project: *It's late, but I'm going **to see** this project **through** to its conclusion.* Useful synonyms are **complete**, **end**, and **finish**. **To see through** also means to understand the real meaning of something: *We **saw through** their disguise. The detective **saw through** the suspect's story.*

to see to means to take care of something: *Please **see to** this task immediately. My mother **saw to** our dinner while we worked outside. **See to** your baby brother while we're gone.* Useful synonyms are **attend to** and **look after**.

seize *verb* — To take hold of: — *The dog **seized** the ball and ran away.*
*The rebels **seized** the capital in a few hours.*

grasp — To seize and hold fast: — *Edward **grasped** the rope and started pulling.*
*I always **grasp** my brother's hand when crossing a street.*

snatch — To seize or grab quickly: — *The dog **snatched** the biscuit in its mouth and
ran out the door.*

For more choices see the entries for CATCH and HOLD.
Antonyms: See the entry for MISS.

---

selfish *adjective* — Thinking only of oneself; not willing to share: — ***Selfish** people are not interested in the feelings of others.*
*The **selfish** boy refused to let anyone else ride his scooter.*

greedy — Selfish; desiring more than one's share: — *The **greedy** child scooped up as much candy
as he could carry.*

possessive — Selfish with one's belongings: — *She is very **possessive** about her CDs and never lends
them to anyone.*

stingy — Not willing to share: — *The **stingy** woman never gave a tip to the delivery boy.*

---

send *verb* — To cause to go from one place to another: — *Laura often **sends** e-mail to her friends.*
*When I got sick, they **sent** me to the school nurse.*

dispatch — To send off quickly: — *The scientist **dispatched** an announcement
of his discovery.*

e-mail — To send a message electronically: — *I **e-mailed** my friend a birthday greeting.*

mail — To send messages or packages: — *We **mailed** our letters at the post office.*

ship — To send by ship, train, truck, or airplane: — *Our new chairs are being **shipped** from the
warehouse today.*

transmit — To send or pass from one person or thing to another: — *The sinking ship **transmitted** an SOS.*
*A television station **transmits** programs.*

---

serious *adjective* — Having a thoughtful manner: — *Kelly had a very **serious** look on her face.*
*Everyone treated the election in a **serious** manner.*

grave — Thoughtful and solemn; serious: — *The principal made a **grave** announcement about
vandalism in the library.*

grim — Stern, frightening, and harsh: — *The judge looked **grim** as he announced the verdict.*

solemn — Serious, grave: — *A funeral is a **solemn** occasion.*
*Art gave his **solemn** oath to tell the truth.*

somber — Dark and gloomy: — *The team was in a **somber** mood after they lost.*

Antonyms: See the entry for FUNNY.

set *adjective*   Fixed or decided; stubborn about changing: *The rules of the game are set. Her mind was set on winning the election no matter what.*

    firm   Not changing: *They had a firm belief that they were right.*

    settled   Decided; agreed upon: *The issue was settled by a vote.*

    stable   Not easily moved, shaken, or changed: *Check to see if that ladder is stable before you climb it.*

WORDS from Words

SET is often combined with other words to form expressions that have special meanings. These expressions also have synonyms. *For example:*

to set aside means to save for a special use: *We set aside money for our trip.* Useful synonyms are **keep** and **save**.

to set forth means to make known: *Ned set forth his reasons for his decision.* Useful synonyms are **declare** and **state**. **Set forth** also means to start to go: *The caravan set forth on its journey.* Useful synonyms are **begin** and **start**.

to set off means to make more prominent by contrast: *Her blue belt set off her red dress.* Useful synonyms are **contrast** and **distinguish**. **Set off** also means to start: *They set off on their bicycles to go to the park.* Useful synonyms are **begin** and **go off**.

to set up means to assemble or prepare for use: *We helped our father set up the tent. We set up a workshop in our garage.* Useful synonyms are **assemble**, **build**, and **erect**.

---

shake *verb*   To move quickly up and down, back and forth, or from side to side: *You have to shake the bottle to mix the salad dressing. We shook our beach towels to get the sand out of them.*

    jiggle   To shake slightly: *My desk jiggles so much I can't write neatly.*

    shiver   To shake; tremble: *Don shivered in the cold room.*

    shudder   To tremble suddenly: *I shuddered when I heard the thunder.*

    tremble   To shake with cold, fear, weakness, or anger: *The frightened bunny trembled and then ran away.*

---

shame *noun*   A painful feeling caused by having done something wrong or foolish: *I blushed with shame after I stumbled on the dance floor. The student felt shame for having cheated.*

    embarrassment   A feeling of shyness or being ashamed: *She turned red with embarrassment when we all shouted "Surprise!"*

    humiliation   A feeling of being ashamed or foolish: *I felt humiliated when I didn't make a single shot during the game.*

    regret   A feeling of sadness or sorrow: *They felt no regret about what they had done.*

shape *noun* | The form of an object: | *An orange has a different **shape** from a banana. The artist drew the **shape** of a bird with chalk on the sidewalk.*

contour | The outline or shape of something: | *The **contour** of the land became rougher as we approached the mountains.*

figure | A form or outline; shape: | *There was a **figure** of a man painted on the wall of the cave.*

profile | A side view, especially an outline of a person's head: | *George Washington's **profile** is on the quarter.*

For more choices see the entry for FORM.

---

sharp¹ *adjective* | Having an edge or point that cuts easily: | *Scissors have **sharp** blades. Some people are said to have a **sharp** tongue. People's feelings can be hurt by **sharp** criticism.*

cutting | Hurting a person's feelings; harsh: | *Her **cutting** comments hurt his feelings.*

pointed | Biting statements referring to a particular person or thing: | *Elijah's **pointed** remarks left no doubt about who he was voting for.*

sharp-edged | Having a keen edge: | *The **sharp-edged** ax cut right through the logs.*

---

sharp² *adjective* | Quick of mind; watchful; aware of things: | *My sister has a **sharp** mind. Keep a **sharp** lookout for trouble.*

alert | Watching carefully: | *You have to be **alert** to solve this puzzle.*

keen | Quick in hearing, seeing, or thinking: | *A dog has a **keen** sense of smell.*

quick | Learning or thinking with speed: | *Adam has a **quick** mind and is very good at spelling.*

For more choices see the entries for SMART and WISE.
Antonyms: See the entries for DUMB and STUPID.

---

sharp³ *adjective* | Having a sudden change in direction: | *The road took a **sharp** turn.*

abrupt | Without warning: | *The bus made an **abrupt** stop at the traffic light.*

rapid | With great speed: | *The **rapid** motion of a hummingbird's wings is too fast to count.*

sudden | Happening without warning: | *A **sudden** rainstorm caught us in the open and soaked us.*

shine *verb* | To give or reflect light: | *The stars shine at night.* |
		We could see a searchlight shining in the distance.
glisten	To shine with reflected light:	*The sunlight glistened off the water.*
glitter	To shine with bright flashes:	*The diamonds in her bracelet glittered in the candlelight.*
		Stars glitter because of the movement of the atmosphere.
sparkle	To shine with quick, bright flashes:	*The jewels sparkled.*
		Her eyes sparkled with mischief.
twinkle	To shine with flashes of light:	*The bright lights of the city twinkled in the distance.*

---

ship *noun* | A large boat: | *A ship can hold more than a boat.* |
| **vessel** | A ship or large boat: | *Several vessels were tied up at the dock.* |

For more choices see the entry for BOAT.

WORD BANK

Sometimes you can make things clearer and more interesting for your reader by naming the particular kind of **SHIP** you mean. Some **ships** are:

aircraft carrier	*ferry*	*paddle steamer*	*supertanker*
barge	*freighter*	*pirate ship*	*tanker*
battleship	*frigate*	*scow*	*transport*
container ship	*galley*	*steamship*	*trawler*
cruiser	*icebreaker*	*steamer*	*tugboat*
destroyer	*ocean liner*	*submarine*	*warship*

---

short *adjective* | Not long or tall: | *We waited a short time to get into the movie.* |
		It is only a short distance to the park.
		Last year Charles was too short to go on the ride, but now he is tall enough.
brief	Short in time:	*We only had time for a brief visit.*
low	Not high or tall:	*We sat on a low bench.*
		A low wall surrounds the playground.
squat	Short and thick; low and broad:	*There was only one squat tree in the dry field.*

Antonyms: See the entry for TALL.

show *verb*   To bring into sight or view: *Gabriella will **show** her drawings to the class tomorrow.*
*His smile **showed** how happy he was.*

   display   To show or exhibit: *The department store displays clothing in its windows.*

   exhibit   To show: *Our best schoolwork is exhibited on the bulletin board.*

   point out   To show; indicate: *Our teacher pointed out the errors on the test.*

   present   To put before an audience; show: *Barry presented a science experiment to the class.*

Antonyms: See the entry for HIDE.

WORDS from Words

SHOW is often combined with other words to form expressions that have special meanings. These expressions also have synonyms. *For example:*

to show off means to behave in a way that calls attention to oneself: *Those boys love **to show off** for each other.* Useful synonyms are **boast** and **brag**.

to show up means to arrive: *They **showed up** late for the party.* Useful synonyms are **arrive**, **come**, and **get there**.

---

shrink *verb*   To make or become smaller: *Our neighborhood seems to **shrink** when everyone leaves for vacation.*
*My wool sweater **shrank** when I washed it in hot water.*

   constrict   To make smaller by pressing together: *The collar of my shirt constricted my neck when I tried to button it.*

   contract   To make or become shorter or smaller: *The snail contracted into its shell.*

   shrivel   To shrink, wrinkle, or wither: *The plants shriveled because it was too hot for them.*

For more choices see the entry for DWINDLE.
Antonyms: See the entries for EXPAND and GROW.

---

shut *verb*   To block or cover up an entrance or opening: *Sid **shut** the window to keep out the breeze.*
*When he was finished reading, Jeremy **shut** the book.*

   bar   To keep out: *Passengers are barred from entering the cockpit on an airliner when it is in flight.*

   slam   To shut with force and a loud noise: *Please don't slam the door.*

For more choices see the entries for CLOSE and LOCK.
Antonyms: See the entry for OPEN.

WORDS from Words

SHUT is often combined with other words to form expressions that have special meanings. These expressions also have synonyms. *For example:*

to shut down means to stop something from operating for a time: *The factory had to shut down because of the strike. They shut down the movie theater so they could put in new seats.* A useful synonym is **close**.

to shut off means to stop the flow, passage, or operation of something: *I shut off the shower. The power will be shut off while the lines are repaired.* Useful synonyms are **end** and **halt**.

to shut out means to keep from entering: *The shades shut out the sunlight.* A useful synonym is **exclude**. In sports, **to shut out** means to defeat a team without letting it score: *We shut out the other school's team six to nothing.* Useful synonyms are **beat** and **defeat**.

---

shy *adjective* — Not comfortable around people: *The shy child stayed away from the party. Lily was too shy to stand in front of the class.*

bashful — Easily embarrassed: *Carlos was too bashful to step out from behind the chair.*

meek — Humble, quiet, and mild-mannered: *The new boy was too meek to ask for directions and went to the wrong classroom.*

timid — Showing a lack of courage; easily frightened: *The timid little boy would not go near the large dog.*

For more choices see the entry for AFRAID.
Antonyms: See the entries for BRAVE and DARING.

---

sick *adjective* — Suffering from disease: *Several people in my class were sick with measles. Jade got a sick feeling from eating too much candy.*

ailing — Feeling ill or sick: *The ailing dog could barely stand up.*

ill — Not healthy or well; sick: *Several of my friends were ill with the flu last winter.*

sickly — Often or always sick: *The sickly child was cured after a week in the hospital.*

---

sickness *noun* — Poor health: *There has been more sickness than usual in our school this winter. A fever is a sign of sickness.*

ailment — An illness; sickness: *The doctor said that rest was all I needed to cure my ailment.*

disease — Something inside that makes a living organism sick: *Germs and viruses cause many diseases. Washing your hands is an effective way to stop diseases from spreading.*

illness — A sickness or disease: *Many illnesses can be cured by taking the right medicine.*

malady — Sickness; illness: *Doctors throughout the world are fighting serious maladies such as malaria and measles.*

sign *noun* — A mark or thing that stands for, shows, or suggests something else: *There are **signs** that warn cars to slow down near our school. A dollar **sign** means money.*

gesture — A movement that expresses a feeling: *Our teacher used the **gesture** of putting her finger to her lips to tell us that she wanted quiet.*

signal — Something that warns, directs, or informs: *A flashing red light is a **signal** to stop.*

symbol — Something that represents something else: *A white dove is a **symbol** for peace.*

WORDS from Words

SIGN is sometimes combined with other words to form expressions that have special meanings. These expressions also have synonyms. *For example:*

to sign up means to sign a document in order to join a group or organization: *We **signed up** for a karate class.* Useful synonyms are **enroll** and **join**.

---

silence *noun* — Lack of sound; complete quiet: *The room was so **silent**, you could hear a pin drop.*

hush — A silence after noise suddenly stops: *A **hush** fell over the audience as the lights went down and the music began.*

quiet — The condition of being silent: *I love the peace and **quiet** of the forest.*

stillness — Quiet and calm silence: *We heard an owl hoot in the **stillness** of the night.*

For more choices see the entry for QUIET.
Antonyms: See the entries for NOISE and RACKET.

---

silly *adjective* — Without judgment or common sense; foolish: *It's **silly** to worry about the sky falling. I felt **silly** wearing a sweater on such a hot day.*

absurd — Silly, foolish, or untrue: *She had an **absurd** idea that someone was spying on her.*

nonsensical — Silly and making no sense: *He has a **nonsensical** way of humming all the time.*

For more choices see the entries for DUMB and STUPID.

---

similar *adjective* — Having many but not all qualities the same: *Our neighbor's house is **similar** to ours. Brooke and Tyler had **similar** ideas about books.*

alike — Like one another; similar: *No two people have fingerprints that are exactly **alike**.*

close — Almost equal: *It was a **close** game, but our team won.*

like — Similar or equal: *My bicycle is **like** hers.*

For more choices see the entry for SAME.

skim *verb* | To read quickly: | Buck **skimmed** the sports section of the newspaper for the football scores.
I need to **skim** through my notes before the test.

browse | To look through or read something in a casual way: | Judy **browsed** through several books before she found one she wanted to read.
I **browse** the Web when I need information for a report.

flip | To turn over quickly: | Jacob **flipped** to the right page.
Let's **flip** a coin to see who goes first.

leaf | To turn pages and glance at them quickly: | We **leafed** through several catalogues looking for sweaters.

---

slack *adjective* | Not tight or firm: | Sabrina pulled on the **slack** rope until it was taut.
After a few minutes in the hot bath my muscles felt **slack**.

limp | Not stiff or firm: | The flowers were very **limp** because they hadn't been watered.

loose | Not fastened firmly: | Several pages in my notebook are **loose**.
I have a **loose** tooth.

Antonyms: See the entries for FIRM, STEADY, and STIFF.

---

slide *verb* | To move smoothly, easily, or quietly: | The skater **slid** silently across the ice.
The desk drawers **slide** open easily.

coast | To ride or slide along without effort or power: | We **coasted** down the hill on our bicycles.

glide | To move smoothly without any effort: | The skier **glided** across the snow.
We saw seagulls **gliding** above the beach.

skid | To slide or slip out of control: | My bike **skidded** on the wet pavement.

skim | To move lightly and swiftly: | The sailboat **skimmed** across the water.

slip | To move smoothly and easily: | Roger **slipped** quietly into the room.
Cory **slipped** the bracelet on her wrist.

---

slow *adjective* | Not fast or quick: | A turtle is **slow**, but a snail is **slower**.
Patrick is **slow** to anger.
The **slow** traffic almost made us late.

gradual | Happening little by little: | The rock climbers made **gradual** progress up the steep cliff.

plodding | Slow, heavy movement: | The **plodding** line of mules carried supplies up the mountain.

sluggish | Slow of movement or action: | The team's play was **sluggish** at the end of a long game.

Antonyms: See the entry for FAST.

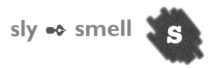

sly *adjective* — Clever and shrewd: — *The **sly** child was caught trying to sneak out of the room. People thought she was **sly** and wouldn't trust her.*

crafty — Skillful at deceiving; cunning: — *The **crafty** student tricked her partner into doing all the work on their report.*

cunning — Good at fooling others; sly: — *The **cunning** cat waited by the bird feeder, but a mockingbird chased it away.*

sneaky — Sly; dishonest: — *The **sneaky** man tried to cheat me.*

tricky — Using tricks: — *His **tricky** behavior didn't fool anyone.*

---

small *adjective* — Not large: — *Ants are **small**. She was **smaller** than her brother, but she wasn't the **smallest** in her family.*

meager — Very little; hardly any: — *The sick child ate a **meager** meal of soup and crackers.*

miniature — Much smaller than usual size: — *Cheryl had **miniature** furniture in her doll house.*

petite — Little; small size: — *Although the woman was **petite**, she was very strong.*

For more choices see the entries for LITTLE, SHORT, and TINY.
Antonyms: See the entries for BIG, GIANT, and LARGE.

---

smart *adjective* — Able to think quickly; mentally alert; having learned a lot: — *My **smart** friend has a lot of books in his library. The **smart** dog learned tricks quickly. Leah is a **smart** girl for her age.*

bright — Smart; clever: — *Karen is so **bright**, she'll probably skip a grade next year.*

clever — Mentally sharp; quick-witted: — *Bruce is a very **clever** fellow.*

intelligent — Able to learn, understand, and reason: — *She is an **intelligent** girl, but she does not try hard enough.*

For more choices see the entries for SHARP² and WISE.
Antonyms: See the entries for DUMB and STUPID.

---

smell *noun* — The quality of something that can be sensed with the nose: — *The **smell** of baking always makes me hungry. The **smell** of burning rubber is very unpleasant.*

aroma — A pleasant or agreeable smell: — *I love the **aroma** of freshly baked cookies.*

fragrance — A sweet or pleasing smell: — *Many flowers have a beautiful **fragrance**.*

odor — Smell; scent: — *She wrinkled her nose when she smelled the **odor** of cabbage cooking.*

scent — A smell: — *The **scent** of roses was in the air.*

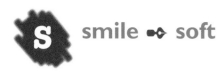

smile •◦ soft

smile *verb* — An expression of the face that shows happiness, amusement, or friendliness:
May Li smiled when she saw the puppy.
Everyone smile for the photographer!

beam — To smile happily:
Celeste beamed when it was announced that she had won the class election.

grin — To smile with amusement:
Keith grinned when he saw my costume.

smirk — To smile in a silly or self-satisfied way:
Wanda smirked at him because she thought she knew the right answer.

Antonyms: See the entry for FROWN.

---

smooth *adjective* — Having a surface that is not uneven or rough:
I like writing on the smooth surface of my desk.
The ride was smooth even though the road is rough.

even — Completely flat; smooth:
The surface of still water is even.
We measured to make sure that the pictures on the wall were even.

polished — Having a smooth or shiny surface:
The polished floor was very smooth.

For more choices see the entry for FLAT.
Antonyms: See the entry for ROUGH.

---

sneak *verb* — To act secretly or slyly:
Did someone sneak an apple from the refrigerator?
Andrea saw a cat sneaking toward the robin's nest.

lurk — To move about quietly; sneak:
The thief lurked in the shadows.
There is a snake lurking in that pile of rocks.

prowl — To move or roam quietly and secretly:
We watched the tiger as it prowled around its cage.

steal — To move or pass secretly and quietly:
The hungry children stole past the baby-sitter to get to the refrigerator.

---

soft *adjective* — Easy to shape; not hard or rough:
It is easy to make things out of soft clay.
Bananas get soft if you leave them out too long.

fluffy — Soft and light; covered with fluff:
Abigail's bed is covered with fluffy pillows.
Everyone loved petting the fluffy puppy.

mushy — Soft and thick:
I had trouble walking through the mushy snow.

squishy — Soft and damp:
My boots sank into the squishy mud.

song *noun* A piece of music that has words set to it:
*The glee club sang two **songs** during graduation.*
I can't remember all the words to that song.

harmony A combination of musical notes that sound pleasing together:
The quartet sings in perfect harmony.

lyrics The words of a song:
I could play the melody, but I couldn't remember the lyrics.

melody A series of musical notes that make up a tune:
He sat at the piano and played a pleasing melody.

music A pleasing combination of sounds:
The orchestra played beautiful music.
Do you know the music from that movie?

tune A song:
The band played some of my favorite tunes.

WORD BANK

Sometimes you can make things clearer for your reader by naming the particular kind of **SONG** you mean. Some types of **songs** are:

air	carol	hymn	round
anthem	chant	lullaby	serenade
aria	country	rap	oldie
ballad	folk song	rock	theme song

soon *adverb* In a short time:
My friend plans to visit us soon.
How soon is lunch?

before long Soon; in a short time:
The bus will be here before long.

promptly Quickly or on time:
Please be at your appointment promptly at four.

shortly In a short time; soon:
The doctor will see you shortly.

sore *noun* A place on the body that has been hurt:
*I have a **sore** on my foot from a blister.*
The sore on my lip has healed.

cut An opening or slit made by something sharp:
The school nurse bandaged the cut on my hand.

hurt Any wound or injury:
The hurt on your arm will go away once the bandage is taken off.

injury Harm or damage done to a person or thing:
The injury from my fall turned out to be very minor.

wound A cut or other injury:
I had a wound on my cheek where the ball hit me.

sour *adjective* | Having a sharp or unpleasant taste: | *The lemonade was too **sour** to drink without adding sugar.*

   bitter | Having a biting, harsh taste: | *The berries had a bitter taste because they weren't ripe.*

   tangy | Having a sharp or strong flavor or odor: | *The tangy taste of that mustard doesn't appeal to me.*

   tart | Having a sharp taste; not sweet: | *Those green apples have a tart taste.*

---

speck *noun* | A very small piece or stain: | *Antonio wiped a **speck** of food off his shirt.*
*The microscope made the **speck** of dust look huge.*

   bit | A small piece or part: | *The glass fell and broke to bits.*

   crumb | A tiny piece of bread, cake, cracker, or cookie: | *I picked up the crumbs on the table after dessert.*

   fleck | A small spot or patch: | *There was a fleck of green paint on the brown door.*

   particle | A very small bit or piece of something: | *I had a particle of dirt in my eye.*

For more choices see the entry for SPOT.

---

speech *noun* | A talk given to an audience: | *Each candidate had to give a **speech** in front of the whole class.*
*Some of the **speeches** were very funny.*

   address | A formal speech: | *The president is going to give a special address tonight.*

   lecture | A talk given to an audience: | *The professor gave an interesting lecture on modern music.*

   talk | An informal speech or lecture: | *The lady gave a talk on the history of our neighborhood.*

---

speed *noun* | The rate of motion: | *We all ran full **speed** to catch the bus.*
*A runner's **speed** is measured with a stopwatch.*

   pace | The rate of speed in walking, running, or moving: | *The marathon started out at a fast pace.*

   rate | An amount or number measured against the amount or number of something else: | *The jet was flying at a rate of 600 miles per hour.*

   velocity | The rate of motion; speed: | *Light travels at a velocity of about 186,000 miles per second.*

spice *noun* — Seeds or other parts of certain plants used to flavor food:

A little spice can make food tasty.
Pepper and cinnamon are spices.

flavoring — Something added to food or drink to give flavor:

The new cereal has chocolate flavoring added to it.

herb — A plant whose parts are used in cooking, in medicine, or for their aroma:

The great flavor of my mother's spaghetti sauce comes from the herbs she puts in it.

seasoning — Something used to bring out the flavor of food:

The only seasonings I use are salt and pepper.

WORD BANK

Sometimes you can make things clearer and more interesting for your reader by naming the particular **SPICE** or **HERB** you mean. Some **spices** and **herbs** are:

basil	curry powder	mint	parsley
black pepper	dill	mustard	peppermint
chili powder	garlic	onion	rosemary
chives	ginseng	oregano	sage
cinnamon	horseradish	paprika	thyme

spill *verb* — To let something fall or flow; to flow out:

Be careful not to spill the sugar.
Water spilled over the side of the boat.

run — To spread:

Water ran all over the kitchen counter.

slop — To spill liquid on:

We slopped water on the floor before cleaning it.

splash — To throw water or other liquid about:

We love to splash each other in the swimming pool.
A passing car splashed us.

For more choices see the entry for FLOW.

spot *noun* — A small mark or area on something that is different from the rest:

We washed the last spot of mud off the car.
A leopard has black spots.

blot — A spot or stain:

He had a blot of gravy on his tie.

dot — A small spot or speck:

The dot on the map showed where the treasure was buried.

smudge — A dirty mark or stain:

Someone's dirty hands left a smudge on the wall.

stain — A small mark left by dirt, food, or other matter:

There was a juice stain on my napkin.

For more choices see the entry for SPECK.

stagger *verb*	To move or cause to move with a swaying motion:	*I was so tired, I could barely **stagger** to my bed.* *Gemma **staggered** with the heavy load of books.*
lurch	To move suddenly in an unsteady manner:	*I almost fell when the train lurched.*
reel	To be thrown off balance; stagger:	*I reeled when the huge man bumped into me.*
totter	To rock or sway as if about to fall:	*The tower of blocks tottered and fell.*

stand[1] *noun*	An opinion or point of view:	*What is your **stand** on the class elections?* *Our teacher took a firm **stand** against cheating.*
attitude	A way of thinking, acting, or feeling:	*She has an enthusiastic attitude about school.* *His attitude has improved this year.*
position	A way of thinking about something:	*The senator explained his position on taxes.*
viewpoint	An attitude or way of thinking; point of view:	*From my viewpoint, this arrangement seems unfair.*

For more choices see the entries for BELIEF and IDEA.

stand[2] *noun*	A place where things are sold:	*We bought fruit at a farmer's **stand**.* *We set up a lemonade **stand** in front of our house.* *We met at the refreshment **stand**.*
booth	A stall where things are sold or shown:	*There many booths at the school fair.*
counter	A long, flat surface on which food is prepared or eaten, or goods are sold:	*We sat at the counter and had a sandwich.* *The woman behind the counter explained how she made the jewelry she was selling.*
stall	A counter or booth where things are shown for sale:	*At the outdoor market, we went from stall to stall buying things for our dinner.*

stand[3] *noun*	A raised place where people sit or stand to watch something:	*We sat in the **stands** at the football game.* *The governor watched the parade from the reviewing **stand**.*
bleachers	A group of seats or benches in rows placed above and behind one another:	*The fans in the bleachers cheered loudly.*
grandstand	The main place where people sit when watching a parade or sports event:	*We sat so far up in the grandstand, I could barely see the field.*
seat	A place to sit:	*We couldn't get seats for the concert.* *I had a window seat on the airplane.*

stand *verb*	To be on your feet or get to your feet:	*I had to **stand** on the bus because there were no seats. We all **stood** for the national anthem.*
get up	To sit up or stand up:	*I **got up** from the dinner table to help wash the dishes.*
rise	To get up from a sitting, kneeling, or lying position:	*Everyone **rose** when the judge entered the court.*

Word Alert

TO STAND also means to be patient about; bear: *I can't **stand** any more talk about soccer. I **stood** his dumb jokes as long as I could.* Synonyms for this meaning of **stand** can be found at the entry for **BEAR**.

WORDS from Words

STAND is often combined with other words to form expressions that have special meanings. These expressions also have synonyms. *For example:*

to stand by means to support or defend: *We **stood by** our friend when he was in trouble.* Useful synonyms are **back** and **support**.

to stand for means to represent: *The contraction "wouldn't" **stands for** "would not." The initials "www" **stand for** "World Wide Web."* A useful synonym is **means**. **To stand for** also means to bear: *I won't **stand for** it anymore!* Synonyms for this meaning of **stand for** can be found at the entry for **BEAR**.

to stand out means to be easy to see: *The purple house **stands out** from all the others.* Useful synonyms are **be noticeable** and **stick out**.

start *verb*	To begin to act, move, or happen:	*When everyone is ready, we can **start**. The movie **started** on time. Our car **starts** with a roar.*
commence	To begin; start:	*The school assembly **commenced** with the national anthem.*
get going	To begin to move; start:	*We have to **get going** early in the morning.*
open	To begin; start:	*Mark **opened** his speech with a joke.*

For more choices see the entry for BEGIN.
Antonyms: See the entry for END.

state *noun* | The condition of a person or thing: | The fans were in a **state** of excitement.
The old house was in a sorry **state**.
Something has to be done about this **state** of affairs.

circumstance | A condition that accompanies an act or event: | If the circumstances were different, the outcome of the election might have changed.
Due to circumstances beyond our control, the meeting was canceled.

condition | The way a person or thing is: | She keeps in good condition by exercising.
The condition of the house was very bad after the fire.

shape | Condition: | The runner was in bad shape after her fall.

situation | A condition or state of affairs; circumstances: | The situation became serious when the river broke through a dam.

---

steady *adjective* | Not shaky; firm; changing little: | The chair was **steady** after its legs were tightened.
Hold the ladder **steady**.
We traveled at a **steady** speed.

solid | Very strong and hard; not weak or loose: | The solid walls of the house were made of adobe.
The ladder was set in a very solid position in a corner.

stable | Not easily moved, shaken, or changed: | The table was very stable after we leveled the legs.

stationary | Standing still; not moving: | They used the North Star as a stationary point to figure their location.

For more choices see the entries for FIRM and STIFF.

---

step *noun* | The distance covered by putting one foot ahead of the other: | It is 231 **steps** from my house to yours.
How many **steps** do think you take in a day?

footstep | A step of the foot: | We counted our footsteps to measure the length of the room.

pace | A single step: | Take two paces forward.

stride | A long step: | It only took a few strides to reach the stage.

WORDS from Words

STEP is often combined with other words to form expressions that have special meanings. These expressions also have synonyms. *For example:*

step by step means gradually advancing from one stage to another: *We learned to cook* **step by step**. Useful synonyms are *gradually* and *inch by inch*.

to step up means to increase or accelerate: *The factory plans* **to step up** *production of its most popular games.* Useful synonyms are *accelerate*, *increase*, and *raise*.

sticky *adjective* — Tending to stick to anything it touches: — *The candy was so **sticky**, we couldn't get it off our fingers. The hot weather made everything **sticky**.*

    gummy — Sticky and damp: — *We use gummy paper tape for wrapping.*

    muggy — Warm and damp: — *We had several muggy days last summer.*

---

stiff *adjective* — Not easily bent: — *My leather belt was **stiff** when it was new.*

    inflexible — Not able to bend: — *Steel is an inflexible material.*

    rigid — Not bending or giving: — *They used a rigid metal pole to keep the tent up.*

For more choices see the entries for FIRM and STEADY.
Antonyms: See the entry for SLACK.

---

stink *verb* — To give off a strong, bad smell: — *Fish **stink** after a short time if they aren't refrigerated. The rotten eggs **stunk** up the room.*

    reek — To produce a strong, bad smell: — *When our dog came home, he reeked of skunk odor.*

    smell bad — To stink or reek: — *The cooking next door smells bad.*

---

stop *verb* — To keep from moving or doing something; to come to an end or halt: — *Please **stop** making so much noise. The cars **stopped** so the students could cross the street.*

    cease — To come or bring to an end; stop: — *The noise ceased. We ceased working on math and began reading.*

    halt — To stop: — *The snowstorm halted traffic on the highway.*

    restrain — To keep from doing something; hold back: — *The barking dog was restrained by his master with a leash.*

For more choices see the entries for END, FINISH, and QUIT.
Antonyms: See the entry for BEGIN.

---

storm *noun* — A strong wind with rain, hail, sleet, or snow: — *The winter **storm** forced the airport to close. After the **storm**, the sky was clear.*

    tempest — A violent, windy storm: — *The tempest created huge waves.*

WORD BANK

Sometimes you can make things clearer and more interesting for your reader by naming the particular kind of **STORM** you mean. Some types of **storms** are:

blizzard	*gale*	*nor'easter*	*squall*
cyclone	*hailstorm*	*rain shower*	*thunderstorm*
deluge	*hurricane*	*rainstorm*	*tornado*
downpour	*monsoon*	*snowstorm*	*typhoon*

story *noun* — An account of something that happened: — *The newspaper had a **story** about a baby elephant.*
*The old man told us **stories** about his childhood.*

anecdote — A short story about an interesting or funny incident or event: — *My grandfather loves to tell anecdotes about his youth.*

narrative — A story or report about something that happened: — *The explorer gave a long narrative of her travels.*

tale — A story: — *This book is filled with thrilling tales about life on old sailing ships.*

yarn — A long story; tale: — *The old sea captain loved to tell yarns about his time at sea.*

For more choices see the entry for REPORT.

---

strange *adjective* — Odd or unusual: — *The food at the new restaurant seemed **strange** to us.*
*A **strange** sound was coming from the basement.*
*Chiara had a **strange** feeling about the incident.*

funny — Strange; odd: — *It's funny that you never told me you went there before.*
He had the funny idea that he could solve the crime.

peculiar — Strange or odd, but in an interesting or curious way: — *Lionel has a peculiar habit of blinking his eyes when he speaks.*

For more choices see the entries for ODD, UNFAMILIAR, and UNUSUAL.
Antonyms: See the entries for COMMON, NORMAL, and USUAL.

---

stray *verb* — To wander away: — *Please don't **stray** from the path.*
*Our dog **strayed** from our yard and got lost.*
*My thoughts **strayed** from the work I was doing.*

drift — To move from place to place without knowing or caring where: — *The man drifted from town to town looking for work.*
I drifted from one hobby to another until I discovered how much I love watching birds.

ramble — To wander about; roam: — *We rambled through the park.*

roam — To move around without any particular place to go; wander: — *I love to roam through the library.*
Last summer we took a week to roam around the woods up north.

wander — To go or move without a particular place to go: — *We wandered though the zoo looking at the animals.*

For more choices see the entry for TRAVEL.

strong *adjective*

Having much power, force, or energy:

A strong wind blew my kite away.
Connor had a strong belief that he was right.

mighty

Great in power, size, or amount:

The Mississippi is a mighty river.
King Arthur was a mighty ruler.

muscular

Having well-developed muscles; strong:

Neil has become muscular from lifting weights.

powerful

Having great strength, influence, or authority:

The governor is a powerful woman.

Antonyms: See the entries for FRAGILE and WEAK.

---

stubborn
adjective

Not yielding; hard to deal with:

The stubborn child refused to admit he was wrong.
My stubborn cold lasted for weeks.

determined

Firm in sticking to a purpose:

The determined puppy kept digging until he found the bone.

headstrong

Insisting on one's own way; stubborn:

The headstrong child wouldn't listen to advice.
The headstrong horse pulled on its bit.

obstinate

Unwilling to change one's mind; stubborn:

The obstinate student wouldn't give in even when the teacher told him he was wrong.

---

study *verb*

To learn by reading about, looking carefully at, or thinking about something:

Our class will study dinosaurs next week.
Bridget studied the face in the painting.

examine

To look at closely and carefully:

Max examined his favorite baseball bat to make sure it wasn't cracked.

go over

To study or review:

We need to go over the lesson before the test.

investigate

To look into carefully to find out the facts:

The detective investigated the crime.

For more choices see the entries for LEARN and LOOK².

---

stupid *adjective*

Lacking common sense or intelligence:

The stupid dog almost wandered into traffic.
I caught myself before I made a stupid remark.

dull

Slow to learn; not intelligent:

A person would have to be pretty dull to miss the point of that joke.

ignorant

Showing lack of knowledge:

Because I grew up in a city, I was ignorant about farm life.

uneducated

Not taught or trained:

The students were uneducated, but they learned fast.

unintelligent

Lacking intelligence or knowledge:

For such a smart person, he sure makes some unintelligent comments.

For more choices see the entries for DUMB and SILLY.
Antonyms: See the entries for SMART and WISE.

subject *noun* — Something thought or talked about: — The **subject** of Andre's report was his family history.

matter — A subject of discussion, interest, or action: — The **matter** we need to decide is where to hold the school dance.
My mother discussed business **matters** on the phone last night.

theme — The main subject or idea of something: — The **theme** of this story is how honesty is rewarded.

topic — What a speech, discussion, or piece of writing is about; subject: — The **topic** of my report is recycling.
I found a chat group on the Web that discusses the **topic** of space travel.

---

sudden *adjective* — Happening without warning: — A **sudden** cloudburst soaked the crowd.
A **sudden** movement startled the rabbit, and it ran away.

abrupt — Without warning; sudden: — The truck made an **abrupt** stop when a deer crossed the road.

unexpected — Without warning; not expected: — My uncle made an **unexpected** visit last weekend.
Audrey had some **unexpected** good luck when she found a dollar on the sidewalk.

For more choices see the entry for QUICK.

---

suffering *noun* — Feeling or experiencing pain or sorrow: — The flood caused widespread **suffering**.
The **suffering** didn't ease until the water finally disappeared.

agony — Great pain or suffering of the mind or body: — My brother was in **agony** because of his toothache.

anguish — Great suffering of the body or mind; agony: — We felt great **anguish** when our dog died.

misery — Great unhappiness or suffering: — Imagine the **misery** of being homeless.

torment — Great pain or suffering: — My ankle caused me so much **torment**, I went to the doctor.

woe — Great sadness or suffering: — The pioneers often suffered the **woes** of loneliness and sickness.

For more choices see the entry for SADNESS.
Antonyms: See the entries for DELIGHT and PLEASURE.

suggest *verb*

To offer as something to think about:

Someone **suggested** that the class go outside.
I **suggest** that we go to the movies.

hint

To give a slight sign or suggestion:

He **hinted** that there would be a surprise, but he wouldn't tell me what it is.

propose

To suggest something to someone else for consideration:

Leon **proposed** that we take turns.
The governor **proposed** building a new dam.

put forward

To express or suggest something out loud:

They **put forward** a solution to the problem.

recommend

To advise; suggest:

The doctor **recommended** some medicine for my cold.

---

sullen *adjective*

Gloomy and silent from anger:

The child was **sullen** after he was punished.
The driver had a **sullen** look on his face after he lost the race.

moody

Tending to change moods often:

She's so **moody** you never know how she will react.

resentful

Feeling anger or bitterness:

The team was **resentful** because they thought the referee favored the other team.

sulky

Angry and silent:

He was **sulky** because he was punished unfairly.

For more choices see the entries for SAD **and** UNHAPPY.
Antonyms: See the entry for HAPPY.

---

support *verb*

To hold up; to help or back:

Two columns **supported** the porch.
Both candidates **support** new laws on safety.

encourage

To give courage, hope, or confidence to; urge on:

The coach **encouraged** every student to try out for the team.

maintain

To take care of:

Specially trained gardeners **maintain** the flowers in the park.

sustain

To keep going; keep up:

His sense of humor **sustained** us through some tough situations.

---

sure *adjective*

Having no doubt:

We were **sure** that she was right.
How can you be **sure** it is going to rain?

certain

Sure; positive:

I was **certain** my answer was correct.

confident

Having trust or faith; sure:

I am **confident** I can win the race.

positive

Certain; sure:

I'm **positive** she said we should meet on this corner.
Are you **positive** you locked the door?

Antonyms: See the entry for HESITANT.

surprise ⟷ swing

surprise *verb* — To cause to feel sudden wonder or amazement:
We were **surprised** at the gifts you brought.
The squirrel **surprised** us when he jumped out from the bushes.

shock — To disturb the mind or emotions of someone:
His rudeness **shocked** all of us.

startle — To frighten suddenly; surprise:
The lightning **startled** my cat.

stun — To shock:
We were **stunned** by the news of the fire.

For more choices see the entry for AMAZE.

---

surrender *verb* — To give up, yield:
The criminal **surrendered** to the sheriff.
As it began to rain harder, we **surrendered** all hope of going camping.

concede — To yield to someone or admit defeat:
The candidate finally **conceded** the election.

submit — To yield to power or authority:
The students **submitted** to their teacher's wishes.

yield — To give up; surrender:
The army **yielded** after a tough battle.

For more choices see the entries for QUIT and STOP.

---

swing *verb* — To move back and forth:
We like to **swing** on an old tire that hangs from a tree.
He **swung** the bat as he walked toward the plate.

dangle — To hang and swing loosely:
A thread **dangled** from my sweater.
We saw an acrobat **dangling** from a rope high above us.

hang — To fasten or be attached so as to move freely back and forth:
The gate **hung** by only one hinge.
Some monkeys can **hang** by their tail.

sway — To move or cause to move back and forth:
The trees were **swaying** in the wind.
The dancers **swayed** to the music.
Shelagh **swayed** the baby in her arms.

take¹ *verb* — To get hold of or grasp; to capture or win by using force or skill:

*Christina **takes** her lunch to school.*
*Our team **took** the championship two years in a row.*

    capture — To catch and hold a person, animal, or thing:

Scientists captured an injured sea lion and nursed it back to health.

    grab — To take hold of suddenly:

Hank grabbed his lunch and ran for the school bus.
Grab that tool for me, will you?

For more choices see the entries for HOLD and SEIZE.

---

take² *verb* — To put up with:

*I can't **take** your rude behavior.*
*Can you **take** being hungry for a little longer?*

    endure — To undergo and survive; put up with:

The mountain climbers endured many snowstorms.

    withstand — To resist the effects of; hold out against:

Pioneers had to withstand many hardships.
The pine trees withstood the cold winter weather.

For more choices see the entry for BEAR.

---

take³ *verb* — To move or remove; subtract:

*I am **taking** my schoolbooks home.*
*If you **take** 5 from 15, you get 10.*

    deduct — To take away or subtract from a total:

The teacher deducts five points for each wrong answer.

    subtract — To take away from:

If you subtract 7 from 11, you will get 4.

For more choices see the entry for REMOVE.

Word Alert

TAKE can mean to obtain or get: *I took a chance that the bus would be late. My mother took my temperature. It's time to take your turn.* Synonyms for this meaning of **take** can be found at the entry for **GET**. **Take** can also mean to carry or transfer: *I usually take my lunch to school. The bus took us to the zoo.* Synonyms for this meaning of **take** can be found at the entry for **CARRY**.

WORDS from Words

TAKE is often combined with other words to form expressions that have special meanings. These expressions also have synonyms. *For example:*

to take after means to look or be like: *Riley **takes after** her father.* Useful synonyms are **favor**, **look like**, and **resemble**.

to take down means to put down in writing: *Leslie **took down** the notes of the meeting.* Useful synonyms are **jot down**, **note**, and **record**.

to take in means to include: *During the emergency we **took in** our neighbors for several days.* Useful synonyms are **accept**, **admit**, and **welcome**.

to take off means to remove or leave: *Seth **took off** his coat. Harold **took off** about an hour ago.* Useful synonyms are **discard**, **remove**, and **leave**. **Take off** also means to rise into the air. *The airplane will **take off** at eight o'clock.* A useful synonym is **lift off** and **launch**. The noun **takeoff** means the act of leaving the ground: *The **takeoff** of the space shuttle went perfectly.* A useful synonym is **launch**.

to take out means to remove: *You need tweezers **to take out** a splinter.* Useful synonyms for this meaning of **take out** can be found at the entry for **REMOVE**. Used informally, **take out** also means to take someone on a date: *My older brother **took out** his girlfriend on Saturday night.* A useful synonym is **escort**. The noun **takeout** means food bought from a restaurant to eat somewhere else: *We had **takeout** for lunch.* A useful synonym is **fast food**.

to take on means to hire: *The store **takes on** extra help during the holidays.* Useful synonyms are **employ** and **engage**.

---

talent *noun*	A natural ability or skill:	*Brad has a **talent** for playing the trumpet.* *Students in this class have many different **talents**.*
aptitude	A natural ability or talent:	*Kylie seems to have an **aptitude** for drawing.*
genius	Great ability to think or invent or create things:	*Pablo Picasso was an artistic **genius**.* *The scientific **genius** of Albert Einstein may never be matched.* *It would take a **genius** to figure out this problem.*
gift	Talent; ability:	*Eric has a musical **gift**.* *Ellie has a **gift** for making friends.*

For more choices see the entry for ABILITY.

talk *verb* — To say words:

*We **talked** until late at night.*
*Everyone was **talking** about the party.*

   chat — To talk in a friendly or relaxed way:

The four friends chatted after school.
What did you chat about?

   chatter — To talk quickly without thought or purpose:

She was so nervous, she couldn't stop chattering.

   converse — To talk together in an informal way:

The players conversed before the game.

   discuss — To talk over; speak about:

The class will discuss the reading assignment tomorrow.
We discussed our plans for the weekend.

   speak — To use or utter words; talk:

Soon my baby brother will learn to speak.
I spoke to my teacher about the homework assignment.
We were speaking about the party.
Sometimes I wish my dog could speak.

For more choices see the entries for COMMUNICATE, SAY, and TELL.

---

tall *adjective* — Higher than average; not short or low:

*The city was full of **tall** buildings.*
*The basketball player was very **tall**.*

   high — At a great distance from the ground:

How high can you throw a ball?
There was a high mountain in the distance.
The airplane flew at a high altitude.

   lofty — Very high; towering:

The lake was surrounded by lofty mountains.
Redwoods are lofty trees.

   towering — Rising high in the air:

We had to lean back to see the top of the towering skyscraper.

Antonyms: See the entry for SHORT.

---

teach *verb* — To help a person learn; show how:

*Our neighbor **teaches** swimming at camp each summer.*
*My sister **taught** our dog how to sit up.*

   educate — To teach or train:

Teachers and parents educate children.
He was educated in France.

   instruct — To show how to do something:

My father instructed me on how to use a computer.

   train — To teach how to do something:

Bo trained with weights to improve his swimming.
We trained our dog to sit up.

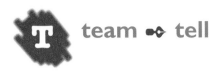

team *noun* — A group that plays or works together:
*The teacher divided the class into **teams** for social studies.*
*Our **team** worked on a science project.*
*The debate **team** is going to the state competition.*
*I want to try out for the baseball **team**.*

crew — A group of people who work together:
The people who operate an airplane, train, or ship are called the crew.
We had a whole crew of your friends over on Saturday.

squad — A small group of people working together:
A squad of police directed traffic.
We divided into squads to play soccer.

unit — A single person, thing, or group that is part of a larger group:
The football team has a defensive unit and an offensive unit.
Our housing development has fifty units.

---

tease *verb* — To make fun of in a playful way:
*The cat might scratch if you **tease** it.*
*My father **teased** me about my haircut.*

make fun of — To tease:
Some mean students made fun of my new glasses.

taunt — To tease or make fun of in an insulting way:
The crowd taunted the other team's star player when she missed a shot.

torment — To cause someone great pain and suffering:
Buzzing mosquitoes tormented us at night.

For more choices see the entry for BOTHER.

---

tell *verb* — To put into words; to reveal something secret:
***Tell** us about your day at school.*
*Don't **tell** anyone about the surprise.*
*Mandy **told** us about summer camp.*

convey — To make known; express:
Her letters conveyed her excitement about the trip.
He conveyed his anger by shaking his fist.

disclose — To make known:
We promised not to disclose her secret to anyone.

inform — To give information to; tell:
They informed us by phone about the time of their arrival.

notify — To tell about something; inform:
Please notify me when my package arrives.
The winner will be notified tomorrow.

For more choices see the entries for DESCRIBE, EXPLAIN, and REPORT.

temporary　Lasting for only a short time:　*There was a **temporary** blackout during the storm.*

　　brief　Short in time:　*There was only time for a brief visit.*
Can you give me a brief summary of what happened?

　　fleeting　Passing very quickly; very brief:　*We had only a fleeting look at the car as it sped past.*
I had a fleeting impression of the bird before it flew away.

　　passing　Not lasting; temporary:　*We had a passing interest in comic books.*
The hula hoop was a passing fad.

Antonyms: See the entry for ETERNAL.

---

test *noun*　A set of problems or tasks:　*We have a spelling **test** almost every week.*
*The **tests** showed that there was little pollution in the air.*

　　examination　A test:　*We studied hard for final examinations.*

　　quiz　A short, informal test:　*We had a surprise quiz in math today.*

---

theft *noun*　The act of stealing:　*The store owner reported the **theft** of some of his merchandise.*
*The prisoner was in jail for **theft**.*

　　burglary　The act of breaking into a house, store, or other place to steal something:　*The burglary was foiled by an alert watchdog.*

　　robbery　The act of robbing; theft:　*The police caught the person who committed the robbery.*

　　stealing　The act of theft:　*Stealing is a crime.*

---

theory *noun*　A group of ideas that explains how something happens; an opinion based on some evidence:　*The **theory** of gravity explains why things fall.*
*The inspector had a **theory** about the crime, but he couldn't prove it.*

　　hypothesis　Something that is suggested as being true for the purpose of argument or further investigation:　*The hypothesis that germs cause disease has led to many of the successes of modern medicine.*
Jeb's hypothesis that it always rains on holidays was disproved by a sunny Fourth of July.

　　idea　A belief; opinion:　*At first, many people laughed at the idea that the world is round.*

　　speculation　Possible reasons or answers for something:　*The speculation that the other team would be tough to beat proved to be true.*
Speculations about the future can be fun, but they are often wrong.

thick *adjective* — Having much space from one side to another:

> The sandwich was so **thick**, I couldn't fit it into my mouth.
> The walls of a castle are **thicker** than the walls of your classroom.
> Deer hide in the **thickest** part of the forest.

bulky — Large size:

> My *bulky* suitcase won't fit in the closet.
> This jacket looks too *bulky* on you.

dense — Packed closely together; thick:

> We were lost for a while in the *dense* woods, but we eventually found the trail.

fat — Having a lot in it; full:

> That collection of folk tales is a *fat* book.

For more choices see the entry for DENSE.
Antonyms: See the entry for THIN.

---

thin *adjective* — Having little space from one side to another:

> The chef cut the carrots into **thin** slices.
> My piece of cake was **thinner** than Sophie's.
> The election was decided by the **thinnest** margin.

lean — With little or no fat, but often strong.

> A runner must have a *lean* body.

skinny — Very thin, in a way that suggests poor health:

> She got so *skinny* that she felt weak.

slender — Not big around; thin:

> The new table has *slender* legs.
> She won the election by a *slender* margin.

slim — Thin, in a good or healthy way:

> Dennis has become *slim* since he started exercising regularly.

For more choices see the entry for NARROW.
Antonyms: See the entries for DENSE and THICK.

---

thing *noun* — Something that can be touched, seen, heard, smelled, or tasted, but is not a human being:

> A book, tree, star, and computer program are **things**.
> Nathaniel put all his **things** in his backpack.

article — A thing or object; item:

> How many *articles* do you have in your bag?
> Several *articles* were missing from the house.

item — A single thing in a group or list:

> Savannah had so many *items* in her backpack, she could never find what she wanted.
> I checked off each *item* on my list.

object — Anything that can be seen or touched:

> What is that *object* in the closet?

think *verb* — To use the mind to form ideas or make decisions: — *Think carefully before you choose.*
Jake thought about the problem before he answered.

    concentrate — To put one's mind on something: — *I concentrated on my homework until I finished it.*

    ponder — To think about something carefully: — *They pondered what to do next.*

    reason — To think or think about clearly: — *I slowly reasoned out the answer to the math problem.*

    reflect — To think seriously and carefully: — *Vincent reflected on what he had accomplished so far.*

For more choices see the entry for CONSIDER.

---

thrill *verb* — To fill with pleasure or excitement: — *Adventure stories thrill Geoff.*
Madison was thrilled when she saw her favorite singer on the street.

    delight — To give great pleasure or joy: — *The clowns delighted the children.*

    excite — To stir up; arouse: — *The team's expert playing excited the fans.*

    please — To give pleasure to: — *My new book pleases me.*

---

throw *verb* — To send through the air: — *My dog is happiest when I throw a ball for him.*
Jake threw his jacket on the floor.

    cast — To throw through the air: — *We cast our fishing lines in the lake.*

    fling — To throw hard or carelessly: — *Just fling your coat on the chair.*
I was in such a hurry, I flung my books down.

    pitch — To throw or toss: — *He pitched nine straight strikes in the first inning.*
Have you ever pitched horseshoes?

    toss — To throw lightly into or through the air: — *Please toss me a towel.*
I love tossing a ball with my brother.

---

tight *adjective* — Held firmly; made so parts are close together: — *I tied the two ropes together with a tight knot.*
We packed the laundry in a tight bundle.

    compact — Tightly packed together: — *Fold your clothes so they are compact enough to fit in a small suitcase.*

    firm — Not easily moved; secure: — *I had a firm grip on the rope.*

    fixed — Fastened tightly; secure: — *The electric lights were fixed to the wall.*

    secure — Firm; steady: — *Are these stairs secure enough to climb?*
Make sure your hold is secure before you try to lift that heavy bag.

time *noun*	The period during which all events, conditions, and actions happen or continue:	*Time is measured in minutes, hours, days, and years. After a **time** we had walked all the way across the park. A short **time** later we came home.*
interval	A time or space between two things:	*The interval between trains is twenty minutes.*
period	A portion of time:	*Our team scored twice in the first period. A day is a period of twenty-four hours.*
term	A definite or limited period of time:	*The term of office for the President of the United States is four years.*

WORDS from Words

TIME is often combined with other words to form expressions that have special meanings. These expressions also have synonyms. *For example:*

ahead of time means before the expected time: *We arrived at the movie **ahead of time** and had to wait for it to begin.* A useful synonym is **early**.

at times means periodically: *Even the best of friends disagree **at times**.* Useful synonyms are **periodically**, **occasionally**, and **sometimes**.

behind the times means old-fashioned or out of date: *The old man's clothes were **behind the times**. Our computer is so **behind the times**, we can't run the new programs.* Useful synonyms are **dated**, **obsolete**, and **outdated**.

in time and **in the nick of time** mean before it is too late: *Please come **in time** for dinner. The hero arrived **in the nick of time** to save the heroine.* Useful synonyms are **promptly** and **punctually**. **In time** can also mean in the correct beat or rhythm: *We clapped **in time** with the music.* A useful synonym is **in rhythm**.

on time means at the correct time: *The plane was **on time**. Were you **on time** for your appointment?* Useful synonyms are **prompt** and **punctual**.

---

tiny *adjective*	Very small:	*The baby mice were tiny. There were only tiny differences between the twins.*
diminutive	Very small; tiny:	*Our puppy has diminutive paws.*
microscopic	So small it can only be seen through a microscope:	*It only takes a microscopic amount of flower pollen to make me sneeze.*
minute	Very small; tiny:	*There were only a few minute crumbs of birthday cake left after the party.*

For more choices see the entries for LITTLE, SHORT, and SMALL.

Antonyms: See the entries for BIG, GIANT, and LARGE.

tip *verb* | To raise one end or side; tilt: | The glass **tipped** over, and water spilled out of it. The old gentleman **tipped** his hat to us when we said hello.

slant | To slope away from a straight line: | The roof of the house slants toward the ground.

incline | To slope or slant: | The street inclines upward as the hill becomes steeper.

lean | To be at a slant: | The walls of the old shack leaned to one side.

list | To lean to one side; tilt: | The sailboat listed as the wind hit its sails.

tilt | To raise one end or side; tip: | The raft tilted and dumped us into the water. She tilts her head when she is listening.

---

tired *adjective* | Weak from too much work or use: | Vance was very **tired** after a day of hiking. The **tired** kitten curled up and went to sleep.

exhausted | Weak or tired: | Bobbie was exhausted after she ran in the cross-country race.

sleepy | Ready for or needing sleep: | It was late, and I felt sleepy.

weary | Very tired: | The weary campers returned after hiking ten miles.

worn-out | Very tired: | We were worn-out from working hard all day.

---

tool *noun* | An object specially made to do work: | My grandfather always said you need the right **tool** for the job. Hammers, saws, and screwdrivers are **tools**.

gadget | A small, useful tool or device: | The workshop was filled with all kinds of gadgets for making things with wood.

implement | An object used to do a particular job; tool: | We used shovels and other gardening implements to prepare our vegetable garden. Prehistoric humans made implements out of stone.

machine | A device made up of many parts that does a particular job: | Cars, lawnmowers, computers, and hair dryers are machines.

utensil | An object or tool that is useful: | All our cooking utensils are stored in the kitchen.

top *noun* | The highest or upper part of something: | The climber planted a flag at the **top** of the mountain.
The **tops** of the books were dusty.

   crest | The highest part of something: | Our old car barely made it over the crest of the hill.

   crown | The highest or top part of anything: | One way to identify that bird is by noting its gray crown.
The crown of my hat was crushed when I packed it.

   peak | The pointed top of a mountain; the highest point or greatest level: | The triumphant climbers placed a flag on the mountain peak.
After months of training, Raoul was at the peak of his performance.

   summit | The highest point: | It took us two hours to hike to the summit of the mountain.

For more choices see the entry for POINT.

---

total *noun* | The whole amount: | Three of us went to the show for a **total** of only six dollars.
My **total** reached eight points before the game was over.

   sum | The whole amount: | The sum of human knowledge was greatly increased by Albert Einstein.

   whole | Having all its parts; entire: | Did you read that whole book?
I could eat the whole cake by myself.

---

tough *adjective* | Not easy to break, cut, or damage: | My backpack is made out of **tough** canvas.
The meat was so **tough**, I couldn't cut it.

   durable | Able to last a long time in spite of wear: | My backpack is very durable.

   hardy | Capable of standing hardship: | This city was founded by hardy pioneers.

   rugged | Very strong and sturdy: | I have rugged boots for hiking.

   sturdy | Strong; hardy: | The sturdy bridge was not damaged by the flood.

Antonyms: See the entry for DELICATE, FRAGILE, and WEAK.

town *noun* — An area with buildings where people live and work: — *A **town** is larger than a village but smaller than a city. My **town** has two schools, a library, and a large park.*

> **community** — A group of people who live together in the same place: — *Our **community** is building a new library next to the post office.*

> **settlement** — A small village or group of houses: — *Many **settlements** grow into towns or cities.*

> **village** — A small group of houses: — *A **village** is smaller than a town but larger than a settlement.*

For more choices see the entry for CITY.

---

trade *verb* — To give something in return for something else: — *I will **trade** my old comics for new ones. Ancient people **traded** all kinds of goods. I enjoy **trading** computer games.*

> **barter** — To trade things for other things without using money: — *Trappers used to **barter** furs for supplies.*

> **exchange** — To give something for something else: — *We **exchanged** jackets to see how they looked. My mother **exchanged** my new shirt because it was too small.*

> **swap** — To exchange or trade: — *We **swapped** sandwiches at lunch.*

> **switch** — To change or shift: — *We **switched** seats so I could see better. Maggie **switched** hats with Moisha.*

---

trap *noun* — A trick used to catch a person or get a person to do something not intended: — *The police set a **trap** for the robbers. They fell into the **trap**.*

> **ambush** — A surprise attack made by people who are hidden: — *My friends set up an **ambush** and pelted me with snowballs.*

> **pitfall** — A trap or hidden danger: — *There are many **pitfalls** in this video game, so be careful.*

> **snare** — A trap: — ***Snares** are used to catch small animals.*

---

trash *noun* — Unwanted things that are thrown away: — *We take the **trash** out on Thursday. The city collects the **trash** and carries it to the dump.*

> **garbage** — Food and other things that are thrown out: — *Some types of **garbage** can be recycled into fertilizer for plants.*

> **refuse** — Anything thrown away as useless or worthless: — *Many cities burn **refuse** in large incinerators.*

> **rubbish** — Useless waste material; trash: — *We removed all the **rubbish** from a vacant lot to make a playing field.*

> **waste** — Material that is left over or has been thrown away: — *We saw a lot of filthy **waste** floating in the river.*

 travel ⚫ trick

travel *verb* — To go from one place to another:
- *I want to **travel** to Europe someday.*
- *Jon **traveled** with his parents to see their relatives.*
- *It takes ten minutes to **travel** from your house to mine.*

journey — To make a trip:
- *Robin wants to journey to the South Pole.*

tour — To travel in or through a place:
- *We toured a castle and an old city.*

voyage — To journey by water or through space:
- *Someday we will be able to voyage to Mars.*

For more choices see the entry for GO.

tree *noun* — A plant with a trunk or stems that is made up of solid, woody tissue:
- *Trees have branches and leaves.*
- *It is pleasant to sit in the shade under a tree on hot days.*

forest — A large number of trees and plants; woods:
- *Many birds nest in the forest.*

timber — Trees; forest:
- *The hills in the park are covered with timber.*

woodland or woods — An area of land that is covered by trees; a forest:
- *Squirrels and deer live in the woodland outside of town.*
- *We sometimes walk in the woods for exercise.*

WORD BANK

Sometimes you can make things clearer and more interesting for your reader by naming the particular kind of **TREE** you mean. Some kinds of **trees** are:

apple	cottonwood	hemlock	pine
beech	cypress	juniper	poplar
birch	dogwood	maple	redwood
cedar	elm	oak	spruce
chestnut	fir	palm	willow

trick *noun* — An action done to fool or cheat someone:
- *Locking your sister out of the house was a dirty trick.*
- *Ronnie likes to play tricks, but he never fools anyone.*

deception — A trick or lie that fools someone:
- *The telephone call was a deception to get her out of the house while we prepared her surprise.*

hoax — A trick or made up story meant to fool people:
- *It turned out that the story about the ghost was a hoax.*

prank — A playful act meant to trick or tease someone:
- *When the cousins get together, they like to play pranks on each other.*

trip *noun* — Traveling or going from one place to another: — *This summer Perry plans to take a **trip** with his friends. Our **trip** took longer than we expected because of the heavy traffic.*

excursion — A short trip made for a special reason or for pleasure: — *Would you like to come on an **excursion** to the zoo tomorrow?*

expedition — A journey made for a special reason: — *Several scientists are going on an **expedition** to find dinosaur bones.*

journey — A long trip: — *Our **journey** to Grandmother's house takes four hours.*

tour — A trip in which many places are visited or many things are seen: — *Our teacher led us on a **tour** of the museum. I would love to go on a **tour** to France.*

Word Alert

TRIP also means to lose one's balance: *I **tripped** over my shoelaces.* Synonyms for this meaning of **trip** are ***fall*** and ***stumble***.

---

trouble *noun* — A difficult or dangerous situation: — *We will all be in **trouble** if the electricity goes out. The noisy class made **trouble** for the teacher.*

adversity — A difficult time or situation: — *The flood victims showed great courage in the face of their **adversity**.*

fix — Trouble; difficulty: — *Trying to finish three late assignments put me in a real **fix**.*

misfortune — An unlucky event or happening: — *It is a great **misfortune** that our star player is sick.*

predicament — An unpleasant or difficult situation: — *Pedro found himself in the **predicament** of having accepted two party invitations for the same time.*

For more choices see the entry for PROBLEM.

---

true *adjective* — Agreeing with the facts; not false: — *The movie was based on a **true** story. Everything I have told you is **true**.*

accurate — Correct, exact, or precise: — *Her statement about what happened is **accurate**. The news stories on the Web were not **accurate**.*

factual — True; accurate: — *The book gave a **factual** account of the historical events.*

valid — Based on facts or evidence; true: — *They ran several experiments to make sure the scientist's theory was **valid**.*

For more choices see the entries for PERFECT and RIGHT.

Antonyms: See the entries for INCORRECT and WRONG or DOUBTFUL and UNCERTAIN.

trust ·◦· turn

trust *noun*   A belief that someone or something is true, honest, or reliable: *I put my **trust** in my friends, and they came through for me.*
*Thank you for your **trust** in this matter.*

    confidence   Trust or faith: *I have confidence in your ability to get the job done.*

    conviction   A strong belief: *It is my conviction that most people are honest.*

    faith   Belief or trust without proof: *I have faith in you.*

---

trust *verb*   To believe to be true, honest, or reliable: *I don't **trust** the weather report.*
*I **trusted** that you would do what you promised.*

    believe   To feel sure someone is true or telling the truth: *I believe his story is true.*
We all believed in her honesty.

    depend   To rely on or trust: *We depend on you to do this job on time.*
Our group depended on each other to get the project finished.

    rely   To trust; depend: *You can always rely on your teacher for help.*
I relied on her information, but it turned out not to be true.

---

try *verb*   To make an effort to do something: *Please **try** to be on time.*
*The team **tried** to score, but their attempt was blocked.*

    attempt   To make an effort; try: *Our dog attempted to jump over the fence again and again.*
It is too complicated for me to attempt to explain.

    endeavor   To make an effort; try: *Our teacher always endeavors to be fair.*

    strive   To make a great effort; try hard: *I always strive to do my best.*

---

turn *verb*   To move around in a circle or part of a circle: *The bus **turned** at the corner.*
*Abigail **turned** the key and unlocked the door.*

    pivot   To turn on a fixed point: *That door squeaks when it pivots on its hinges.*
The basketball player pivoted and shot a basket.

    revolve   To spin or turn around a central point: *Since the accident, the wheels on my bike don't revolve properly.*
Nine planets revolve around the sun.

    rotate   To turn or cause to turn around an axis: *The top rotated so fast it was a blur.*
A gyroscope is stable because it rotates.

    spin   To turn around quickly: *The car's tires spun in the mud.*

    twirl   To spin around quickly: *The skater twirled on the ice.*

WORDS from Words

TURN is often combined with other words to form expressions that have special meanings. These expressions also have synonyms. *For example:*

to turn down means to refuse: *The principal turned down our request to count the votes another time.* Useful synonyms are **deny**, **refuse**, and **reject**.

to turn in means to give or return: *I turned in the library books yesterday. Has everyone turned in their homework?* Useful synonyms are **hand in** or **submit**.

to turn off means to stop something from flowing or operating: *Kyle turned off the computer.* Useful synonyms are **stop** and **switch off**.

to turn out means to produce: *The factory turns out thousands of cars each year.* Useful synonyms are **generate** and **make**. **Turn out** also means to show up: *A large crowd turned out to watch the game.* Useful synonyms are **assemble**, **gather**, and **come**.

---

type *noun*	A group of things that are alike:	*An eagle is a **type** of bird.* *Do you like that **type** of music?* *You find all **types** of people in a city.*
category	A group or class of things:	*The music collection in the library is shelved by category.*
class	A group of persons or things that are alike in some way:	*Cat owners form a large class of people in this country.*
kind	A group of things that are alike in some way:	*Whales are a kind of mammal.* *Our school has many different kinds of clubs.*
sort	A group of people or things that are the same in some way; kind; type:	*That sort of insect might sting you.* *What sort of work does your father do?*

ugly *adjective* — Not pleasing to look at:

*Adrian thought the painting was **ugly**.*
*The **ugly** duckling became a beautiful swan.*

hideous — Very ugly; unattractive:

The movie features a hideous monster.
That color is hideous.

homely — Having a plain appearance; not handsome or pretty:

Our old cat is homely, but we love him.

unattractive — Not attractive; ugly:

He wore an unattractive hat until someone made fun of it.

unbecoming — Not flattering or attractive:

Those unbecoming clothes make you look pale and unhealthy.

Antonyms: See the entries for BEAUTIFUL, HANDSOME, and MAGNIFICENT.

---

unbelievable *adjective* — Hard to believe:

*Her story about UFOs was **unbelievable**.*
*There is an **unbelievable** number of insects in the world.*

inconceivable — Not believable or thinkable:

It was inconceivable that I would do well on that test because I didn't have time to study.

incredible — Hard or impossible to believe:

He told an incredible story about diving to the bottom of the ocean.

For more choices see the entry for DOUBTFUL.
Antonyms: See the entry for TRUE.

uncertain
adjective

Not known or not knowing for sure:

*The outcome of the game is **uncertain**.*
*I was **uncertain** where I had left my books.*

ambiguous — Having more than one meaning; not clear:

We couldn't figure out what the ambiguous wording of your note meant.

indefinite — Not clear, set, or exact; vague:

Our plans for next week are indefinite.

unclear — Not clear; uncertain; vague:

We made mistakes because the directions were unclear.
It is unclear exactly what you want us to do.

vague — Not definite or clear:

We could only see vague shapes in the fog.
I have only a vague idea of what I want to do tomorrow.

For more choices see the entry for DOUBTFUL.
Antonyms: See the entry for TRUE.

---

under *preposition* — Lower than:

*The book fell **under** my desk.*
*Diana dove **under** the surface of the water.*

below — In a lower place than; beneath:

My friend lives on the floor below our apartment.

beneath — Lower than; under:

The subway runs beneath the streets.
We have a basement beneath our house.

underneath — In a place or position lower than; under:

My homework was underneath all my books.

---

understand *verb* — To get the meaning of:

*I didn't **understand** the directions.*
*The teacher explained the lesson until she was sure I **understood**.*

fathom — To get to the bottom of; understand:

I could never fathom algebra.

follow — To pay attention and understand:

We followed the directions and arrived right on time.
Do you follow what I mean?

get — To understand:

I don't get the point of your story.

realize — To understand completely:

We realized that we were late when we heard the bell ring for class.

see — To understand:

Mariah finally saw the answer to the problem.
Do you see the problem?
I see what you mean.

For more choices see the entry for KNOW.

undo *verb* | To loosen something that is fastened or tied: | You have to **undo** the ribbon before you can open the present.
Bianca **undid** the knots in her shoelaces.

cancel | To decide not to do, have, or go: | The game was canceled because of rain.
I canceled my order when I realized I wasn't hungry.

reverse | To change to the opposite: | The teacher reversed the order of the line by starting at the back and working forward.
The outcome of the game was reversed by the referee.

wipe out | To destroy totally: | Their three goals in the second period wiped out our lead.
An epidemic could wipe out the entire town.

For more choices see the entries for ERASE and REMOVE.

---

unequal *adjective* | Not the same; uneven: | It was an **unequal** contest because we had fewer players.
My pants look silly because the legs are **unequal**.

lopsided | Larger or heavier on one side than on the other; leaning to one side: | The lopsided shack looked like it was about to fall down.
Larry straightened the lopsided pictures on the wall.

uneven | Not level; not equal: | A bulldozer smoothed the uneven ground.
The baseball game between the teachers and the students was an uneven contest.

Antonyms: See the entries for EQUAL and SAME.

---

unfair *adjective* | Not fair or just: | The bully took **unfair** advantage of the smaller students.
Everyone thought the decision was **unfair**.

one-sided | Favoring only one side; unfair: | All her arguments were so one-sided, nobody believed her.

unjust | Not just or fair: | Punishing someone for no reason is unjust.

unreasonable | Not reasonable; unfair: | She has an unreasonable dislike of cats.

Antonyms: See the entry for FAIR.

---

unfamiliar *adjective* | Not well known: | The **unfamiliar** insect didn't look like any I had seen before.
The handwriting on the envelope was **unfamiliar**.

exotic | Foreign, strange, or unusual: | Her parents collect exotic plants.

foreign | Of or from another country: | We tried foreign food at the festival, and it was delicious.

unknown | Not known; unfamiliar: | They planned to explore unknown territory.

For more choices see the entries for ODD, STRANGE, and UNUSUAL.
Antonyms: See the entries for COMMON, NORMAL, and USUAL.

unfavorable
adjective

| | Not favorable, harmful: | Tomorrow's weather forecast is **unfavorable** for going to the beach. The safety inspector gave our fire alarm system an **unfavorable** report. |

adverse — Not helpful to what is wanted; not favorable: — They closed the airport because the snowy weather was adverse to safe flying.

detrimental — Harmful: — Smoking is detrimental to your health.

negative — Not helpful: — If you have a negative attitude, you will never get anything done.

For more choices see the entry for BAD³.

---

unfriendly
adjective

| | Feeling or showing dislike: | Our neighbors seemed **unfriendly** until we got to know them. The **unfriendly** dog growled at Gavin. |

aloof — Showing little concern or friendliness: — The aloof girl stood apart from the other students.

distant — Not friendly: — The two friends have been distant toward each other ever since their quarrel.

unsociable — Not friendly or sociable: — Grizzly bears are unsociable and spend most of their time alone.

Antonyms: See the entries for FRIENDLY, KIND, and NICE.

---

unhappy
adjective

| | Without happiness or joy: | My brother is **unhappy** about moving. Shannon looked **unhappy** after losing the race. |

blue — Unhappy; discouraged: — Helen felt blue the first few days away from home.

desolate — Miserable; cheerless: — Ike was desolate until his puppy was found.

gloomy — Having low spirits; sorrowful: — I was gloomy for weeks after my best friend moved away.

miserable — Extremely unhappy: — Angelina was miserable after her brother left home. Everyone felt miserable waiting for the bus in the cold rain.

wretched — Very unhappy or uncomfortable: — The flu made me feel wretched.

For more choices see the entry for SAD and SULLEN.
Antonyms: See the entry for HAPPY.

unhealthy
adjective
Not having good health:
*The child looked **unhealthy** from staying indoors.*
*Your plants won't look so **unhealthy** if you water them.*

   ill
Not healthy or well:
Several of my friends missed school because they were ill last week.

   sick
Suffering from a disease or poor health:
My father was sick with flu and stayed home.
The roller coaster made me feel sick.

   unwell
Sick; ill:
Charles is feeling unwell and can't come to the party.

---

unimportant
adjective
Of no special value, meaning, or interest; not important:
*What time we start is **unimportant** as long as we finish the job.*
*We chatted about **unimportant** things before class.*

   irrelevant
Having no connection to something of immediate concern; unimportant:
Your irrelevant comment has nothing to do with the problem we are trying to solve.

   insignificant
Having little or no importance or meaning:
Our problems seem insignificant compared to others.

   petty
Not important; insignificant:
He worried too much about petty problems.

   trifling
Small in amount or importance:
The difference in their heights was trifling.

For more choices see the entry MINOR.
Antonyms: See the entries for KEY and MAIN.

---

unique *adjective*
Not having an equal; the only one of its kind:
*Each snowflake has a **unique** shape.*
*Walking on the moon was a **unique** achievement.*

   characteristic
A quality that helps identify a person or thing:
Dogs have a characteristic bark.

   distinctive
Easy to recognize; characteristic:
I easily recognized her distinctive laugh.

   individual
Characteristic of a particular person or thing:
She has a very individual way of dressing.

   separate
Set apart:
We made separate choices at the candy store.

---

universal
adjective
Shared by all:
*There was **universal** joy when a cure for polio was announced.*
*Food and shelter seem to be **universal** needs.*

   general
For all:
The movie is suitable for a general audience.

   unlimited
Without any limits:
Your card gives you unlimited use of the library.

   widespread
Happening to many people or over a large area:
There was a widespread belief that the contest had not been fair.
The cold weather was widespread.

unlucky *adjective* | Not having good luck: | *It was an **unlucky** day for me when I lost my backpack. Kenneth was **unlucky** at dodge ball, but he always won at tether ball.*

doomed | Sure to fail or die: | *Our project was doomed because we tried to do too much at one time.*

unfortunate | Not fortunate; unlucky: | *Falling into the mud was an unfortunate accident.*

Antonyms: See the entry for LUCKY.

---

unnatural *adjective* | Different from what is usual in nature: | *It is **unnatural** for this area to receive so little rain. Her smile seemed forced and **unnatural** in the photograph.*

abnormal | Not normal or usual: | *The doctor said that her abnormal temperature was caused by chicken pox.*

artificial | Made by people, not natural: | *The artificial flowers looked fake.*

synthetic | Artificial; made by people: | *Plastic is a synthetic material made from oil.*

For more choices see the entries for RARE and UNUSUAL.
Antonyms: See the entries for COMMON, NORMAL, and USUAL.

---

untidy *adjective* | Not neat: | *I couldn't find any socks that matched in my **untidy** drawer. After the game, the locker room was an **untidy** mess.*

slovenly | Untidy or careless, especially in dress or habits: | *His slovenly dress kept him from getting a job.*

unkempt | Untidy; neglected: | *Weeds made our garden look unkempt.*

For more choices see the entries for DIRTY and MESSY.
Antonyms: See the entries for CLEAN and NEAT.

---

unusual *adjective* | Not usual, common, or ordinary: | *The **unusual** flower stood out from all the rest. It is **unusual** for them not to arrive on time.*

exceptional | Not ordinary; unusual: | *An exceptional amount of snow fell this winter.*

extraordinary | Very unusual; beyond the ordinary: | *The view from the top of the tallest building in the city was extraordinary.*

freakish | Unusual or odd: | *In a freakish accident today, a bird hit a power line and blacked out half the city.*

uncommon | Not happening often: | *Snowstorms are uncommon in this area.*

For more choices see the entries for INCREDIBLE, ODD, STRANGE, and UNFAMILIAR.
Antonyms: See the entries for COMMON, NORMAL, and USUAL.

U up ⟷ urge

up *adverb* — From a lower to a higher place or degree; in a higher place or condition: — We climbed **up** the stairs.
The price didn't go **up**.
The sun came **up** this morning.
The bird flew **up** into the tree.

   above — In or to a higher place: — The moon seemed to float *above* the clouds.

   aloft — Far above the ground; high up: — Several kites were *aloft* over the park.

   high — At or to a high place: — The acrobats swung *high* above the audience.

   overhead — Above one's head: — Airplanes circled *overhead*, waiting to land.

   upward — From a lower to a higher place: — The balloon flew *upward* into the sky.

Antonyms: See the entry for DOWN.

---

upset *adjective* — Feeling uneasy; distressed: — Tina was **upset** when no one came to the party.

   anxious — Uneasy or fearful of what may happen: — Melinda is *anxious* about her first day at the new school.

   concerned — Troubled or worried: — Mom was *concerned* when my brother did not come home for supper.

   worried — Uneasy or troubled about something: — Jack was *worried* that the river would flood.

For more choices see the entry for NERVOUS.
Antonyms: See the entries for CALM and QUIET.

---

upset *verb* — To turn or knock over: — I accidentally **upset** my glass of milk.
We had to swim when the wind **upset** our boat.

   capsize — To turn upside down: — The strong wind *capsized* our sailboat.

   overturn — To turn or throw over; upset: — I *overturned* my desk when I stood up suddenly.

   tip — To knock or turn over: — I accidentally *tipped* my soda over.

---

urge *verb* — To try to convince or persuade: — We **urged** Veronica to run for class president.
The crowd was **urging** on the team with cheers.

   drive — To force into some act or condition: — The noise was *driving* me crazy.

   prod — To make do something; urge: — Our teacher *prodded* me to answer the math problem on the board.

   spur — To urge on: — The crowd *spurred* the runners on.

For more choices see the entries for ENCOURAGE and PERSUADE.
Antonyms: See the entry for DISCOURAGE.

urgent *adjective* | Needing immediate attention: | *There was an **urgent** message for her to call home.*
*The hospital announced there was an **urgent** need for blood donors.*

critical | Having to do with a crisis: | *Farmers faced a critical shortage of water during the drought.*

dire | Very urgent: | *The flood was a dire emergency.*
We were in dire need of help.

pressing | Important; urgent: | *I must hurry because I am late for a pressing engagement.*

For more choices see the entry for IMPORTANT.

---

use¹ *verb* | To put into service for a particular purpose: | *May I **use** the pencil sharpener?*
Use a dictionary to help you learn to spell.

employ | To use: | *Scientists employ toothbrushes to uncover dinosaur bones.*

utilize | To make use of: | *Satellites are utilized to predict the weather.*

---

use² *verb* | To go through a supply of something; to finish: | *If you **use** all your money now, you will have none left for later.*
*We **used** all the paints for our project.*

consume | To use up or destroy: | *We consumed all the sodas and had to get more.*
The fire consumed hundreds of acres of forest.

deplete | To use up: | *Heavy pumping has depleted the water supply in many places.*

exhaust | To use up completely: | *Our supplies were exhausted so we replaced them before we went camping.*

finish | To use up completely: | *I finished the milk and threw away the carton.*

---

useful *adjective* | Serving a good use or purpose: | *A screwdriver is a **useful** tool.*
*Evan made a **useful** suggestion.*

handy | Easy to use or handle: | *I keep all my school supplies in a handy case.*

helpful | Giving help; useful: | *My teacher gave me some helpful advice.*
A calculator can be a helpful tool.

practical | Easy to use, do, or put into effect: | *An umbrella is practical in the rain.*

Antonyms: See the entry for USELESS.

useless *adjective* — Serving no use; worthless: — *Our useless old computer hasn't worked in years. We threw away some useless junk.*

hopeless — Having or giving no hope: — *Even though the situation appeared hopeless, they kept trying to find an answer.*

worthless — Not good or useful; without value or worth: — *The old washing machine was worthless.*

Antonyms: See the entry for USEFUL.

---

usual *adjective* — Common or expected: — *He arrived at school at the usual time. Snow is usual this time of year.*

average — Usual; typical: — *We have had an average amount of rainfall so far this month.*

customary — Usual: — *It is customary for our family to celebrate my mother's birthday at a restaurant.*

habitual — Commonly occurring or used; usual: — *Jesse took his habitual seat next to Dora.*

For more choices see the entries for COMMON, REGULAR, and NORMAL.
Antonyms: See the entries for RARE and UNUSUAL.

---

usually *adverb* — Commonly or customarily: — *He usually arrives at school late. The game usually begins with a kickoff. You can usually find me studying in the library in the afternoon.*

customarily — Usually: — *Multiplication is customarily taught in elementary school.*

generally — Almost always; usually: — *The team generally practices after school. The weather is generally hot and dry in summer.*

habitually — Commonly occurring or used; usually: — *My father habitually reads the newspaper each morning.*

ordinarily — In normal conditions or circumstances; usually: — *Ordinarily, the movie starts at eight o'clock. Sean ordinarily goes to his locker between classes to get his books.*

For more choices see the entry for OFTEN.
Antonyms: See the entries for RARELY and SCARCELY.

value¹ *noun* | The worth or importance of something: | *Don't underestimate the **value** of a good education.*
*Meg places great **value** on her friendship with Julia.*

significance | Special value or meaning: | *Your choice of what to study in college could have great significance on your future success.*
What is the significance of this old map?

usefulness | Practical value; helpfulness: | *Don't underrate her usefulness to our team.*

For more choices see the entry for WORTH.

---

value² *noun* | The worth of something in money: | *The **value** of our house has gone up.*
*There is almost no **value** in your old comic books.*

cost | The amount of money paid or charged for something: | *The cost of those shoes is very reasonable.*

price | The amount of money for which something is sold or offered for sale: | *What is the price of that bicycle?*
I paid a fair price for this computer game.

---

vanish *verb* | To go out of sight or existence: | *The sun **vanished** behind a cloud.*
*The cat **vanished** at the first sight of the dog.*

disappear | To go out of sight: | *The road disappeared into the tunnel.*
Dinosaurs disappeared about 65 million years ago.

fade | To become gradually fainter, dimmer, or weaker: | *The light slowly faded as the sun set.*
The sound of the passing train faded away.

go away | To leave; vanish: | *Has your headache gone away?*
Our cat went away and didn't reappear for a week.

Antonyms: See the entry for COME.

vehicle *noun* | A means of carrying people or goods: | *The highways are filled with* **vehicles**. *A* **vehicle** *knocked over a street sign, but no one was hurt.*

automobile | A vehicle, usually with four wheels, powered by an engine: | *Automobiles are used mainly to carry passengers.*

bus | A large motor vehicle with rows of seats for carrying passengers: | *Our class rode a school bus to the museum.*

car | An automobile: | *The parking lot has space for several hundred cars.*

truck | A large motor vehicle used to carry heavy loads: | *A truck brought our furniture to our new home.*

Word Alert

The word **VEHICLE** is sometimes combined with other words to define the **vehicle** more clearly. For example, cars and trucks are **motor vehicles**. Rockets and satellites are **space vehicles**.

---

very *adverb* | To a high degree or great extent: | *We were* **very** *happy when our team won. It was* **very** *cold on the icy street.*

absolutely | Without any doubt: | *You are absolutely right that 72 minus 41 equals 31. She was absolutely certain she knew the way.*

extremely | Very: | *We were extremely happy to see our old friends again.*

greatly | Very much; highly: | *We greatly appreciate the time you have taken to show us around.*

immensely | Very; greatly: | *Our puppy was immensely pleased to see us when we came home. We enjoyed the party immensely.*

---

vicious *adjective* | Showing a strong desire to hurt someone: | *Don't believe that* **vicious** *lie. The* **vicious** *dog tugged at his chain.*

hateful | Marked by hatred: | *His hateful behavior toward smaller children cost him many friends.*

malicious | Wishing to cause harm or pain: | *This malicious gossip must stop.*

spiteful | Filled with ill feelings toward others: | *When she was angry, she said some spiteful things that she regretted later.*

For more choices see the entries for CRUEL and MEAN.

victory *noun* — The defeat of an opponent: — *Yesterday's game ended in a victory for our team.* *The general led his army to victory.*

    conquest — The act of conquering something: — *The conquest of smallpox took decades.*

    success — A favorable end; a hoped-for result: — *We are very pleased with the success of our team.*

    triumph — A great success or victory: — *The discovery of a polio vaccine was a great triumph for medical science.*

    win — A victory or success: — *Our team has four wins and two losses this year.*

    Antonyms: See the entry for LOSS.

---

view *noun* — The act of looking or seeing: — *We had our first view of the ocean as we came over the hill.* *Benjamin stood in front of the crowd so he could get the best view.*

    glimpse — A quick look; glance: — *We caught a glimpse of the bus as it passed.*
    scene — View; sight: — *The scene of the park from our window is beautiful.*
    sight — Something seen or worth seeing: — *The sunset over the ocean was a beautiful sight.*

---

villain *noun* — A wicked or evil person: — *The villains in the story tried to kidnap the puppies.*

    beast — A coarse or cruel person: — *They called the ugly man a beast, but actually he was very kind.*

    brute — A cruel person: — *That brute tried to kick my dog.*
    monster — A wicked, cruel person: — *She behaved like a monster when she threw a tantrum.*

---

violent *adjective* — Acting with great force: — *The violent hurricane stayed out to sea.* *He gave the rope a violent jerk.*

    destructive — Causing great damage: — *A destructive wind knocked down several trees in the park.*

    intense — Very great or strong: — *Even though the burn I got from the stove was small, it caused intense pain.* *The forest fire was so intense that the firefighters couldn't get near it.*

    rough — Marked by or showing force or violence: — *The other team earned penalties for its rough play.*

visible *adjective* | Able to be seen: | Our house is **visible** from the street.
The airplane was barely **visible** in the thick clouds.

    apparent | Easily seen or understood: | It was apparent from their cheers that the audience liked the show.

    clear | Easily seen, heard, or understood: | Your directions were very clear.
We had a clear view of the stage.

    observable | Able to be seen or noticed: | Only part of the backyard is observable from our window.

    plain | Clearly seen or heard: | My lost book bag was in plain sight.
My friends made it plain that they did not agree with me.

---

visit *verb* | To go or come to see: | Abigail **visits** her grandmother for the holidays.
Would you like to **visit** the museum?

    call on | To go to see: | We called on my aunt yesterday.
We will call on our friends at their house.

    go to see | To visit: | Russ is going to see his uncle in another town.

    report to | To present oneself: | The coach told us to report to the gym.
We reported to work on time.

    stay with | To visit for a short time: | We stayed with friends during our vacation.
I will stay with my grandparents next month.

---

volunteer *verb* | To offer to do something of one's own free will: | Several of us **volunteered** to help at the hospital.
She **volunteered** by raising her hand.

    contribute | To give: | Many people contribute time and money to charities.

    donate | To give; contribute: | We donated food to the food bank to help people who don't have enough to eat.

    offer | To show a desire to give something; volunteer: | We offered to help at the nursing home.

For more choices see the entry for GIVE.

---

vote *noun* | A formal expression of a wish or choice: | The class will **vote** on whether to go to the park or on the boat ride.
We **voted** by raising our hands.

    ballot | A printed form used in voting: | Ballots are counted to see who won the election.

    election | The act of choosing by voting: | There is an election for President of the United States every four years.

wait *verb*

To stay in place:

We **waited** until Kyle and Lauren caught up with us.
Let's **wait** until the rain stops.

linger

To stay on as if not
wanting to leave:

We linger*ed* after class to talk to the teacher.
The fans lingered at the stadium to get autographs
from the players.

remain

To stay behind or
in the same place:

Kevin remained in our classroom while we
went to the library.
A few leaves remain on the trees through
the whole winter.

stay

To continue in one
place; not leave:

Sometimes I just like to stay at home.
We stayed at the park until it got dark.

Antonyms: See the entries for GO and TRAVEL.

---

walk *noun*

The act of traveling on foot
at a normal, slow pace:

The long **walk** in the woods was very refreshing.
We will go for another **walk** this afternoon.

gait

A way of walking
or running:

The horse's gait changed from a trot to a gallop.

hike

A long walk:

Our hike through the woods took two hours.

stroll

A slow, relaxed walk:

We went for a stroll in the park.

tread

The way or sound
of walking:

I heard your tread on the stairs.

walk *verb* — To move on foot at a normal pace:

*We **walked** to the store instead of taking the bus.*
*You **walk** so fast, I have to run to keep up.*

go on foot — To travel by walking:

*No cars were allowed so we **went on foot**.*

march — To walk with regular steps:

*The band **marched** down the street.*

stride — To walk with long steps, usually with a purpose:

*We watched him **stride** down the aisle toward the stage.*

stroll — To walk in a relaxed or leisurely manner:

*Amy and Sally **strolled** through the park.*

strut — To walk in a vain or very proud way:

*Joe proudly **strutted** up and down in his new clothes.*

trudge — To walk slowly and with effort:

*The tired hikers **trudged** through the mud.*

---

want *verb* — To feel an impulse to have or do something; to have a desire or wish for:

*Anna **wants** to be a doctor.*
*Daniel **wanted** butter on his popcorn.*

crave — To want badly:

*Sue **craved** ice cream so much that she ran all the way to the store.*

desire — To have a strong wish for:

*Molly **desired** a trip to the seashore.*

long — To want very much; yearn:

*Carrie **longed** to see her old friends again.*

wish — To have a longing or strong need for:

*Gary **wished** he had a brother.*

yearn — To feel a strong and deep desire:

*Grandpa **yearned** for the warm days of summer.*

---

warm *adjective* — Somewhat hot; not cold:

*A blanket kept Caitlin **warm**.*
*It was a **warm** afternoon with bright sunshine.*

lukewarm — Slightly warm; neither hot nor cold:

*I washed my cut with **lukewarm** water before putting a bandage on it.*

tepid — Slightly warm:

*I was so busy that by the time I drank my tea it was **tepid**.*
*Our water heater broke, and I had to shower in **tepid** water.*

For more choices see the entry for HOT.
Antonyms: See the entries for COLD and RAW.

warn *verb* | To tell beforehand about something that might happen: | The policeman **warned** us that the road ahead was blocked. Birds often **warn** each other that danger is present by calling loudly.

alert | To warn: | The weather service **alerted** us to the danger of severe thunderstorms.

caution | To warn: | The signs **cautioned** about the danger of swimming in the rough surf.

---

wash *noun* | To clean with water: | I always **wash** my hands before eating. Our class **washed** cars to raise money for charity.

clean | To make free from dirt: | It took hours to **clean** my room. We **cleaned** the floor last.

cleanse | To make clean: | I **cleansed** my face with a special soap.

scour | To clean or polish by rubbing hard: | Terry **scoured** the pots and pans with cleanser.

scrub | To rub in order to wash or clean: | I always **scrub** my hands carefully after I work in the garden.

---

waste *verb* | To use or spend in a careless way: | We **wasted** hours looking for the right address. Don't **waste** your money on junk.

discard | To throw away: | Each spring we **discard** all our worn-out clothes.

squander | To spend foolishly: | He **squandered** every cent he earned on video games.

throw away | To get rid of; discard: | We used to **throw away** old newspapers, but now we recycle them.

For more choices see the entry for LOSE¹.

---

watch¹ *verb* | To look at a person or thing carefully: | We **watched** the sky, looking for meteorites. Taylor will **watch** the movie and review it for the school newspaper.

look at | To turn one's eyes or attention toward; examine: | Would you **look at** the computer to see what's wrong? **Look at** the camera when the photographer takes your picture.

observe | To make a careful study of: | Astronomers **observed** a comet hitting Jupiter.

view | To look at or see: | Our class **viewed** many beautiful paintings at the museum.

For more choices see the entries for LOOK¹, PEEK, and SEE.

watch[2] *verb*	To guard or take care of:	Madison has to **watch** her baby brother while her parents are out. Please **watch** my apartment while I'm on vacation.	
look after	To take care of:	Will you look after my cat while I'm away?	
mind	To take care of:	The baby-sitter minded the children while their parents were out.	
tend	To take care of; look after:	I plan to tend my garden this summer.	

wave *noun*	To signal by moving one's hand or an object back and forth:	Kaylee **waved** to her friends across the street. The Queen will **wave** to the crowd. The crowd **waved** little flags at the ball game.
gesture	To move the head or hands to show what a person is thinking or feeling:	The speaker gestured to make his point.
motion	To move a part of the body as a signal:	The coach motioned to us with his arm.
signal	To make a signal to:	We tried to signal our friend that someone was behind him, but he got hit with a snowball anyway.

way *noun*	A course of action for doing or getting something; how something is done:	She styled her hair in a new **way**. He waved in a friendly **way**. Is there a **way** to fix my computer?
fashion	Manner or way:	Our class walked to the auditorium in an orderly fashion.
manner	The way in which something is done:	The meeting was conducted in an official manner.
method	A way of doing something:	What method did you use to cook this chicken?

WORDS from Words

WAY is often combined with other words to form expressions that have special meanings. These expressions also have synonyms. For example:

by the way is an expression used to bring up a new topic that is usually related to what is being discussed: *By the way, our teacher wants to see you this afternoon about your report.* A useful synonym is **incidentally**.

to give way means to withdraw: *The outnumbered defenders slowly gave way to their attackers.* Useful synonyms are **retreat** and **withdraw**. **To give way** can also mean to collapse: *That table almost gave way under the heavy load.* Useful synonyms are **break down**, **fail**, and **fall**.

under way means moving, happening, or being carried out: *The ship got under way as soon as the anchor was pulled up. The game had been under way for half an hour by the time we got there.* Useful synonyms are **going**, **in motion**, and **moving**.

weak *adjective* — Not having enough strength, force, or power: — *Elizabeth felt **weak** because she hadn't eaten all day.* *The chair is too **weak** to hold you.*

   faint — Not clear or strong; weak: — *We could pick up only a faint signal on our radio.* *There was a faint light ahead.*

   feeble — Not strong; weak: — *The tired kitten made a feeble attempt to play and then fell asleep.*

   helpless — Not able to take care of oneself: — *I felt helpless the first time I turned on a computer.* *The helpless baby lay in the crib.*

For more choices see the entries for DELICATE and FRAGILE.
Antonyms: See the entries for STRONG, TOUGH, and POWERFUL.

---

wear *verb* — To have on the body: — *We all **wore** costumes for Halloween.* *James and Ashley **wear** mittens in winter.*

   don — To put on: — *I donned my new hat and went outside.*

   dress up — To put on clothing that is fancier than usually worn: — *Everyone dressed up for the party.*

   get into — To put on clothing: — *We got into costume before the play.*

   put on — To wear something: — *I put on rubber gloves and washed the dishes.*

---

well *adverb* — In a good or satisfactory way: — *Everything went **well** at the rehearsal for the school play.* *Bobby played the piano **well** at his recital.*

   agreeably — In a pleasant way: — *The exchange student answered all our questions about her homeland agreeably.* *We settled our argument agreeably.*

   nicely — In a pleasant or agreeable way: — *The children behaved nicely at the party.*

   properly — In a correct or suitable way: — *You have to eat properly if you want to stay healthy.*

---

wet *adjective* — Covered or moist with water or another liquid: — *The streets were **wet** after the rain.* *The paint is still **wet**.* *The **wet** sponge is on the sink.* *Her hair was **wet** after she went swimming.*

   drenched — Completely wet; soaked: — *The downpour drenched us.*

   soaked — Very wet: — *Our dog was soaked by the lawn sprinkler.*

   soggy — Very wet or damp; soaked: — *The ground is still soggy from the flood.*

   sopping — Extremely wet; dripping: — *Even though she ran through the thunderstorm, Lisa's clothes were sopping by the time she got home.*

For more choices see the entry for DAMP.
Antonyms: See the entry for DRY.

whisper *verb*	To say or speak very softly:	*I whispered a secret to my friend.* *They were whispering in the library.*
murmur	To make or say with a low, soft sound:	*They were murmuring to each other when I entered the room.*
speak softly	To use words in a low tone; whisper:	*We spoke softly so we wouldn't disturb other people.*

wide *adjective*	Filling much space from side to side; not narrow:	*We crossed a wide river on a ferry.* *The wide box barely fit through the doorway.*
broad	Large from side to side; wide:	*The city is crisscrossed by broad avenues.*
vast	Very great in extent, size, or amount:	*We could see a vast plain from the top of the mountain.* *A vast crowd gathered to see the parade.*

For more choices see the entries for ROOMY and LARGE.
Antonyms: See the entry for NARROW.

wild *adjective*	Living or growing naturally; not controlled by people:	*Tigers, lions, and bears are wild animals.* *The rain forest is filled with wild plants.*
natural	Found in nature; not made by people:	*This park is built around a natural rock formation.* *Wool and cotton are natural fibers; nylon is not.*
unruly	Hard to control or manage:	*The police were called to manage the unruly mob.* *Sandra's hair was unruly after walking in the wind.*
untamed	Not gentle or tame:	*They couldn't find any signs of other humans in the untamed wilderness.*

will *noun*	A firm purpose:	*Ashley had a strong will to win.* *You have the talent but lack the will to succeed.*
determination	A definite and firm purpose:	*Their determination to succeed made them work harder.*
inclination	A natural tendency; liking:	*My inclination is to finish the work first and then relax.*
willpower	Strength of will; determination:	*It takes lots of willpower to refuse a tempting dessert.*

win *verb*	To do better than any other in a race or contest:	*Our team will win if they play hard.* *Liam won two races.*
defeat	To win a victory over:	*Our team defeated our rivals.*
succeed	To have a good result; do well:	*Our plan succeeded, and we won the game.* *Frances succeeded in memorizing the poem.*
triumph	To succeed or win:	*Our school's relay team triumphed in the state finals.*

Antonyms: See the entry for LOSE[2].

wise *adjective* — Having good judgment and intelligence:

*It is **wise** not to tire yourself out.*
*The teacher gave us **wise** advice about taking the test.*
*The chief was a **wise** old man.*

prudent — Having or showing good judgment and caution:

He made the prudent choice to save some of his allowance rather than spend it all right away.
It's best to be prudent when riding a bike around cars.

sensible — Having or showing good sense; wise:

She is the right candidate for treasurer because she is so sensible.

sound — Based on facts, truth, or good sense:

They made a sound decision not to skate on thin ice.
She has very sound judgment.

For more choices see the entries for SHARP² and SMART.
Antonyms: See the entries for DUMB and STUPID.

---

wish *noun* — A feeling of wanting something:

*Steve's **wish** is to become an astronaut.*
*Sometimes **wishes** come true.*

craving — A wish; a strong desire:

I have a strong craving for potato chips.

hope — A strong wish and belief that something will happen:

Angela's high test scores gave her hope about getting into a good college.
We had high hopes for winning the competition.

itch — A restless, uneasy feeling or desire:

After we've stayed in a place for a while, we develop an itch to move on.

For more choices see the entry for DESIRE.

---

witness *noun* — A person who saw or heard something and can tell what happened:

*The **witness** explained how the car got into a ditch.*

eyewitness — A person who has seen something happen:

The eyewitness was asked to testify about the accident in court.

observer — A person who sees or notices:

He was an innocent observer of the argument.
The official observer advised us to make some changes before the race.

onlooker — A person who watches without taking part:

Several onlookers watched the workers build a skyscraper.

spectator — A person who watches something but does not take part:

The spectators were asked to hold their applause until all the winners had been announced.

woman *noun* — An adult female person: — *When a girl grows up, she becomes a woman.*
Our biology teacher and our coach are women.

female — A person or animal that gives birth to young or produces eggs: — *The surgeon was a female.*
Among lions, the female does most of the hunting.

lady — Any woman: — *A lady called and left a message.*

maid — A girl or young unmarried woman: — *Jesse will be the maid of honor at her older sister's wedding.*

For more choices see the entries for HUMANITY, MAN, and PERSON.

---

wonderful *adjective* — Causing wonder; remarkable: — *They had a wonderful time at the theater.*
The jugglers did wonderful tricks.

amazing — Causing great surprise or astonishment: — *The magician performed an amazing feat.*
Maurice told us an amazing story.

astonishing — Amazing; surprising: — *The new teacher has taught us an astonishing amount of math in a very short time.*

fantastic — Very good; excellent: — *I found fantastic information for my report on the Web.*

incredible — Amazing; astonishing: — *She spends an incredible amount of time training for swim meets.*

marvelous — Causing wonder or amazement: — *The symphony orchestra gave a marvelous performance.*

---

work[1] *noun* — The use of a person's energy or ability to do something: — *The students had a lot of work to do.*
It took some work to build our club house, but it was worth it.

effort — Hard work: — *Carrying the groceries into the house took a lot of effort.*
His efforts in math improved his grade.

labor — Hard work; toil: — *A lot of labor went into building that wall.*
Tony was tired after a day of labor.

toil — Hard and exhausting effort or work: — *The hero in the story had to toil in the fields to earn a living.*

For more choices see the entry for ACTION.
Antonyms: See the entries for ENTERTAINMENT, HOBBY, and LEISURE.

work[2] *noun* — What a person does to earn money: — *What kind of* **work** *does your mother do? I am looking for* **work** *for this summer.*

employment — The work a person does: — *After the factory closed, the workers had to find new* **employment**.

job — A position of work; employment: — *I have a* **job** *making deliveries for the grocery store after school.*

occupation — The work a person does to earn a living: — *Her* **occupation** *is teaching.*

profession — An occupation that requires special education and training: — *Teaching and medicine are* **professions** *that require years of preparation.*

For more choices see the entry for JOB.

---

work *verb* — To use one's energy or ability in order to do or get something: — *I* **worked** *very hard on my term paper. My mother* **works** *as a lawyer.*

labor — To do hard work: — *The construction workers* **labored** *extra hours to get the building finished on time.*

operate — To go or run; work; function: — *The new program* **operates** *well on my computer. How do you* **operate** *this phone?*

run — To operate; work: — *My grandfather* **ran** *huge boilers that heated the hospital.*

toil — To do hard or exhausting work: — *We* **toiled** *for hours cleaning up the yard.*

WORDS from Words

WORK is often combined with other words to form expressions that have special meanings. These expressions also have synonyms. *For example:*

out of work means to be without a job: *Several people were* **out of work** *until the new plant opened.* Useful synonyms are **jobless** and **unemployed**.

work out means to plan or solve: *They* **worked out** *several math problems on the board. You will have to* **work out** *your own schedule. I hope things* **work out** *the way you want.* Useful synonyms are **plan**, **resolve**, and **solve**. A **workout** is exercise or practice: *The dancers had a tough* **workout** *today.*

Work is also combined with other words to form names for things that are related to working. A **workman** or **worker** is a person who works. A **workbench** is a heavy table used by someone who works with tools, such as a carpenter or mechanic. A **workbook** is a book in which a student does written work. A **workstation** is an area where work is done in an office or school, often on a computer.

worry *noun* | Something that causes an uneasy or troubled feeling: | My brother doesn't have a **worry** in the world. *They let their **worries** get them down.*

    anxiety | A feeling of fearful worry or uneasiness about what may happen: | *Many people have* anxiety *about going to the dentist.*

    apprehension | A fear of what may happen; worry: | *I felt* apprehension *about the history test.*

    care | A feeling of worry: | *He had so many* cares *he couldn't sleep.*

    concern | Serious interest or worry: | *We were filled with* concern *when you didn't call. We discussed our* concerns *with the principal.*

For more choices see the entry for FEAR.

---

worry *verb* | To feel or cause to feel uneasy or troubled: | *We **worried** that you might not show up. Don't let me **worry** you.*

    concern | To worry; trouble: | *Your bad cough* concerned *us.*

    distress | To cause pain, sorrow, or misery: | *The news of the plane crash* distressed *us.*

    disturb | To make uneasy or nervous: | *Don't let her strange behavior* disturb *you.*

    trouble | To disturb or make uncomfortable: | *Does the argument still* trouble *you? Wayne was* troubled *by bad dreams.*

    upset | To make nervous and worried: | *The bad news* upset *me.*

---

worth *noun* | The quality that makes a person or thing good or useful: | *This book has real **worth**. Our dog proved its **worth** by chasing away a raccoon.*

    importance | Great value or meaning: | *Your term paper will be of great* importance *in deciding your grade in this class.*

    merit | Goodness, worth, or value: | *Her suggestions have great* merit.

For more choices see the entry for VALUE.

---

wrong *adjective* | Not correct or true: | *You got a low grade because there were too many **wrong** answers on your homework. Tom was **wrong** about the weather.*

    erroneous | Wrong; mistaken: | *They reached an* erroneous *conclusion because they didn't have all the facts.*

    mistaken | In error; wrong: | *We were* mistaken *about the time of our meeting.*

    untrue | Not true; false: | *The rumor was* untrue.

For more choices see the entry for INCORRECT.
Antonyms: See the entries for CORRECT, RIGHT, and TRUE.

x-ray *noun* — A kind of radiation that can pass through substances; a photograph made with x-rays: — *An **x-ray** can show the inside of your body. Security guards use **x-rays** to check baggage at airports.*

CAT scan or CT scan — A series of x-ray images that show a cross-section of a person or thing: — *Scientists took a CAT scan of an ancient Egyptian mummy to see what they could learn.*

Word Alert

X-RAY is often used as a verb. For example: *The doctor **x-rayed** my ankle to make sure it wasn't broken. The dentist will **x-ray** your teeth during your next checkup.*

yank *verb* — To pull with a sharp, sudden motion: — *I gave the door a **yank**, and it flew open. She **yanked** the rope to ring the bell.*

snatch — To seize or grab suddenly or quickly: — *We all tried to snatch the gold ring on the merry-go-round. I was so busy I barely had time to snatch a sandwich for lunch.*

tug — To pull on something: — *The child tugged on my sleeve to get attention. She tugs on her hair when she gets nervous.*

wrench — To twist or pull with a hard, sharp motion: — *I wrenched a sandwich from the tray before it was passed to the next table.*

For more choices see the entries for JERK and PULL.

261

yell ↔ youth

yell *verb*	To call loudly, shout, or cry:	The crowd **yelled** when our team scored. My sister **yells** at me when she gets mad.
bellow	To make a loud, deep sound; roar:	The elephant **bellowed** and then charged. The coach **bellowed** at the team to get them moving.
cheer	To give a shout of happiness, encouragement, or praise.	The fans **cheered** when their team scored.
shout	To call loudly:	Carlos **shouted** to his friends across the busy street. He had to **shout** to be heard.
roar	To make a loud, deep sound or cry:	The hungry lion **roared**. The crowd **roared** with approval.

For more choices see the entries for CALL and SCREAM.

yet *adverb*	Up to the present time:	We haven't finished painting my room **yet**. Please don't leave **yet**.
finally	At the end; at last:	We **finally** made it. **Finally**, the boring assembly ended.
so far	Until now:	The movie has been entertaining **so far**.
sometimes	At some times; on certain occasions:	**Sometimes** they serve ice cream in the cafeteria.
thus far	Yet; until now:	No one has been hurt in the novel **thus far**.

young *adjective*	Not completely developed; of or for children:	My parents said I was too **young** to fly alone. A **young** horse is called a colt.
immature	Not having reached full growth; not mature:	The **immature** apples were sour. Your **immature** comments are embarrassing.
juvenile	Of or for children or young people; childish:	Our library has a good selection of **juvenile** books. Our teacher scolded us for our **juvenile** behavior.
youthful	The condition or quality of being young:	The new players have plenty of **youthful** enthusiasm but not much experience.

For more choices see the entry for CHILDISH.
Antonyms: See the entry for OLD.

youth *noun*	The fact or quality of being a young person:	Several **youths** were standing outside the gym. In his **youth**, our teacher was a champion tennis player.
adolescence	The time in life when one changes from a child to an adult:	**Adolescence** lasts from about age twelve to age twenty.
childhood	The period of life when one is a child:	**Childhood** lasts from the ages of two or three years to about twelve.

For more choices see the entry for CHILD.

zero *noun* — No quantity or amount:

Both teams had scored zero points at the end of the first period.
As the fog closed in, visibility was reduced to zero.

    none — Not one; nothing; not any:

I reached into the box of cookies, but there were none left.
None of the lost explorers were ever found.

    nothing — Not anything; no thing:

We found nothing that we wanted at the store.
There was nothing left after the children got finished with the birthday cake.

---

zest *noun* — An exciting or lively quality:

The lemon juice added zest to my soda.
Good music adds zest to a party.

    flavor — A special or main quality; a particular taste:

The preview gave us the flavor of the movie.
Red pepper gives food a spicy flavor.

    spice — Something that adds interest or excitement:

There is an old saying that "variety is the spice of life."
The music ought to add spice to our party.

    tang — A sharp or strong taste or odor:

There was the tang of lemon scent in the air.

---

zip *verb* — To close with a zipper:

Zip your backpack or your books will fall out.
Kathy zipped up her jacket when she went outside.

    close — To shut:

Jeremy closed his jacket against the cold wind.

    fasten — To close so it will not come open:

I had to stop to fasten my boots.

---

zone *noun* — An area with some special quality:

You have to reach the end zone to score.
The cars slowed for the school zone.

    district — An area that is part of a larger area:

Our county is divided into many voting districts.
My father works in the financial district of the city.

    neighborhood — A small area or district where people live:

Our neighborhood is one of the oldest in the town.

    region — A large area or territory:

The western region of our country has high mountains.

 **zoom**

zoom *verb*	To move or climb suddenly and quickly:	*A jet airplane **zoomed** overhead.* *I love to **zoom** around on my bicycle.*
dart	To move suddenly or quickly:	*Our cat **darted** through the door and ran outside.* *Josh **darted** from room to room looking for his jacket.*
speed	To go or cause to go quickly:	*We **sped** down the hill on our bicycles.* *Don't **speed** or you'll cause an accident.*
streak	To move at great speed:	*The jet **streaked** past overhead.* *I **streaked** down the hall because I was late for class.*

For more choices see the entries for HURRY and RUN.

Word Alert

ZOOM IN means to move a camera lens forward quickly, which brings the subject closer: *The camera zoomed in for a close-up.*

Every synonym mentioned in the thesaurus is also listed alphabetically in the *index*. In the *index*, all words in CAPITAL LETTERS are *entry words*. These are the words that are listed alphabetically and defined in the thesaurus. Every synonym found in the thesaurus is listed in the *index* in lowercase letters. Under each word in lowercase letters is the word *See* followed by an *entry word* in CAPITAL LETTERS. This is the *entry word* under which you will find the synonym you are looking up. If the synonym doesn't appear in the entry itself, it can be found in the special feature that accompanies that entry.

Index

A

abandon
See BACK
abandon
See GIVE
abandon
See LEAVE
abandon
See QUIT
abide by
See FOLLOW²
ABILITY
ABLE
abnormal
See UNNATURAL
abolish
See DO
ABOUT (*adverb*)
ABOUT (*preposition*)
above
See UP
abrupt
See SHARP³
abrupt
See SUDDEN
ABSENT
ABSOLUTE
absolutely
See VERY
absorbing
See INTERESTING
absurd
See SILLY
abundant
See PLENTIFUL
academy
See SCHOOL
accelerate
See STEP
accept
See TAKE
accident
See DISASTER

acclaim
See PRAISE
accompany
See GO
accomplish
See CARRY
accomplish
See DO
accomplish
See FINISH
accomplishment
See ACT
accord
See PEACE
accordion
See MUSIC
account
See REPORT
accumulate
See GATHER
accurate
See TRUE
accuse
See BLAME
ace
See EXPERT
ACHE
ache
See HURT
ache
See PAIN
achieve
See DO
achievement
See ACT
acknowledge
See ADMIT²
acquaint
See INTRODUCE
acquire
See GET
acquire
See LEARN
acre
See MEASUREMENT
ACT (*noun*)

ACT (*verb*)
act on
See ACT
act out
See ACT
act up
See ACT
act upon
See ACT
ACTION
actions
See ACTION
active
See ALIVE
active
See LIVELY
activity
See HOBBY
actor
See ART
actress
See ART
actual
See REAL
adage
See SAYING
adapt
See CHANGE
additional
See MORE
address
See SPEECH
adequate
See ENOUGH
adjacent
See NEAR
adjust
See CORRECT
admirable
See GOOD
admire
See LOOK
admire
See PRAISE
ADMIT¹ (*to let in*)
ADMIT² (*to confess*)

admit
See LET
admit
See TAKE
adolescence
See YOUTH
adorable
See PRETTY
adore
See LOVE
adored
See POPULAR
adorn
See DECORATE
ADULT (*adjective*)
ADULT (*noun*)
adult
See MATURE
advance
See MOVE
adventurous
See DARING
adversary
See ENEMY
adverse
See UNFAVORABLE
adversity
See TROUBLE
affection
See LOVE
affix
See FASTEN
affluent
See RICH
affront
See INSULT
AFRAID
after-school snack
See MEAL
age
See PERIOD
aged
See OLD
agitated
See KEY
agitated
See RESTLESS

agony
See SUFFERING
AGREE
agreeable
See NICE
agreeably
See WELL
AGREEMENT
agreement
See PEACE
ahead
See EARLY
ahead of time
See TIME
aid
See ASSIST
aid
See HELP
ailing
See SICK
ailment
See SICKNESS
aim
See INTEND
aim
See PURPOSE
air
See SONG
aircraft carrier
See SHIP
ajar
See OPEN
alarm
See SCARE
ALERT
alert
See SHARP²
alert
See WARN
alien
See FOREIGN
alike
See SIMILAR
ALIVE
allow
See LET

allow to enter
See ADMIT¹
ALMOST
almost
See GOOD
aloft
See UP
ALONE
aloof
See UNFRIENDLY
alter
See CHANGE
alternative
See CHOICE
although
See BUT
altitude
See HEIGHT
AMAZE
amazing
See INCORRECT
amazing
See WONDERFUL
ambiguous
See UNCERTAIN
ambush
See ATTACK
ambush
See TRAP
amend
See CHANGE
amiable
See FRIENDLY
amid
See BETWEEN
among
See BETWEEN
AMOUNT
amount
See NUMBER²
amount to
See MAKE²
ample
See ENOUGH
ample
See LARGE

a amuse �∘ bear

amuse
　See ENTERTAIN
amusement
　See ENTERTAINMENT
amusing
　See FUNNY
ANCIENT
anecdote
　See STORY
ANGER
anger
　See INFURIATE
Angora
　See CAT
ANGRY
anguish
　See SUFFERING
ANIMAL
animated
　See ALIVE
announce
　See INTRODUCE
announce
　See REPORT
annoy
　See BOTHER
annoy
　See IRRITATE
another
　See MORE
ANSWER (verb)
ANSWER¹ (reply)
ANSWER² (result)
answer
　See KEY
ant
　See INSECT
anthem
　See MUSIC
anthem
　See SONG
anticipate
　See HOPE
anticipate
　See LOOK
antique
　See ANCIENT
antiquity
　See PAST
anxiety
　See WORRY
anxious
　See UPSET
anyway
　See LEAST
apathy
　See INDIFFERENCE
apex
　See POINT
apologize
　See MAKE
apparel
　See CLOTHES

apparent
　See VISIBLE
appealing
　See INTERESTING
appear
　See COME
appear
　See LOOK³
appearance
　See LOOK
appetizing
　See DELICIOUS
applause
　See PRAISE
apple
　See TREE
APPRECIATE
appreciative
　See GRATEFUL
apprehend
　See CATCH
apprehension
　See WORRY
apprehensive
　See NERVOUS
approach
　See COME
APPROPRIATE
appropriate
　See FITTING
appropriate
　See POINT
approval
　See PRAISE
approve
　See PRAISE
approximately
　See ABOUT
aptitude
　See TALENT
Arabian
　See HORSE
Arabic numeral
　See NUMBER
area
　See PLACE
ARGUE
ARGUMENT
aria
　See SONG
arid
　See DRY
arise
　See COME
armistice
　See PEACE
aroma
　See SMELL
around
　See ABOUT
ARRANGE
arrange
　See PREPARE

arrangement
　See ORDER
arrest
　See CATCH
arrive
　See COME
arrive
　See GET
arrive
　See SHOW
arrive at
　See REACH
arrogant
　See PROUD²
ART
arthropod
　See INSECT
article
　See THING
artificial
　See UNNATURAL
artisan
　See ART
artist
　See ART
as a rule
　See RULE
as good as
　See GOOD
ascend
　See CLIMB
ASK
ask
　See INVITE
asleep
　See NUMB
assault
　See ATTACK
assemble
　See BUILD
assemble
　See GATHER
assemble
　See GET
assemble
　See SET
assemble
　See TURN
assent
　See AGREE
assert
　See DECLARE
assert
　See INSIST
assignment
　See DUTY
ASSIST
assist
　See HELP
associate
　See FRIEND
astonish
　See AMAZE

astonishing
　See INCORRECT
astonishing
　See WONDERFUL
astound
　See AMAZE
at a loss
　See LOSS
at a loss for words
　See LOSS
at any rate
　See LEAST
at ease
　See EASE
at least
　See LEAST
at one time
　See ONCE
at the rear of
　See BACK
at times
　See TIME
ATOM
attach
　See FASTEN
ATTACK
attain
　See REACH
attempt
　See TRY
attend
　See GET
attend
　See GO
attend to
　See SEE
attention
　See CAUTION
attention
　See INTEREST
attentive
　See ALERT
attire
　See CLOTHES
attitude
　See STAND¹
attractive
　See HANDSOME
author
　See ART
authorize
　See LET
automobile
　See VEHICLE
automobile racing
　See GAME
available
　See HAND
average
　See MEAN
average
　See USUAL
avid
　See EAGER

AVOID
avoid
　See GET
award
　See PRIZE
awareness
　See KNOWLEDGE
away
　See ABSENT
AWFUL
AWKWARD

baby
　See CHILD
baby
　See PAMPER
babyish
　See CHILDISH
BACK
back
　See HELP
back
　See STAND
back and forth
　See BACK
back down
　See BACK
back out
　See BACK
back up
　See BACK
backgammon
　See GAME
backpack
　See PACK
BAD¹ (defective)
BAD² (evil)
BAD³ (harmful)
BAD⁴ (disobedient)
badminton
　See GAME
baffle
　See PUZZLE
baffled
　See LOSS
bag
　See PACK
baggy
　See LOOSE
ballad
　See SONG
ballot
　See VOTE
ban
　See FORBID
band
　See GROUP

band
　See MUSIC
bang
　See KNOCK
bang
　See NOISE
bang
　See RATTLE
banjo
　See MUSIC
banquet
　See MEAL
bar
　See FORBID
bar
　See SHUT
bare
　See EMPTY
barely
　See ONLY
barely
　See SCARCELY
bargain
　See AGREEMENT
barge
　See SHIP
BARREN
barter
　See TRADE
baseball
　See GAME
bashful
　See SHY
BASIC
basil
　See SPICE
basketball
　See GAME
bassoon
　See MUSIC
battle
　See FIGHT
battleship
　See SHIP
be careful
　See LOOK
be cordial
　See GET
be defeated
　See LOSE²
be friendly with
　See GET
be in stitches
　See LAUGH
be noticeable
　See STAND
be watchful
　See LOOK
beam
　See SMILE
BEAR
bear
　See CARRY

　Entries are in CAPITAL LETTERS. Synonyms are in lowercase letters.

bear with
　See BEAR
beast
　See ANIMAL
beast
　See VILLAIN
beat
　See DEFEAT
beat
　See HIT
beat
　See SHUT
BEAUTIFUL
bee
　See INSECT
beech
　See TREE
beetle
　See INSECT
before
　See EARLY
before long
　See RUN
before long
　See SOON
beforehand
　See EARLY
BEGIN
begin
　See BREAK
begin
　See SET
begin slowly
　See EASE
BEGINNING
BEHAVIOR
behind
　See BACK
behind one's back
　See BACK
behind the times
　See TIME
behold
　See SEE
BELIEF
believe
　See TRUST
bellow
　See YELL
belly laugh
　See LAUGH
beloved
　See POPULAR
below
　See DOWN
below
　See UNDER
BEND
beneath
　See DOWN
beneath
　See UNDER
bequeath
　See PASS

beside the point
　See POINT
bestow
　See GIVE
betray
　See LET
BETWEEN
bewilder
　See CONFUSE
bewildered
　See LOSS
bias
　See PREJUDICE
bicker
　See ARGUE
BIG
bill
　See LAW
billiards
　See GAME
binary system
　See NUMBER
bind
　See FASTEN
bingo
　See GAME
birch
　See TREE
bit
　See ATOM
bit
　See HORSE
bit
　See MEASUREMENT
bit
　See SPECK
biting
　See RAW
bitter
　See RAW
bitter
　See SOUR
black
　See COLOR
black out
　See PASS
black pepper
　See SPICE
BLAME
blank
　See EMPTY
blaze
　See BURN
bleachers
　See STAND[3]
bleak
　See RAW
blend
　See MIX
blizzard
　See STORM
block
　See PREVENT

bloodhound
　See DOG
bloom
　See FLOWER
blossom
　See FLOWER
blot
　See SPOT
blue
　See COLOR
blue
　See UNHAPPY
bluegrass
　See MUSIC
blues
　See MUSIC
blunder
　See MISTAKE
boarding school
　See SCHOOL
BOAST
boast
　See SHOW
BOAT
boating
　See GAME
bobcat
　See CAT
BODY
bold
　See BRAVE
bolt
　See LOCK
bong
　See NOISE
boom
　See NOISE
booth
　See STAND[2]
border
　See EDGE
boring
　See DULL
BOSS
BOTHER
bother
　See IRRITATE
bound
　See JUMP
boundary
　See EDGE
bow
　See FRONT
bow
　See KNOT
bowling
　See GAME
BOX
boyfriend
　See FRIEND
brace
　See GROUP
brace
　See HOLD

brag
　See BOAST
brag
　See SHOW
braid
　See KNOT
brain
　See MIND
brains
　See INTELLIGENCE
brass band
　See MUSIC
BRAVE
bravery
　See COURAGE
BREAK (*noun*)
BREAK (*verb*)
break
　See DISOBEY
break down
　See BREAK
break down
　See WAY
break in
　See INTERRUPT
break off
　See BREAK
break out
　See BREAK
break up
　See BREAK
break up
　See LAUGH
breakable
　See FRAGILE
breakfast
　See MEAL
bridle
　See HORSE
brief
　See SHORT
brief
　See TEMPORARY
brig
　See JAIL
BRIGHT
bright
　See SMART
brilliant
　See BRIGHT
BRING
bring about
　See BRING
bring on
　See BRING
bring out
　See BRING
bring together
　See ROUND
bring up
　See BRING
brisk
　See QUICK

brittle
　See FRAGILE
broad
　See WIDE
broke
　See POOR
bronco
　See HORSE
brown
　See COLOR
browse
　See SKIM
brunch
　See MEAL
brutal
　See FIERCE
brute
　See VILLAIN
bubble
　See LAUGH
bud
　See FLOWER
buddy
　See FRIEND
bug
　See FAULT
bug
　See INSECT
BUILD
build
　See BODY
build
　See SET
bulky
　See THICK
bulldog
　See DOG
bumble
　See MISS
bump
　See CRASH
bump
　See RUN
bumpy
　See JAGGED
bunch
　See GROUP
bundle
　See PACK
bungalow
　See CABIN
burble
　See NOISE
burglary
　See THEFT
BURN
burrow
　See CAVE
bus
　See VEHICLE
bush
　See PLANT[1]
bushel
　See MEASUREMENT

BUSINESS[1]
　(*occupation*)
BUSINESS[2] (*company*)
BUSY (*in use*)
BUSY (*occupied*)
BUT (*conjunction*)
BUT (*preposition*)
butterfly
　See INSECT
by the way
　See WAY
byte
　See MEASUREMENT

CABIN
cabin cruiser
　See BOAT
cackle
　See LAUGH
caddis fly
　See INSECT
calamity
　See DISASTER
calf
　See CHILD
calico
　See CAT
CALL
call
　See DROP
call on
　See VISIT
call together
　See ROUND
CALM
calm
　See EASE
calm
　See QUIET
camouflage
　See CONCEAL
canal boat
　See BOAT
cancel
　See UNDO
canine
　See DOG
canoe
　See BOAT
cantata
　See MUSIC
capability
　See ABILITY
capable
　See ABLE
capsize
　See UPSET

Entries are in CAPITAL LETTERS. Synonyms are in lowercase letters.

Index 267

captivating ↔ come at

captivating
See INTERESTING
capture
See CATCH
capture
See TAKE¹
capture the flag
See GAME
car
See VEHICLE
carat
See MEASUREMENT
cardinal
See KEY
cardinal number
See NUMBER
cards
See GAME
care
See CAUTION
care
See WORRY
care for
See LIKE
CAREFUL
CARELESS
caress
See PET
caring
See KIND
carol
See SONG
carriage horse
See HORSE
CARRY
carry on
See CARRY
carry out
See CARRY
carry out
See DO
carry out
See OBEY
carton
See BOX
carve
See CUT
case
See BOX
case
See EXAMPLE
cash
See MONEY
cast
See THROW
castanets
See MUSIC
castle
See HOUSE
casual
See INFORMAL
CAT
CAT scan
See X-RAY

cat's cradle
See GAME
catalog
See LIST
catastrophe
See DISASTER
CATCH
catch
See COME
catch on
See CATCH
catch up
See CATCH
category
See TYPE
cause
See REASON
cause
See BRING
CAUTION
caution
See WARN
cautious
See CAREFUL
CAVE
cavern
See CAVE
cavity
See HOLE
cease
See LEAVE
cease
See STOP
cease to work
See BREAK
cedar
See TREE
CELEBRATE
celebrated
See FAMOUS
celebration
See CEREMONY
celebration
See PARTY
cello
See MUSIC
cent
See MONEY
centavo
See MONEY
center
See MIDDLE
centime
See MONEY
centimeter
See MEASUREMENT
central
See MAIN
century
See MEASUREMENT
CEREMONY
certain
See PARTICULAR

certain
See SURE
challenge
See DARE
chamber orchestra
See MUSIC
CHAMPION
chance
See LUCK
chance
See POSSIBILITY
CHANGE
chant
See SONG
chaos
See DISORDER
chaos
See JUMBLE
character
See PERSONALITY
characteristic
See QUALITY
characteristic
See UNIQUE
charades
See GAME
charge
See ATTACK
charger
See HORSE
charity
See KINDNESS
charter
See RENT
chase
See GO
chase
See HUNT
chat
See TALK
chateau
See HOUSE
chatter
See TALK
CHEAP¹ (inexpensive)
CHEAP² (shabby)
cheat
See DECEIVE
check
See END
check
See ENSURE
check
See INSPECT
check
See PREVENT
checkers
See GAME
cheer
See YELL
cheerful
See HAPPY
cheetah
See CAT

cherish
See APPRECIATE
cherish
See LOVE
chess
See GAME
chestnut
See TREE
chick
See CHILD
chief
See KEY
chiefly
See MOSTLY
Chihuahua
See DOG
CHILD
childhood
See YOUTH
CHILDISH
childlike
See CHILDISH
chili powder
See SPICE
chilly
See COLD
chives
See SPICE
CHOICE
CHOOSE
choose
See PICK
chop
See CUT
chorale
See MUSIC
chore
See JOB
chortle
See LAUGH
chow
See MEAL
chrysanthemum
See FLOWER
chuckle
See LAUGH
chug
See NOISE
cicada
See INSECT
cinch
See HORSE
cinnamon
See SPICE
circular
See ROUND
circumstance
See STATE
circus horse
See HORSE
cite
See QUOTE
CITY

civil
See POLITE
claim
See DECLARE
claim
See INSIST
clammy
See DAMP
clamor
See NOISE
clarify
See EXPLAIN
clarinet
See MUSIC
clasp
See HOLD
class
See TYPE
classify
See ARRANGE
clatter
See RATTLE
CLEAN (adjective)
CLEAN (verb)
clean
See WASH
cleanse
See CLEAN
cleanse
See WASH
clear
See OBVIOUS
clear
See PLAIN
clear
See VISIBLE
clever
See SMART
cleverness
See INTELLIGENCE
CLIMB
clip
See CUT
cloak
See CONCEAL
CLOSE
close
See END
close
See NEAR
close
See SHUT
close
See SIMILAR
close
See ZIP
closing
See LAST
CLOTHES
clothing
See CLOTHES
clown around
See CUT

cluck
See NOISE
clue
See KEY
clumsy
See AWKWARD
clutch
See HOLD
clutter
See MESS
cluttered
See MESSY
coarse
See ROUGH
coast
See SLIDE
coax
See PERSUADE
cocker spaniel
See DOG
cockroach
See INSECT
code
See LAW
COLD
collect
See GATHER
collected
See CALM
college
See SCHOOL
collide
See CRASH
collie
See DOG
colony
See COUNTRY
colony
See GROUP
COLOR
colossal
See GIANT
colt
See CHILD
colt
See HORSE
combat
See FIGHT
combine
See JOIN
COME
come
See SHOW
come
See TURN
come across
See COME
come across
See FIND
come across
See RUN
come at
See COME

268 Index

Entries are in CAPITAL LETTERS. Synonyms are in lowercase letters.

Entries are in CAPITAL LETTERS. Synonyms are in lowercase letters.

Index   269

CRAZY

crazy
  See DULL
create
  See MAKE[1]
creativity
  See IMAGINATION
creator
  See ART
creature
  See ANIMAL
creed
  See RELIGION
creep
  See CRAWL
crest
  See TOP
crew
  See TEAM
cricket
  See INSECT
CRIME
critical
  See URGENT
criticize
  See BLAME
crop
  See CUT
crow
  See LAUGH
CROWD
crowd
  See GROUP
crowd
  See PACK
crown
  See TOP
crucial
  See IMPORTANT
CRUEL
cruiser
  See SHIP
crumb
  See SPECK
crunch
  See NOISE
CRY
cry
  See CALL
CT scan
  See X-RAY
cub
  See CHILD
cube root
  See NUMBER
cunning
  See SLY
cup
  See MEASUREMENT
cure
  See HEAL
curiosity
  See INTEREST

CURIOUS

curious
  See ODD
currency
  See MONEY
current
  See MODERN
curry comb
  See HORSE
curry powder
  See SPICE
curve
  See BEND
custom
  See HABIT
customarily
  See USUALLY
customary
  See USUAL
CUT
cut
  See SORE
cut back
  See CUT
cut down
  See CUT
cut off
  See CUT
cut off
  See INTERRUPT
cut out
  See CUT
cut up
  See CUT
cute
  See PRETTY
cutting
  See SHARP[1]
cyclone
  See STORM
cymbals
  See MUSIC
cypress
  See TREE

D

dachshund
  See DOG
daffodil
  See FLOWER
dainty
  See DELICATE
daisy
  See FLOWER
damage
  See INJURE
damage
  See LOSS

damaging
  See BAD[3]
DAMP
dancer
  See ART
DANGER
DANGEROUS
dangle
  See SWING
DARE
DARING
DARK
dart
  See ZOOM
dash
  See RUN
DATA
dated
  See OLD
dated
  See TIME
day
  See MEASUREMENT
DEAD
DEADLY
deafening
  See LOUD
deal
  See AGREEMENT
debate
  See ARGUMENT
debate
  See DISCUSS
decade
  See MEASUREMENT
deceased
  See DEAD
deceitful
  See DISHONEST
DECEIVE
deceive
  See LIE[1]
deception
  See LIE (noun)
deception
  See TRICK
decibel
  See MEASUREMENT
DECIDE
decide
  See PICK
decide against
  See RULE
decimal system
  See NUMBER
DECLARE
declare
  See SAY
declare
  See SET
decline
  See FALL

decline
  See REFUSE
DECORATE
DECREASE
decrease
  See CUT
decrease
  See DWINDLE
decree
  See RULE
deduct
  See TAKE[3]
deed
  See ACT
DEFEAT
defeat
  See LOSS
defeat
  See SHUT
defeat
  See WIN
defect
  See FAULT
defective
  See BAD[1]
defective
  See IMPERFECT
DEFEND
deficient
  See INCOMPLETE
define
  See EXPLAIN
definite
  See RIGHT
defy
  See DARE
degree
  See MEASUREMENT
dejected
  See SAD
DELAY
delay
  See HESITATION
delay
  See PAUSE
delayed
  See LATE
delete
  See ERASE
DELICATE
DELICIOUS
DELIGHT
delight
  See ENTERTAIN
delight
  See PLEASE
delight
  See THRILL
delight in
  See LIKE
deliver
  See BRING
deliver
  See DROP

deliver
  See HAND
deliver
  See SAVE
deluge
  See STORM
demand
  See INSIST
demanding
  See HARD
demeanor
  See LOOK
democracy
  See COUNTRY
demolish
  See DESTROY
demolish
  See RUIN
denominator
  See NUMBER
denounce
  See DISAPPROVE
DENSE
dense
  See THICK
deny
  See CONTRADICT
deny
  See TURN
depart
  See LEAVE
depend
  See TRUST
dependable
  See RESPONSIBLE
depict
  See DESCRIBE
deplete
  See RUN
deplete
  See USE[2]
deposit
  See PUT
depressed
  See SAD
derive
  See DESCEND
DESCEND (originate)
descend
  See DIVE
descend
  See DROP
DESCRIBE
describe
  See EXPLAIN
DESERVE
design
  See FORM
design
  See INVENT
designer
  See ART
DESIRE

desire
  See GREED
desire
  See WANT
desolate
  See BARREN
desolate
  See UNHAPPY
despise
  See HATE
destiny
  See FATE
destitute
  See POOR
DESTROY
destroy
  See RUIN
destroyer
  See SHIP
destructive
  See VIOLENT
detach
  See CUT
detect
  See DISCOVER
deter
  See DISCOURAGE
determination
  See WILL
determine
  See CHOOSE
determine
  See DECIDE
DETERMINED
determined
  See STUBBORN
detest
  See HATE
detrimental
  See UNFAVORABLE
develop
  See GROW
develop
  See HAPPEN
devious
  See DISHONEST
devise
  See INVENT
devoted
  See FAITHFUL
devotion
  See LOVE
devour
  See EAT
devout
  See RELIGIOUS
dice
  See CUT
dictatorship
  See COUNTRY
DIE
differ
  See DISAGREE

Entries are in CAPITAL LETTERS. Synonyms are in lowercase letters.

Entries are in CAPITAL LETTERS. Synonyms are in lowercase letters.

embarrassment
See SHAME
EMOTION
EMPHASIZE
empire
See COUNTRY
employ
See HIRE
employ
See TAKE
employ
See USE[1]
employed
See BUSY
employer
See BOSS
employment
See WORK[2]
empress
See QUEEN
EMPTY
encounter
See MEET[1]
encounter
See RUN
ENCOURAGE
encourage
See SUPPORT
END (noun)
END (verb)
end
See BREAK
end
See COME
end
See DO
end
See PURPOSE
end
See RESULT
end
See SEE
end
See SHUT
endeavor
See TRY
ending
See END
endless
See ETERNAL
endow
See GIVE
endure
See BEAR
endure
See CONTINUE
endure
See GET
endure
See PASS
endure
See TAKE[2]
ENEMY

energetic
See LIVELY
ENERGY
engage
See HIRE
engage
See TAKE
engaged
See BUSY
enjoy
See LIKE
enjoyment
See PLEASURE
enlarge
See EXPAND
enormous
See BIG
ENOUGH
enrage
See INFURIATE
enraged
See ANGRY
enroll
See JOIN
enroll
See SIGN
ensemble
See MUSIC
ENSURE
entangle
See MIX
ENTER
enter
See GET
enter
See JOIN
enter
See KEY
ENTERTAIN
entertain
See PLAY
ENTERTAINMENT
entertainment
See PLAY
ENTHUSIASM
enthusiastic
See EAGER
entire
See COMPLETE
entrance
See DOOR
entree
See MEAL
entry
See DOOR
envious
See JEALOUS
environment
See NATURE
ENVY
EQUAL
equal
See COME

equal
See MAKE[2]
equivalent
See EQUAL
era
See PERIOD
ERASE
erect
See BUILD
erect
See SET
errand
See JOB
erroneous
See WRONG
error
See MISTAKE
erupt
See BREAK
ESCAPE
escape
See BREAK
escape
See RUN
escort
See GO
escort
See LEAD
escort
See TAKE
essential
See NECESSARY
estate
See HOUSE
esteem
See RESPECT
estimate
See GUESS
ETERNAL
euro
See MONEY
evade
See AVOID
evade
See GET
evaluate
See CONSIDER
even
See EQUAL
even
See ROUND
even
See SMOOTH
even number
See NUMBER
EVENT
everlasting
See ETERNAL
everyday
See NORMAL
evidence
See INFORMATION
evidence
See PROOF

evident
See OBVIOUS
evil
See BAD[2]
exact
See CAREFUL
exact
See PERFECT
exaggerate
See BOAST
exaggerate
See DO
examination
See TEST
examine
See GO
examine
See INSPECT
examine
See LOOK
examine
See STUDY
EXAMPLE
excellent
See GOOD
excellent
See GREAT
except
See BUT
exceptional
See UNUSUAL
EXCESSIVE
exchange
See TRADE
excite
See THRILL
exclaim
See CALL
exclude
See FORBID
exclude
See RULE
exclude
See SHUT
excursion
See TRIP
excuse
See FORGIVE
excuse
See LET
execute
See DO
exertion
See ACTION
exhaust
See RUN
exhaust
See USE[2]
exhausted
See TIRED
exhibit
See SHOW
existing
See REAL

exit
See DOOR
exit
See LEAVE
exotic
See FOREIGN
exotic
See UNFAMILIAR
EXPAND
expect
See HOPE
expect
See INTEND
expect
See LOOK
expedition
See JOURNEY
expedition
See TRIP
EXPENSIVE
EXPERT
expire
See DIE
expired
See DEAD
EXPLAIN
explanation
See REASON
explore
See LOOK[2]
exponent
See NUMBER
expose
See REVEAL
express
See SAY
expression
See SAYING
exquisite
See BEAUTIFUL
EXTEND
extend
See LENGTHEN
extensive
See LARGE
extensive
See ROOMY
exterior
See OUTSIDE
external
See OUTSIDE
extra
See MORE
extract
See REMOVE
extraordinary
See UNUSUAL
extravagant
See EXCESSIVE
extremely
See VERY
eyewitness
See WITNESS

fable
See LEGEND
facing
See OPPOSITE
fact
See INFORMATION
factory
See PLANT[2]
facts
See DATA
factual
See TRUE
fad
See FASHION
fade
See VANISH
fail
See BREAK
fail
See FALL
fail
See LET
faint
See DIM
faint
See PASS
faint
See WEAK
FAIR
faith
See RELIGION
faith
See TRUST
FAITHFUL
FAKE
fake
See PRETEND
FALL
fall
See TRIP
fall
See WAY
fall back
See FALL
fall back on
See FALL
fall behind
See FALL
fall short
See FALL
fall through
See FALL
false
See FAKE
false
See INCORRECT
falsehood
See LIE (noun)

Entries are in CAPITAL LETTERS. Synonyms are in lowercase letters.

falter
  See HESITATE
familiar
  See COMMON
FAMILY
famished
  See HUNGRY
FAMOUS
fanatic
  See CRAZY
fancy
  See IMAGINATION
fanfare
  See MUSIC
fantastic
  See WONDERFUL
fantasy
  See IMAGINATION
FAR
faraway
  See FAR
fare
  See MEAL
fascinating
  See INTERESTING
FASHION
fashion
  See MAKE[1]
fashion
  See WAY
FAST
fast food
  See TAKE
FASTEN
fasten
  See CLOSE
fasten
  See ZIP
fat
  See THICK
fatal
  See DEADLY
FATE
fathom
  See MEASUREMENT
fathom
  See UNDERSTAND
FAULT
fault
  See BLAME
faultless
  See RIGHT
faulty
  See IMPERFECT
favor
  See TAKE
fawn
  See CHILD
FEAR
fearful
  See AFRAID
fearless
  See DARING

feast
  See EAT
feast
  See MEAL
feat
  See ACT
feature
  See EMPHASIZE
feature
  See QUALITY
federation
  See COUNTRY
feeble
  See WEAK
feed
  See EAT
feeling
  See EMOTION
feign
  See PRETEND
fellow
  See MAN
female
  See WOMAN
ferocious
  See FIERCE
ferry
  See SHIP
fertile
  See PRODUCTIVE
festivity
  See PARTY
feud
  See QUARREL
FEW
fewest
  See LEAST
fib
  See LIE[1]
fidgety
  See NERVOUS
field hockey
  See GAME
FIERCE
fiery
  See HOT
fife
  See MUSIC
FIGHT
fight
  See QUARREL
figure
  See BODY
figure
  See NUMBER[1]
figure
  See SHAPE
figures
  See DATA
file
  See BACK
FILL
filly

  See HORSE
filter
  See PASS
filthy
  See DIRTY
final
  See LAST[1]
finale
  See END
finally
  See RUN
finally
  See YET
FIND
find
  See COME
find out
  See LEARN
fine
  See GOOD
FINISH
finish
  See BREAK
finish
  See CARRY
finish
  See CATCH
finish
  See END
finish
  See GET
finish
  See ROUND
finish
  See SEE
finish
  See USE[2]
fir
  See TREE
firefly
  See INSECT
FIRM
firm
  See BUSINESS[2]
firm
  See DETERMINED
firm
  See SET
firm
  See TIGHT
first
  See ORIGINAL
fishing
  See GAME
fishing boat
  See BOAT
fit
  See APPROPRIATE
FITTING
FIX
fix
  See PREPARE
fix
  See TROUBLE

fixed
  See TIGHT
flabbergasted
  See LOSS
FLAT
flatboat
  See BOAT
flavor
  See ZEST
flavoring
  See SPICE
flaw
  See FAULT
flawed
  See IMPERFECT
flawless
  See PERFECT
flea
  See INSECT
fleck
  See SPECK
flee
  See BREAK
flee
  See ESCAPE
flee
  See RUN
fleeing
  See RUN
fleet
  See FAST
fleeting
  See TEMPORARY
flimsy
  See DELICATE
fling
  See THROW
flip
  See SKIM
flock
  See GROUP
flood
  See RUN
flourish
  See MAKE
FLOW
FLOWER
flower
  See PLANT[1]
fluffy
  See SOFT
flush
  See FLOW
fluster
  See EMBARRASS
flute
  See MUSIC
FLY
foal
  See HORSE
foe
  See ENEMY
FOG
folk

  See PEOPLE
folk group
  See MUSIC
folk music
  See MUSIC
folk song
  See SONG
folklore
  See LEGEND
folktale
  See LEGEND
FOLLOW[1] *(pursue)*
FOLLOW[2] *(obey)*
follow
  See ACT
follow
  See CARRY
follow
  See GO
follow
  See OBEY
follow
  See UNDERSTAND
following
  See NEXT
fondness
  See LOVE
fool
  See DECEIVE
fool around
  See CUT
foolish
  See DULL
foot
  See MEASUREMENT
football
  See GAME
footstep
  See STEP
for good
  See GOOD
FORBID
FORCE
forceful
  See POWERFUL
forecast
  See PREDICT
FOREIGN
foreign
  See UNFAMILIAR
foresee
  See PREDICT
forest
  See TREE
foretell
  See PREDICT
forever
  See GOOD
forfeit
  See LOSE[2]
FORGET
forget
  See LEAVE

FORGIVE
FORM
former
  See PAST
formerly
  See ONCE
fortunate
  See LUCKY
fortune
  See FATE
fortune
  See LUCK
foul
  See DIRTY
fox terrier
  See DOG
fraction
  See NUMBER
FRAGILE
fragrance
  See SMELL
frail
  See DELICATE
franc
  See MONEY
frayed
  See RAGGED
freakish
  See UNUSUAL
FREE
free
  See LET
free
  See LOOSE
free time
  See LEISURE
FREEDOM
freezing
  See COLD
freighter
  See SHIP
French horn
  See MUSIC
frequent
  See COMMON
frequently
  See OFTEN
FRESH
fresh
  See CLEAN
FRIEND
FRIENDLY
frigate
  See SHIP
fright
  See FEAR
frighten
  See SCARE
frightened
  See AFRAID
FRIGHTENING
frightening
  See AWFUL

Entries are in CAPITAL LETTERS. Synonyms are in lowercase letters.

Index 273

frigid ↔ ground

frigid
See COLD

fringe
See EDGE

from side to side
See BACK

FRONT

frosty
See COLD

FROWN

fugue
See MUSIC

fulfill
See PASS

full
See COMPLETE

full-grown
See ADULT

full-grown
See MATURE

fumble
See MISS

fun
See PLEASURE

function
See ACT

function
See OPERATE

fundamental
See BASIC

fundamental
See KEY

funds
See MONEY

FUNNY

funny
See STRANGE

furious
See ANGRY

furlong
See MEASUREMENT

furnish
See GIVE

fury
See RAGE

gadget
See TOOL

gag
See JOKE

gaggle
See GROUP

gain
See EARN

gain entry
See GET

gait
See WALK

gale
See STORM

gallant
See DARING

galley
See SHIP

gallon
See MEASUREMENT

GAME

gang
See GROUP

garbage
See TRASH

garlic
See SPICE

garment
See CLOTHES

GASP

gateway
See DOOR

GATHER

gather
See GET

gather
See PICK

gather
See ROUND

gather
See TURN

gathering
See PARTY

gathering
See ROUND

gaze
See LOOK¹

general
See UNIVERSAL

generally
See USUALLY

generate
See TURN

genius
See EXPERT

genius
See TALENT

GENTLE

gentleman
See MAN

genuine
See PURE

genuine
See REAL

geranium
See FLOWER

German shepherd
See DOG

gesture
See SIGN

gesture
See WAVE

GET

get
See UNDERSTAND

get along
See GET

get away
See ESCAPE

get away with
See GET

get back
See GET

get by
See MAKE

get going
See START

get in
See GET

get in touch with
See COMMUNICATE

get into
See WEAR

get out
See GET

get out of bed
See GET

get ready
See PREPARE

get there
See SHOW

get through
See GET

get to
See REACH

get to one's feet
See GET

get together
See GET

get up
See GET

get up
See STAND (verb)

GIANT

GIFT

gift
See ABILITY

gift
See TALENT

gigantic
See BIG

giggle
See LAUGH

gin rummy
See GAME

ginseng
See SPICE

girlfriend
See FRIEND

GIVE

give
See DROP

give
See HAND

give access
See ADMIT¹

give away
See GIVE

give back
See GIVE

give back
See RETURN²

give in
See GIVE

give out
See GIVE

give up
See GIVE

give up
See PASS

give up
See QUIT

give way
See WAY

glad
See HAPPY

glance
See PEEK

glare
See FROWN

gleaming
See BRIGHT

glee
See DELIGHT

glide
See FLY

glide
See SLIDE

glimpse
See PEEK

glimpse
See VIEW

glisten
See SHINE

glitter
See SHINE

gloat
See BOAST

gloomy
See DARK

gloomy
See UNHAPPY

glorious
See MAGNIFICENT

glowing
See BRIGHT

glug
See NOISE

gnat
See INSECT

GO

go
See LEAVE

go after
See GO

go along
See GO

go around
See GO

go away
See VANISH

go back
See GO

go back
See RETURN¹

go fish
See GAME

go in
See ENTER

go in
See GO

go into
See ENTER

go into
See GO

go off
See SET

go on
See CONTINUE

go on
See GO

go on foot
See WALK

go out
See GO

go over
See STUDY

go through
See GO

go to see
See VISIT

goal
See PURPOSE

going
See WAY

golf
See GAME

gondola
See BOAT

gone
See ABSENT

gong
See MUSIC

GOOD

good
See DELICIOUS

good will
See KINDNESS

good-looking
See HANDSOME

gorgeous
See BEAUTIFUL

gossip
See RUMOR

GOVERN

grab
See TAKE¹

GRACEFUL

GRACIOUS

gradual
See SLOW

gradually
See STEP

grain
See ATOM

gram
See MEASUREMENT

grammar school
See SCHOOL

grand
See MAGNIFICENT

grandstand
See STAND³

granny
See KNOT

grant
See GIVE

grasp
See CATCH

grasp
See KNOW

grasp
See SEIZE

grasshopper
See INSECT

GRATEFUL

gratify
See PLEASE

grave
See SERIOUS

gray
See COLOR

GREAT

Great Dane
See DOG

GREATEST

greatest
See MOST

greatly
See VERY

GREED

greed
See ENVY

greedy
See SELFISH

green
See COLOR

green
See RAW

greyhound
See DOG

grief
See SADNESS

grim
See SERIOUS

grimace
See FROWN

grimy
See DIRTY

grin
See SMILE

grip
See HOLD

gripe
See COMPLAIN

gripping
See INTERESTING

ground
See DIRT

Entries are in CAPITAL LETTERS. Synonyms are in lowercase letters.

grounds
  See LAND
GROUP
GROW
grown-up
  See ADULT
grown-up
  See MATURE
grumble
  See COMPLAIN
guard
  See DEFEND
guarded
  See SAFE
GUESS
guffaw
  See LAUGH
GUIDE
guide
  See KEY
guilder
  See MONEY
guitar
  See MUSIC
gulp
  See DRINK
gummy
  See STICKY
gunboat
  See BOAT
guy
  See MAN
gymnastics
  See GAME

HABIT
habitual
  See USUAL
habitually
  See USUALLY
hacienda
  See HOUSE
hack
  See HORSE
hail
  See CALL
hailstorm
  See STORM
halt
  See SHUT
halt
  See STOP
halter
  See HORSE
hammer
  See HIT
HAND

hand back
  See RETURN[2]
hand down
  See HAND
hand down
  See PASS
hand in
  See HAND
hand in
  See TURN
hand out
  See GIVE
hand out
  See HAND
hand out
  See PASS
hand over
  See HAND
handball
  See GAME
handicap
  See DISADVANTAGE
HANDSOME
handy
  See USEFUL
hang
  See SWING
hangman
  See GAME
hangman
  See KNOT
HAPPEN
happen
  See GO
happen suddenly
  See BREAK
happiness
  See DELIGHT
HAPPY
harass
  See PICK
HARD
hard
  See FIRM
hardly
  See SCARCELY
hardy
  See TOUGH
harm
  See INJURE
harmful
  See BAD[3]
harmonica
  See MUSIC
harmony
  See PEACE
harmony
  See SONG
harness
  See HOLD
harness
  See HORSE
harp

See MUSIC
hasten
  See HURRY
HATE
hateful
  See VICIOUS
haughty
  See PROUD[2]
haul
  See PULL
have
  See CONTAIN
have
  See OWN
hazard
  See DANGER
hazardous
  See DANGEROUS
haze
  See FOG
hazy
  See DIM
head
  See BOSS
head
  See FRONT
head off
  See PREVENT
headstrong
  See STUBBORN
HEAL
hearsay
  See RUMOR
heart
  See MIDDLE
heartless
  See CRUEL
HEAVY
heed
  See ACT
heed
  See FOLLOW[2]
heedless
  See RECKLESS
HEIGHT
HELP
help
  See ASSIST
helpful
  See USEFUL
helpless
  See WEAK
hemlock
  See TREE
herb
  See SPICE
herd
  See GROUP
heroic
  See BRAVE
heroism
  See COURAGE
hertz

See MEASUREMENT
HESITANT
HESITATE
HESITATION
hidden
  See MYSTERIOUS
HIDE
hide-and-seek
  See GAME
hideous
  See UGLY
high
  See TALL
high
  See UP
high school
  See SCHOOL
high-priced
  See EXPENSIVE
highest
  See GREATEST
highlight
  See EMPHASIZE
hike
  See WALK
hilarious
  See FUNNY
hinder
  See HOLD
hinder
  See PREVENT
hint
  See SUGGEST
HIRE
hire
  See RENT
history
  See PAST
HIT
hit
  See RUN
hitch
  See KNOT
hoax
  See TRICK
HOBBY
hoist
  See RAISE
HOLD
hold
  See CONTAIN
hold
  See KEEP
hold back
  See HOLD
hold out
  See HOLD
hold up
  See HOLD
HOLE
hollow
  See HOLE
home

See HOUSE
homely
  See UGLY
homesick
  See LONELY
HONEST
honk
  See NOISE
honor
  See CELEBRATE
honor
  See PRIZE
honorable
  See HONEST
hoot
  See NOISE
hop
  See JUMP
HOPE
hope
  See WISH
hopeless
  See USELESS
hopscotch
  See GAME
horde
  See CROWD
horizontal
  See FLAT
hornet
  See INSECT
horrible
  See AWFUL
HORSE
horsepower
  See MEASUREMENT
horseradish
  See SPICE
HOT
hound
  See DOG
hour
  See MEASUREMENT
HOUSE
houseboat
  See BOAT
housefly
  See INSECT
household
  See FAMILY
however
  See BUT
howl
  See CRY
howl
  See LAUGH
hue
  See COLOR
huge
  See BIG
human
  See PERSON
human being

See PERSON
humane
  See KIND
HUMANITY
humankind
  See HUMANITY
humans
  See PEOPLE
HUMBLE
humiliate
  See EMBARRASS
humiliation
  See SHAME
humor
  See PAMPER
humorous
  See FUNNY
hunger
  See GREED
HUNGRY
HUNT
hurricane
  See STORM
hurried
  See QUICK
HURRY
hurrying
  See RUN
HURT
hurt
  See ACHE
hurt
  See SORE
hurtful
  See BAD[3]
hush
  See SILENCE
husky
  See DOG
hustle
  See HURRY
HUT
hydrofoil
  See BOAT
hymn
  See MUSIC
hymn
  See SONG
hypothesis
  See THEORY

ice hockey
  See GAME
ice pack
  See PACK
ice skating
  See GAME

Entries are in CAPITAL LETTERS. Synonyms are in lowercase letters.

Index 275

icebreaker
  See SHIP
icy
  See COLD
IDEA
idea
  See THEORY
IDEAL
ideal
  See PERFECT
identical
  See SAME
identify
  See DISCOVER
identity
  See PERSONALITY
idle
  See LAZY
ignite
  See BURN
ignorant
  See STUPID
ignore
  See DISOBEY
ignore
  See LEAVE
ill
  See SICK
ill
  See UNHEALTHY
illness
  See SICKNESS
illustrator
  See ART
image
  See PICTURE
imaginary number
  See NUMBER
IMAGINATION
imaginative
  See ORIGINAL
imagine
  See GUESS
imagine
  See MAKE
IMITATE
imitation
  See FAKE
immature
  See CHILDISH
immature
  See YOUNG
IMMEDIATE
immediate
  See NEAR
immense
  See BIG
immensely
  See VERY
impartial
  See FAIR
IMPERFECT
imperfection
  See FAULT

impetuous
  See RECKLESS
implement
  See TOOL
IMPOLITE
impolite
  See RUDE
importance
  See WORTH
IMPORTANT
imported
  See FOREIGN
impossible
  See DOUBTFUL
impress
  See AMAZE
impudent
  See BAD⁴
impurity
  See POLLUTION
in advance
  See EARLY
in any case
  See LEAST
in back of
  See BACK
in between
  See BETWEEN
in motion
  See WAY
in person
  See PERSON
in public
  See PUBLIC
in rhythm
  See TIME
in the end
  See RUN
in the long run
  See RUN
in the nick of time
  See TIME
in the short run
  See RUN
in time
  See TIME
in use
  See BUSY
inaccurate
  See INCORRECT
inactive
  See LAZY
inadequate
  See BAD¹
inattention
  See INDIFFERENCE
inborn
  See NATURAL
incense
  See INFURIATE
incessant
  See CONTINUAL
inch
  See CRAWL

inch
  See MEASUREMENT
inch by inch
  See STEP
incident
  See EVENT
incidentally
  See WAY
inclination
  See WILL
incline
  See TIP
include
  See CONTAIN
INCOMPLETE
inconceivable
  See UNBELIEVABLE
inconsiderate
  See IMPOLITE
INCORRECT
increase
  See EXPAND
increase
  See STEP
incredible
  See UNBELIEVABLE
incredible
  See WONDERFUL
indefinite
  See UNCERTAIN
independence
  See FREEDOM
independent
  See FREE
index
  See LIST
indicate
  See POINT
INDIFFERENCE
indispensable
  See NECESSARY
individual
  See PERSON
individual
  See PERSONAL
individual
  See UNIQUE
indulge
  See PAMPER
industry
  See BUSINESS¹
inexpensive
  See CHEAP¹
infantile
  See CHILDISH
inferior
  See BAD¹
infertile
  See BARREN
infinity
  See NUMBER
inflexible
  See STIFF

influence
  See PERSUADE
influential
  See POWERFUL
inform
  See TELL
INFORMAL
INFORMATION
infrequent
  See RARE
infrequently
  See RARELY
INFURIATE
inhabit
  See LIVE
initial
  See ORIGINAL
initiate
  See BEGIN
INJURE
injury
  See SORE
innards
  See INSIDE
inner
  See INSIDE
input
  See ENTER
input
  See KEY
inquire
  See ASK
inquisitive
  See CURIOUS
insane
  See CRAZY
INSECT
INSIDE (adjective)
INSIDE (noun)
inside
  See MIDDLE
insides
  See INSIDE
insignificant
  See UNIMPORTANT
INSIST
INSPECT
inspire
  See ENCOURAGE
inspiring
  See INTERESTING
instance
  See EXAMPLE
instant
  See IMMEDIATE
instinctive
  See NATURAL
instruct
  See ORDER
instruct
  See TEACH
INSULT (noun)
INSULT (verb)

insulting
  See SARCASTIC
integer
  See NUMBER
intellect
  See INTELLIGENCE
intellect
  See MIND
INTELLIGENCE
intelligence
  See MIND
intelligent
  See SMART
INTEND
intense
  See VIOLENT
intent
  See DETERMINED
intention
  See PLAN
interchangeable
  See EQUAL
INTEREST
interested
  See CURIOUS
INTERESTING
interfere
  See INTERRUPT
interior
  See INSIDE
interlude
  See BREAK
intermission
  See BREAK
internal
  See INSIDE
interpret
  See EXPLAIN
interrogate
  See ASK
INTERRUPT
interrupt
  See DISRUPT
interrupt
  See PAUSE
interruption
  See PAUSE
intersect
  See MEET
intersection
  See MEET
interval
  See TIME
intimate
  See PERSONAL
intolerance
  See PREJUDICE
intricate
  See COMPLICATED
INTRODUCE
introductory
  See BASIC
invade
  See ATTACK

INVENT
investigate
  See LOOK
investigate
  See STUDY
INVITE
involve
  See MIX
irate
  See ANGRY
iris
  See FLOWER
Irish setter
  See DOG
irregular
  See JAGGED
irrelevant
  See UNIMPORTANT
IRRITATE
irritate
  See BOTHER
irritation
  See ANGER
isolated
  See ALONE
issue
  See GIVE
issue
  See PASS
issue
  See QUESTION
itch
  See WISH
item
  See THING

jacks
  See GAME
JAGGED
jaguar
  See CAT
JAIL
jazz
  See MUSIC
jazz band
  See MUSIC
JEALOUS
jealousy
  See ENVY
JERK
jest
  See JOKE
jiggle
  See SHAKE
jingle
  See RATTLE
JOB

Entries are in CAPITAL LETTERS. Synonyms are in lowercase letters.

LOST
LOUD
LOVE (noun)
LOVE (verb)
lovely
  See BEAUTIFUL
lovely
  See GRACEFUL
low
  See SHORT
loyal
  See FAITHFUL
LUCK
LUCKY
lug
  See CARRY
lukewarm
  See WARM
lull
  See BREAK
lullaby
  See SONG
lunch
  See MEAL
lurch
  See JERK
lurch
  See STAGGER
lurk
  See SNEAK
lush
  See PRODUCTIVE
luxuriant
  See PRODUCTIVE
LUXURIOUS
lynx
  See CAT
lyrics
  See SONG

machine
  See TOOL
mad
  See ANGRY
mad
  See CRAZY
madden
  See INFURIATE
magistrate
  See JUDGE
MAGNIFICENT
maid
  See WOMAN
mail
  See SEND
mailboat
  See BOAT

MAIN
mainly
  See MOSTLY
maintain
  See CONSERVE
maintain
  See SUPPORT
Majesty
  See KING
major
  See KEY
majority
  See MOST
MAKE¹ (create)
MAKE² (total)
make
  See EARN
make
  See FORCE
make
  See TURN
make believe
  See MAKE
make do
  See DO
make fun of
  See TEASE
make it
  See MAKE
make off with
  See MAKE
make sure
  See ENSURE
make up
  See MAKE
malady
  See SICKNESS
male
  See MAN
malicious
  See CRUEL
malicious
  See MEAN
malicious
  See VICIOUS
MAN
man
  See HUMANITY
man-hour
  See MEASUREMENT
manage
  See CONTROL
manage
  See GET
manage
  See LEAD
manager
  See BOSS
mankind
  See HUMANITY
manner
  See BEHAVIOR
manner
  See WAY

manor
  See HOUSE
mansion
  See HOUSE
mantis
  See INSECT
Manx
  See CAT
MANY
maple
  See TREE
march
  See MUSIC
march
  See WALK
marching band
  See MUSIC
mare
  See HORSE
marigold
  See FLOWER
marimba
  See MUSIC
mark
  See MONEY
mark
  See POINT
marvelous
  See WONDERFUL
mask
  See HIDE
massive
  See HEAVY
massive
  See LARGE
master
  See EXPERT
master
  See LEARN
matching
  See SAME
matter
  See SUBJECT
MATURE
mature
  See ADULT
mature
  See GROW
maximum
  See GREATEST
maximum
  See MOST
MAYBE
meager
  See SMALL
MEAL
MEAN
meandering
  See ROUND
means
  See STAND
MEASUREMENT
meek
  See SHY

MEET¹ (encounter)
MEET² (contact)
meet
  See CONTEST
meet
  See RUN
melancholy
  See SAD
melancholy
  See SADNESS
MELODY
melody
  See SONG
MELT
mend
  See FIX
mend
  See HEAL
mention
  See BRING
mention
  See QUOTE
mention
  See SAY
mercy
  See PITY
merely
  See ONLY
merge
  See MIX
merit
  See DESERVE
merit
  See QUALITY
merit
  See WORTH
merry
  See JOLLY
MESS
mess
  See JUMBLE
mess
  See MEAL
mess up
  See JUMBLE
MESSAGE
MESSY
meter
  See MEASUREMENT
method
  See WAY
metric ton
  See MEASUREMENT
metropolis
  See CITY
microscopic
  See TINY
MIDDLE
middle
  See MEAN
middle school
  See SCHOOL
midge
  See INSECT

midnight snack
  See MEAL
mighty
  See GIANT
mighty
  See STRONG
military band
  See MUSIC
millennium
  See MEASUREMENT
millimeter
  See MEASUREMENT
mimic
  See IMITATE
MIND
mind
  See INTELLIGENCE
mind
  See WATCH²
mindless
  See CARELESS
miniature
  See SMALL
MINOR
minor
  See POINT
mint
  See SPICE
minuet
  See MUSIC
minute
  See MEASUREMENT
minute
  See TINY
misbehave
  See ACT
mischievous
  See NAUGHTY
miserable
  See UNHAPPY
misery
  See SUFFERING
misfortune
  See DISASTER
misfortune
  See TROUBLE
mislaid
  See LOST
mislay
  See LOSE¹
mislead
  See DECEIVE
mislead
  See LIE¹
misplace
  See LOSE¹
misplaced
  See LOST
MISS
miss
  See FALL
miss
  See PASS

miss
  See WANT
missing
  See ABSENT
missing
  See LOST
mist
  See FOG
MISTAKE
mistake
  See MIX
mistaken
  See INCORRECT
mistaken
  See WRONG
misunderstand
  See MIX
MIX
mix up
  See MIX
mob
  See CROWD
mob
  See GROUP
mocking
  See SARCASTIC
model
  See IDEAL
MODERN
modest
  See HUMBLE
modify
  See CHANGE
moist
  See DAMP
monarch
  See KING
monarchy
  See COUNTRY
MONEY
monotonous
  See DULL
monsoon
  See STORM
monster
  See VILLAIN
monstrous
  See GIANT
month
  See MEASUREMENT
moody
  See SULLEN
MORAL
MORE
mortal
  See DEADLY
mosquito
  See INSECT
MOST
most recent
  See LAST²
MOSTLY

Entries are in CAPITAL LETTERS. Synonyms are in lowercase letters.

Entries are in CAPITAL LETTERS. Synonyms are in lowercase letters.

ordinarily
See USUALLY
ordinary
See REGULAR
öre
See MONEY
oregano
See SPICE
organ
See MUSIC
organism
See ANIMAL
organize
See ARRANGE
organized
See NEAT
organs
See INSIDE
origin
See BEGINNING
ORIGINAL
original
See NEW
originality
See IMAGINATION
originate
See BEGIN
originate
See DESCEND
originate
See INVENT
ornament
See DECORATE
ornate
See LUXURIOUS
out of action
See ACTION
out of work
See WORK
out-of-date
See ANCIENT
outboard
See BOAT
outcome
See COME
outcome
See EFFECT
outcome
See RESULT
outdated
See TIME
outdoor
See OUTSIDE
outdoors
See NATURE
outer
See OUTSIDE
outlandish
See ODD
outline
See FORM
outrage
See ANGER

outrage
See INSULT
outrigger
See BOAT
OUTSIDE (*adjective*)
OUTSIDE (*noun*)
outstanding
See GREAT
overdo
See DO
overdue
See LATE
overhead
See UP
overlook
See FORGET
overlook
See LEAVE
oversee
See LOOK
oversight
See MISTAKE
overtake
See CATCH
overture
See MUSIC
overturn
See UPSET
overwork
See DO
OWN

pace
See SPEED
pace
See STEP
PACK (*noun*)
PACK (*verb*)
pack
See FILL
pack
See GROUP
package
See PACK
packhorse
See HORSE
pact
See AGREEMENT
paddle steamer
See SHIP
padlock
See LOCK
PAIN
painter
See ART
pal
See FRIEND

palm
See TREE
palomino
See HORSE
PAMPER
panic
See FEAR
pansy
See FLOWER
pant
See GASP
panther
See CAT
pantomime
See GAME
paprika
See SPICE
parched
See DRY
pardon
See FORGIVE
pardon
See LET
parsley
See SPICE
part
See PIECE
partiality
See PREJUDICE
particle
See ATOM
particle
See SPECK
PARTICULAR
PARTY
PASS (*noun*)
PASS (*verb*)
pass
See GO
pass
See HAND
pass away
See DIE
pass away
See PASS
pass on
See DIE
pass on
See HAND
pass on
See PASS
pass out
See HAND
pass out
See PASS
pass over
See PASS
pass over
See RUN
pass through
See PASS
pass up
See PASS

passing
See TEMPORARY
passion
See ENTHUSIASM
PAST
pastime
See HOBBY
patch
See FIX
PATIENT
patrol boat
See BOAT
pattern
See FORM
pattern
See ORDER
PAUSE (*noun*)
PAUSE (*verb*)
pause
See BREAK
pause
See HESITATION
PEACE
peace
See QUIET
peaceful
See QUIET
peacefulness
See QUIET
peak
See TOP
peculiar
See STRANGE
PEEK
peep
See PEEK
peer
See LOOK¹
penalize
See PUNISH
pence
See MONEY
penetrate
See ENTER
penitentiary
See JAIL
penniless
See POOR
penny
See MONEY
PEOPLE
pep
See ENERGY
peppermint
See SPICE
perceive
See KNOW
perceive
See NOTICE
percentage
See NUMBER
PERFECT
perform
See ACT

perform
See COME
performance
See ACT
perhaps
See MAYBE
peril
See DANGER
PERIOD
period
See TIME
periodically
See TIME
perish
See DIE
permanently
See GOOD
permit
See LET
permit
See PASS
perpetual
See CONTINUAL
Persian
See CAT
persist
See CARRY
persist
See GET
persist
See HOLD
PERSON
PERSONAL
PERSONALITY
PERSUADE
peseta
See MONEY
peso
See MONEY
pester
See IRRITATE
pester
See PICK
PET
petite
See SMALL
petty
See UNIMPORTANT
petunia
See FLOWER
pfennig
See MONEY
photograph
See PICTURE
piano
See MUSIC
piaster
See MONEY
piccolo
See MUSIC
PICK
pick on
See PICK

pick out
See PICK
pick up
See LEARN
pick up
See RAISE
PICTURE
picture
See DESCRIBE
PIECE
piglet
See CHILD
pilfer
See MAKE
piñata
See GAME
pine
See TREE
pink
See COLOR
pint
See MEASUREMENT
pinto
See HORSE
pious
See RELIGIOUS
pirate ship
See SHIP
pit
See HOLE
pitch
See THROW
pitfall
See TRAP
PITY
pivot
See TURN
PLACE
place
See PUT
PLAIN
plain
See OBVIOUS
plain
See VISIBLE
plait
See KNOT
PLAN
plan
See INTEND
plan
See WORK
planet
See EARTH
PLANT¹ (*bush*)
PLANT² (*factory*)
plantation
See HOUSE
PLAY (*noun*)
PLAY (*verb*)
playwright
See ART
pleasant
See COMFORTABLE

Entries are in CAPITAL LETTERS. Synonyms are in lowercase letters.

pleasant
See NICE
PLEASE
please
See THRILL
pleasing
See HAPPY
PLEASURE
pledge
See PROMISE
PLENTIFUL
plenty
See MANY
plodding
See SLOW
plummet
See DROP
plunge
See DIVE
pod
See GROUP
poet
See ART
POINT
point
See PURPOSE
point out
See POINT
point out
See SHOW
pointed
See SHARP¹
pointer
See DOG
poker
See GAME
polished
See SMOOTH
POLITE
pollute
See DIRTY
POLLUTION
polo
See GAME
ponder
See THINK
pony
See HORSE
poodle
See DOG
pool
See GAME
POOR
poor
See CHEAP²
pop
See MUSIC
poplar
See TREE
poppy
See FLOWER
POPULAR
portion
See PIECE

portrait
See PICTURE
portray
See PLAY
pose
See PRETEND
position
See STAND¹
positive
See SURE
possess
See OWN
possessive
See SELFISH
POSSIBILITY
POSSIBLE
possibly
See MAYBE
postpone
See PAUSE
potential
See POSSIBLE
pound
See HIT
pound
See MEASUREMENT
pound
See MONEY
pour
See FLOW
power
See NUMBER
POWERFUL
powerful
See STRONG
practical
See USEFUL
practically
See ALMOST
practically
See GOOD
practice
See HABIT
PRAISE (noun)
PRAISE (verb)
praise
See RESPECT
prank
See JOKE
prank
See TRICK
preceding
See PAST
precise
See RIGHT
predicament
See TROUBLE
PREDICT
PREJUDICE
preliminary
See BASIC
PREPARE
prepared
See READY

present
See BRING
present
See GIFT
present
See GIVE
present
See INTRODUCE
present
See SHOW
preserve
See CONSERVE
press
See PUSH
pressing
See URGENT
PRETEND
pretend
See MAKE
PRETTY
prevail
See MAKE
PREVENT
previously
See ONCE
price
See VALUE²
PRIDE
pride
See GROUP
primary
See BASIC
primary
See MAIN
primary school
See SCHOOL
prime number
See NUMBER
principal
See MAIN
principle
See RULE
prison
See JAIL
private
See PERSONAL
PRIZE
prize
See APPRECIATE
probable
See POSSIBLE
PROBLEM
proceed
See CARRY
proceed
See GO
prod
See URGE
produce
See BRING
produce
See MAKE¹
PRODUCTIVE

profession
See BUSINESS¹
profession
See WORK²
profile
See SHAPE
profuse
See PLENTIFUL
progress
See GO
prohibit
See FORBID
prolong
See EXTEND
prolong
See LENGTHEN
prolonged
See LONG
prominent
See FAMOUS
prominent
See IMPORTANT
PROMISE
prompt
See IMMEDIATE
prompt
See TIME
promptly
See SOON
promptly
See TIME
PROOF
prop up
See HOLD
propel
See MOVE
proper
See APPROPRIATE
proper
See POINT
properly
See WELL
property
See LAND
prophesy
See PREDICT
proportion
See MEASUREMENT
propose
See INTEND
propose
See SUGGEST
prospect
See POSSIBILITY
prosperous
See RICH
PROTECT
protected
See SAFE
protest
See COMPLAIN
protest
See OBJECT

PROUD¹ (dignified)
PROUD² (vain)
proverb
See SAYING
provide
See OFFER
province
See COUNTRY
provoke
See DARE
provoke
See IRRITATE
prowl
See SNEAK
prudent
See WISE
prune
See CUT
PT boat
See BOAT
PUBLIC
publicly
See PUBLIC
puff
See GASP
PULL
punch
See HIT
punctual
See IMMEDIATE
punctual
See TIME
punctually
See TIME
PUNISH
punt
See BOAT
pup
See CHILD
puppy
See CHILD
puppy
See DOG
PURE
pure
See FRESH
purple
See COLOR
PURPOSE
purposeful
See DETERMINED
pursue
See FOLLOW¹
pursue
See HUNT
pursuit
See HOBBY
PUSH
PUT
put forward
See SUGGEST
put off
See DELAY

put on
See WEAR
put up with
See BEAR
PUZZLE
puzzle
See CONFUSE
puzzle
See MYSTERY
puzzling
See MYSTERIOUS

qualified
See ABLE
QUALITY
quantity
See AMOUNT
quantity
See NUMBER²
QUARREL
quarrel
See ARGUE
quart
See MEASUREMENT
quarter
See MONEY
quarter horse
See HORSE
quartet
See MUSIC
QUEEN
query
See QUESTION
QUESTION
question
See ASK
question
See DOUBT
question
See MYSTERY
questionable
See DOUBTFUL
QUICK
quick
See SHARP²
QUIET (adjective)
QUIET (noun)
quiet
See SILENCE
QUIT
quit
See BACK
quit
See LEAVE
quiz
See TEST
QUOTE

Entries are in CAPITAL LETTERS. Synonyms are in lowercase letters.

Index 281

Entries are in CAPITAL LETTERS. Synonyms are in lowercase letters.

sharp-edged
See SHARP[1]
shatter
See BREAK
shed
See HUT
shekel
See MONEY
shelter
See PROTECT
shepherd
See GUIDE
Shetland sheepdog
See DOG
shield
See DEFEND
shift
See MOVE
shilling
See MONEY
SHINE
shiny
See BRIGHT
SHIP
ship
See SEND
shiver
See SHAKE
shoal
See GROUP
shock
See SURPRISE
shocked
See LOSS
shop
See PLANT[2]
SHORT
shortcoming
See DISADVANTAGE
shortcut
See CUT
shorthair
See CAT
shortly
See RUN
shortly
See SOON
shoulder pack
See PACK
shout
See LET
shout
See YELL
shove
See PUSH
SHOW
show
See BRING
show
See PLAY
show
See POINT
show off
See SHOW

show the way
See GUIDE
show up
See SHOW
shower
See RAIN
shriek
See LAUGH
shriek
See SCREAM
SHRINK
shrivel
See SHRINK
shrub
See PLANT[1]
shudder
See SHAKE
SHUT
shut down
See SHUT
shut off
See SHUT
shut out
See SHUT
SHY
Siamese
See CAT
SICK
sick
See UNHEALTHY
sickly
See SICK
SICKNESS
side
See EDGE
sidestep
See AVOID
sideways
See BACK
sight
See VIEW
SIGN
sign up
See SIGN
signal
See SIGN
signal
See WAVE
significance
See VALUE[1]
significant
See IMPORTANT
SILENCE
silent
See QUIET
silhouette
See BODY
SILLY
SIMILAR
Simon says
See GAME
simple
See EASY

simple
See PLAIN
singe
See BURN
singer
See ART
sink
See DROP
sip
See DRINK
site
See PLACE
situation
See STATE
sizable
See LARGE
size
See MEASUREMENT
skid
See SLIDE
skiff
See BOAT
skiing
See GAME
skill
See ABILITY
skill
See ART
SKIM
skim
See SLIDE
skinny
See THIN
skip
See LEAVE
SLACK
slack
See LOOSE
slacken
See EASE
slam
See SHUT
slander
See INSULT
slant
See TIP
slap one's thighs
See LAUGH
sleepy
See TIRED
slender
See THIN
slice
See CUT
SLIDE
slight
See LITTLE
slight
See MINOR
slightest
See LEAST
slim
See THIN

slip
See KNOT
slip
See MISTAKE
slip
See SLIDE
slop
See SPILL
sloppy
See MESSY
slovenly
See UNTIDY
SLOW
sluggish
See LAZY
sluggish
See SLOW
slur
See INSULT
SLY
SMALL
smallest
See LEAST
SMART
smart
See ACHE
smart
See HURT
smash
See BREAK
smash
See CRASH
SMELL
smell bad
See STINK
SMILE
smirk
See SMILE
smog
See FOG
SMOOTH
smudge
See SPOT
snakes and ladders
See GAME
snapdragon
See FLOWER
snare
See TRAP
snarl
See KNOT
snatch
See MAKE
snatch
See SEIZE
snatch
See YANK
SNEAK
sneaky
See SLY
sneering
See SARCASTIC
snicker
See LAUGH

snigger
See LAUGH
snort
See LAUGH
snowstorm
See STORM
snug
See COMFORTABLE
snug
See NARROW
so far
See YET
soaked
See WET
soar
See FLY
sob
See CRY
soccer
See GAME
sociable
See FRIENDLY
social
See PARTY
SOFT
soft
See GENTLE
softball
See GAME
soggy
See WET
soil
See DIRT
soil
See DIRTY
soiled
See DIRTY
solemn
See SERIOUS
solid
See DENSE
solid
See FIRM
solid
See STEADY
solitaire
See GAME
solitary
See LONELY
solitary
See ONLY
solo
See ALONE
solution
See ANSWER[2]
solve
See WORK
somber
See SERIOUS
sometimes
See TIME
sometimes
See YET

sonata
See MUSIC
SONG
song
See MELODY
SOON
soon
See RUN
soothe
See EASE
sopping
See WET
SORE
soreness
See PAIN
sorrow
See SADNESS
sort
See ARRANGE
sort
See TYPE
soul
See MUSIC
sound
See NOISE
sound
See WISE
soundless
See QUIET
SOUR
source
See BEGINNING
sovereign
See QUEEN
space vehicles
See VEHICLE
spacious
See ROOMY
span
See PERIOD
spare time
See LEISURE
sparkle
See SHINE
speak
See LET
speak
See TALK
speak softly
See WHISPER
speak to
See COMMUNICATE
speak with
See COMMUNICATE
special
See DIFFERENT
specific
See PARTICULAR
specific
See RIGHT
SPECK
speck
See ATOM

Entries are in CAPITAL LETTERS. Synonyms are in lowercase letters.

spectator
 See WITNESS
speculation
 See THEORY
SPEECH
SPEED
speed
 See ZOOM
speedboat
 See BOAT
speedy
 See QUICK
spherical
 See ROUND
SPICE
spice
 See ZEST
SPILL
spill over
 See RUN
spin
 See TURN
spin the bottle
 See GAME
spirit
 See ENERGY
spiritual
 See RELIGIOUS
spiteful
 See VICIOUS
splash
 See SPILL
splat
 See NOISE
splendid
 See MAGNIFICENT
splice
 See KNOT
split
 See DIVIDE
split one's sides
 See LAUGH
sploosh
 See NOISE
spooky
 See FRIGHTENING
sport
 See GAME
SPOT
spot
 See FIND
spot
 See SEE
spotless
 See CLEAN
spread
 See MEAL
sprinkle
 See RAIN
sprint
 See RUN
spruce
 See TREE

spur
 See URGE
squabble
 See QUARREL
squad
 See TEAM
squall
 See STORM
squander
 See WASTE
square
 See KNOT
square root
 See NUMBER
squat
 See SHORT
squeal
 See SCREAM
squeeze
 See PACK
squishy
 See SOFT
St. Bernard
 See DOG
stable
 See HORSE
stable
 See SET
stable
 See STEADY
STAGGER
stain
 See SPOT
stalk
 See HUNT
stall
 See HORSE
stall
 See STAND[2]
stallion
 See HORSE
STAND[1] *(position)*
STAND[2] *(booth)*
STAND[3] *(bleachers)*
STAND *(verb)*
stand
 See BEAR
stand by
 See STAND
stand for
 See STAND
stand out
 See STAND
stand up
 See GET
standard
 See IDEAL
standard
 See NORMAL
stare
 See LOOK[1]
START
start
 See BEGINNING

start
 See FRONT
start
 See SET
startle
 See SCARE
startle
 See SURPRISE
starving
 See HUNGRY
STATE
state
 See COUNTRY
state
 See DECLARE
state
 See EXPLAIN
state
 See SET
statement
 See MESSAGE
statement
 See REMARK
stationary
 See STEADY
statute
 See LAW
stay
 See LIVE
stay
 See WAIT
stay with
 See VISIT
STEADY
steady
 See FIRM
steal
 See MAKE
steal
 See SNEAK
stealing
 See THEFT
steamboat
 See BOAT
steamer
 See SHIP
steamship
 See SHIP
steed
 See HORSE
steel band
 See MUSIC
steer
 See GUIDE
STEP
step by step
 See STEP
step up
 See STEP
stick out
 See STAND
STICKY
STIFF

still
 See QUIET
stillness
 See SILENCE
stimulate
 See ENCOURAGE
stimulated
 See KEY
stingy
 See SELFISH
STINK
stir
 See MIX
stirrup
 See HORSE
STOP
stop
 See BREAK
stop
 See GIVE
stop
 See TURN
store
 See BACK
store
 See BUSINESS[2]
store
 See KEEP
STORM
STORY
stout
 See HEAVY
strain
 See PASS
STRANGE
strategy
 See PLAN
STRAY
stray
 See GO
streak
 See ZOOM
stream
 See FLOW
strengthen
 See BACK
stress
 See EMPHASIZE
stretch
 See LENGTHEN
stretch
 See PERIOD
stretch out
 See EXTEND
stretch out
 See LIE[2]
stride
 See STEP
stride
 See WALK
strike
 See HIT
string quartet
 See MUSIC

strive
 See TRY
stroke
 See PET
stroll
 See WALK
STRONG
strong
 See POWERFUL
strut
 See WALK
STUBBORN
STUDY
stuff
 See FILL
stumble
 See TRIP
stun
 See SURPRISE
STUPID
sturdy
 See TOUGH
style
 See FASHION
subdue
 See DEFEAT
SUBJECT
subject
 See QUESTION
submarine
 See SHIP
submit
 See GIVE
submit
 See HAND
submit
 See SURRENDER
submit
 See TURN
subtract
 See TAKE[3]
succeed
 See COME
succeed
 See FOLLOW[1]
succeed
 See MAKE
succeed
 See WIN
success
 See VICTORY
SUDDEN
sudden
 See SHARP[3]
suffer
 See HURT
SUFFERING
sufficient
 See ENOUGH
SUGGEST
suggest
 See BRING
suitable
 See FITTING

suitable
 See POINT
suite
 See MUSIC
sulky
 See SULLEN
SULLEN
sum
 See AMOUNT
sum
 See NUMBER[2]
sum
 See TOTAL
summarize
 See REPORT
summary
 See REPORT
summit
 See TOP
summon
 See INVITE
sumptuous
 See LUXURIOUS
sunflower
 See FLOWER
supertanker
 See SHIP
supervise
 See CONTROL
supervise
 See LEAD
supervise
 See LOOK
supervisor
 See BOSS
supper
 See MEAL
supply
 See OFFER
SUPPORT
support
 See BACK
support
 See HOLD
support
 See STAND
supreme
 See GREATEST
SURE
SURPRISE
SURRENDER
surrender
 See GIVE
survey
 See INSPECT
survive
 See MAKE
survive
 See PASS
suspect
 See DOUBT
suspend
 See DELAY

Entries are in CAPITAL LETTERS. Synonyms are in lowercase letters.

suspend
See LEAVE

sustain
See SUPPORT

swallow
See DRINK

swamp
See RUN

swap
See TRADE

swarm
See CROWD

swarm
See GROUP

sway
See PERSUADE

sway
See SWING

sweet
See NICE

sweet
See PRETTY

swell
See EXPAND

swift
See FAST

swimming
See GAME

SWING

switch
See TRADE

switch off
See TURN

swoop
See DIVE

symbol
See SIGN

sympathetic
See KIND

sympathy
See KINDNESS

sympathy
See PITY

symphony
See MUSIC

symphony
orchestra
See MUSIC

synthesizer
See MUSIC

synthetic
See UNNATURAL

tabby
See CAT

tag
See GAME

tail
See GO

TAKE¹ (capture)

TAKE² (withstand)

TAKE³ (subtract)

take action
See ACTION

take after
See TAKE

take away
See REMOVE

take back
See BACK

take care
See LOOK

take down
See TAKE

take in
See TAKE

take leave of
See SEE

take off
See TAKE

take on
See TAKE

take out
See TAKE

take place
See HAPPEN

takeoff
See TAKE

takeout
See TAKE

tale
See STORY

TALENT

TALK

talk
See SPEECH

talk about
See DISCUSS

TALL

tame
See GENTLE

tang
See ZEST

tangle
See KNOT

tangy
See SOUR

tanker
See SHIP

tantrum
See RAGE

tap
See KNOCK

tardy
See LATE

tarry
See DELAY

tart
See SOUR

task
See DUTY

task
See JOB

tasty
See DELICIOUS

tattered
See RAGGED

taunt
See TEASE

TEACH

TEAM

tear
See JERK

TEASE

tease
See PICK

technique
See ART

telephone
See GAME

TELL

tell
See COME

tell
See GIVE

temper
See ANGER

tempest
See STORM

TEMPORARY

tend
See WATCH²

tender
See GENTLE

tennis
See GAME

tense
See NERVOUS

tepid
See WARM

term
See TIME

termites
See INSECT

terrible
See AWFUL

terrier
See DOG

terrified
See AFRAID

terrify
See SCARE

territory
See COUNTRY

terror
See FEAR

TEST

thankful
See GRATEFUL

thaw
See MELT

THEFT

theme
See SUBJECT

theme song
See SONG

THEORY

THICK

thick
See DENSE

THIN

thin
See DWINDLE

THING

THINK

think of
See REMEMBER

thoroughbred
See HORSE

thought
See IDEA

thoughtless
See CARELESS

threat
See DANGER

THRILL

thrill
See DELIGHT

throb
See ACHE

throng
See CROWD

THROW

throw away
See WASTE

thrust
See PUSH

thump
See KNOCK

thunderstorm
See STORM

thus far
See YET

thyme
See SPICE

tidy
See NEAT

tie
See KNOT

tiger
See CAT

TIGHT

tight
See DENSE

tight
See NARROW

tilt
See TIP

timber
See TREE

TIME

timeless
See ETERNAL

timid
See SHY

tiniest
See LEAST

tint
See COLOR

TINY

TIP

tip
See POINT

tip
See UPSET

TIRED

tiring
See DULL

titter
See LAUGH

to the point
See POINT

toil
See WORK

tolerant
See PATIENT

tolerate
See BEAR

tomcat
See CAT

ton
See MEASUREMENT

tone
See COLOR

TOOL

TOP

topic
See SUBJECT

topple
See FALL

torment
See SUFFERING

torment
See TEASE

torn
See RAGGED

tornado
See STORM

torrid
See HOT

toss
See THROW

TOTAL

total
See ABSOLUTE

total
See COME

total
See COMPLETE

total
See MAKE²

tote
See CARRY

totter
See STAGGER

TOUGH

tough
See HARD

tour
See JOURNEY

tour
See TRAVEL

tour
See TRIP

tournament
See CONTEST

tow
See PULL

towering
See TALL

TOWN

toxic
See DEADLY

track
See HUNT

track and field
See GAME

TRADE

trail
See FALL

trail
See FOLLOW¹

trail
See HUNT

train
See TEACH

training
See EDUCATION

tranquillity
See QUIET

transfer
See BRING

transfer
See DROP

transfer
See HAND

transform
See CHANGE

transmit
See SEND

transport
See BRING

transport
See SHIP

TRAP

trap
See CATCH

TRASH

TRAVEL

trawler
See SHIP

tread
See WALK

treasure
See APPRECIATE

treaty
See AGREEMENT

TREE

tree
See PLANT¹

tremble
See SHAKE

triangle

Entries are in CAPITAL LETTERS. Synonyms are in lowercase letters.

See MUSIC
TRICK
trick
  See DECEIVE
trickle through
  See PASS
tricky
  See SLY
trifling
  See UNIMPORTANT
trim
  See CUT
trim
  See DECORATE
trio
  See MUSIC
TRIP
trip
  See JOURNEY
triumph
  See VICTORY
triumph
  See WIN
trivial
  See MINOR
trombone
  See MUSIC
troop
  See GROUP
trot
  See JOG
TROUBLE
trouble
  See WORRY
truce
  See PEACE
truck
  See VEHICLE
trudge
  See WALK
TRUE
true
  See FAITHFUL
true
  See REAL
trumpet
  See MUSIC
TRUST (noun)
TRUST (verb)
trustworthy
  See RESPONSIBLE
truthful
  See HONEST
TRY
trying to avoid
  See RUN
tuba
  See MUSIC
tug
  See YANK
tug of war
  See GAME
tugboat
  See SHIP

tulip
  See FLOWER
tumble
  See FALL
tune
  See MELODY
tune
  See SONG
tunnel
  See CAVE
turmoil
  See DISORDER
TURN
turn down
  See REFUSE
turn down
  See TURN
turn in
  See TURN
turn off
  See TURN
turn out
  See COME
turn out
  See TURN
turn to
  See FALL
twinge
  See PAIN
twinkle
  See SHINE
twirl
  See TURN
twist
  See BEND
twitter
  See LAUGH
twitter
  See NOISE
TYPE
type in
  See ENTER
type in
  See KEY
typhoon
  See STORM
typical
  See REGULAR

UGLY
ultimate
  See GREATEST
ultimate
  See LAST[1]
umiak
  See BOAT
unassuming
  See HUMBLE
unattractive
  See UGLY

unbecoming
  See UGLY
UNBELIEVABLE
unbelievable
  See INCORRECT
unbiased
  See FAIR
UNCERTAIN
uncertain
  See HESITANT
unclear
  See UNCERTAIN
uncommon
  See RARE
uncommon
  See UNUSUAL
uncomplicated
  See EASY
uncomplicated
  See PLAIN
unconcern
  See INDIFFERENCE
uncoordinated
  See AWKWARD
uncover
  See COME
uncovered
  See OPEN
UNDER
under
  See DOWN
under way
  See WAY
underneath
  See UNDER
UNDERSTAND
understand
  See CATCH
understanding
  See PATIENT
undiluted
  See PURE
UNDO
undue
  See EXCESSIVE
unearth
  See DISCOVER
uneasy
  See RESTLESS
uneducated
  See STUPID
unemployed
  See WORK
UNEQUAL
uneven
  See JAGGED
uneven
  See UNEQUAL
unexpected
  See SUDDEN
UNFAIR
UNFAMILIAR
UNFAVORABLE

unfeeling
  See CRUEL
unfinished
  See INCOMPLETE
unfortunate
  See UNLUCKY
UNFRIENDLY
ungainly
  See AWKWARD
unhappiness
  See SADNESS
UNHAPPY
UNHEALTHY
UNIMPORTANT
unimportant
  See POINT
unintelligent
  See STUPID
uninteresting
  See DULL
UNIQUE
unique
  See PARTICULAR
unit
  See TEAM
unite
  See JOIN
unite
  See MEET[2]
UNIVERSAL
university
  See SCHOOL
unjust
  See UNFAIR
unkempt
  See UNTIDY
unkind
  See CRUEL
unknown
  See UNFAMILIAR
unlike
  See DIFFERENT
unlikely
  See DOUBTFUL
unlimited
  See UNIVERSAL
unlit
  See DARK
unlocked
  See OPEN
UNLUCKY
UNNATURAL
unoccupied
  See EMPTY
unreasonable
  See UNFAIR
unruly
  See BAD[4]
unruly
  See NAUGHTY
unruly
  See WILD
unsafe
  See DANGEROUS

unskilled
  See RAW
unsociable
  See UNFRIENDLY
unsoiled
  See CLEAN
unspoiled
  See FRESH
unsure
  See LOSS
untamed
  See WILD
UNTIDY
untrained
  See RAW
untrue
  See WRONG
untruth
  See LIE (noun)
untruthful
  See DISHONEST
UNUSUAL
unwell
  See UNHEALTHY
UP
up-to-date
  See MODERN
upright
  See HONEST
upright
  See MORAL
uproar
  See RACKET
UPSET (adjective)
UPSET (verb)
upset
  See DISRUPT
upset
  See WORRY
upward
  See UP
URGE
urge
  See INSIST
URGENT
USE[1] (utilize)
USE[2] (deplete)
use up
  See RUN
USEFUL
usefulness
  See VALUE[1]
USELESS
useless
  See GOOD
usher
  See GUIDE
USUAL
USUALLY
utensil
  See TOOL
utilize
  See USE[1]

utmost
  See GREATEST
utter
  See ABSOLUTE
utter
  See SAY

vacant
  See EMPTY
vague
  See UNCERTAIN
vain
  See PROUD[2]
valid
  See TRUE
valor
  See COURAGE
valuable
  See EXPENSIVE
valuables
  See MONEY
VALUE[1] (usefulness)
VALUE[2] (price)
value
  See APPRECIATE
VANISH
vanity
  See PRIDE
various
  See DIFFERENT
vast
  See WIDE
vault
  See JUMP
VEHICLE
veil
  See CONCEAL
velocity
  See SPEED
verification
  See PROOF
VERY
vessel
  See SHIP
VICIOUS
victor
  See CHAMPION
VICTORY
VIEW
view
  See BELIEF
view
  See WATCH[1]
viewpoint
  See STAND[1]
vigilance
  See CAUTION
vigilant
  See ALERT

Entries are in CAPITAL LETTERS. Synonyms are in lowercase letters.

Index 287

vigor
  See ENERGY
vigorous
  See LIVELY
villa
  See HOUSE
village
  See TOWN
VILLAIN
viola
  See MUSIC
violate
  See DISOBEY
violation
  See CRIME
VIOLENT
violet
  See COLOR
violet
  See FLOWER
violin
  See MUSIC
virtuoso
  See ART
virtuous
  See MORAL
VISIBLE
VISIT
visit
  See DROP
vitality
  See ENERGY
volt
  See MEASUREMENT
VOLUNTEER
volunteer
  See OFFER
VOTE
vow
  See PROMISE
voyage
  See JOURNEY
voyage
  See TRAVEL

wail
  See CRY
WAIT
wake up
  See COME
wake up
  See GET
WALK (noun)
WALK (verb)
waltz
  See MUSIC

wander
  See GO
wander
  See STRAY
WANT
war
  See FIGHT
war-horse
  See HORSE
WARM
WARN
warship
  See SHIP
wary
  See CAREFUL
WASH
wash
  See CLEAN
washed
  See CLEAN
wasp
  See INSECT
WASTE
waste
  See TRASH
WATCH¹ (observe)
WATCH² (look after)
watchful
  See ALERT
waterless
  See DRY
watt
  See MEASUREMENT
WAVE
waver
  See HESITATE
wavering
  See HESITANT
WAY
WEAK
weakness
  See DISADVANTAGE
wealth
  See MONEY
wealthy
  See RICH
WEAR
weary
  See TIRED
wee
  See LITTLE
week
  See MEASUREMENT
weep
  See CRY
weigh
  See CONSIDER
weighty
  See HEAVY
weird
  See ODD

welcome
  See TAKE
WELL
well-groomed
  See NEAT
well-known
  See COMMON
well-liked
  See POPULAR
WET
wet
  See DAMP
whaleboat
  See BOAT
wham
  See NOISE
wheeze
  See GASP
WHISPER
white
  See COLOR
whole
  See COMPLETE
whole
  See TOTAL
whole number
  See NUMBER
whomp
  See NOISE
whoop
  See LAUGH
whoosh
  See NOISE
wicked
  See BAD²
WIDE
widespread
  See UNIVERSAL
WILD
wildcat
  See CAT
wilderness
  See NATURE
WILL
will
  See PASS
willow
  See TREE
willpower
  See WILL
WIN
win
  See EARN
win
  See VICTORY
wind
  See BEND
winding
  See ROUND
winner
  See CHAMPION

wipe out
  See UNDO
wisdom
  See KNOWLEDGE
WISE
WISH
wish
  See HOPE
wish
  See WANT
withdraw
  See BACK
withdraw
  See FALL
withdraw
  See GIVE
withdraw
  See REMOVE
withstand
  See TAKE²
WITNESS
witty
  See FUNNY
wizard
  See EXPERT
woe
  See SUFFERING
wolfhound
  See DOG
WOMAN
WONDERFUL
woodland
  See TREE
woods
  See TREE
word
  See PROMISE
WORK¹ (labor)
WORK² (job)
WORK (verb)
work
  See ACT
work
  See OPERATE
work out
  See WORK
workable
  See POSSIBLE
workbench
  See WORK
workbook
  See WORK
worker
  See WORK
workhorse
  See HORSE
workman
  See WORK
workout
  See WORK
workshop
  See PLANT²

workstation
  See WORK
world
  See EARTH
worn-out
  See RAGGED
worn-out
  See TIRED
worried
  See UPSET
WORRY (noun)
WORRY (verb)
WORTH
worth
  See QUALITY
worthless
  See CHEAP²
worthless
  See GOOD
worthless
  See USELESS
wound
  See INJURE
wound
  See SORE
wrath
  See RAGE
wreck
  See DESTROY
wreck
  See RUIN
wrench
  See YANK
wretched
  See UNHAPPY
writer
  See ART
WRONG
wrong
  See BAD²

X-RAY
xylophone
  See MUSIC

yacht
  See BOAT
YANK
yard
  See MEASUREMENT

yarn
  See STORY
year
  See MEASUREMENT
yearling
  See HORSE
yearn
  See WANT
YELL
yellow
  See COLOR
yen
  See DESIRE
yen
  See MONEY
YET
yet
  See BUT
yield
  See GIVE
yield
  See LOSE²
yield
  See SURRENDER
yoke
  See GROUP
YOUNG
youngster
  See CHILD
YOUTH
youthful
  See YOUNG

zap
  See NOISE
zeal
  See ENTHUSIASM
ZERO
ZEST
zing
  See NOISE
ZIP
zloty
  See MONEY
ZONE
ZOOM
zoom in
  See ZOOM

Entries are in CAPITAL LETTERS. Synonyms are in lowercase letters.